PERSPECTIVES ON RESTORATION DRAMA

MANCHESTER
UNIVERSITY PRESS

SUSAN J. OWEN

Perspectives on
Restoration drama

Manchester University Press
Manchester and New York

distributed exclusively in the USA by Palgrave

The right of Susan J. Owen to be identified as the author of this work has been
asserted by her in accordance with the Copyright, Designs and Patents Act 1988

Published by Manchester University Press
Oxford Road, Manchester M13 9NR, UK
and Room 400, 175 Fifth Avenue, New York, NY 10010, USA
http://www.manchesteruniversitypress.co.uk

Distributed exclusively in the USA
by Palgrave, 175 Fifth Avenue, New York, NY 10010, USA

Distributed exclusively in Canada
by UBC Press, University of British Columbia, 2029 West Mall,
Vancouver, BC, Canada V6T 1Z2

British Library Cataloguing-in-Publication Data
A catalogue record for this book is available from the British Library

Library of Congress Cataloging-in-Publication Data applied for

ISBN 0 7190 4966 0 *hardback*
    0 7190 4967 9 *paperback*

First published 2002
10 09 08 07 06 05 04 03 02   10 9 8 7 6 5 4 3 2 1

Typeset in Bulmer
by Koinonia, Manchester
Printed in Great Britain
by Bell & Bain Ltd, Glasgow

CONTENTS

ACKNOWLEDGEMENTS

I would like to thank the University of Sheffield for giving me study leave during which this book was completed. Thanks are also due to all my colleagues in the field of Restoration drama for their invaluable comments. I am also grateful to Neil Roberts for his support in the final stages of this work, and to Anita Roy and Matthew Frost, my successive editors. I would like to thank Mike Macnair for his help and encouragement, and to express my love and thanks to my daughters, Alice and Jenny. Finally, my thanks go to all the friends of Bill Wilson who helped me during the period in which this book was written. This book is dedicated to them.

University of Sheffield

Introduction

Contrary to widely held belief, the Restoration period was a time of dramatic variety, innovation and vitality. This book offers perspectives on that variety through readings of selected plays, each play being 'situated' in its dramatic and social contexts.

Restoration theatre was affected by big social contradictions, involving sex and gender, as well as political power. Everyone has heard of the so-called merry monarch and his mistresses, of whom Nell Gwyn is the best known. Under Charles II there was a burgeoning of libertinism. If John Wilmot, Earl of Rochester, was the best-known exponent, the chief practitioners were the Stuarts, Charles II and his brother and heir, James. The period after 1660 also saw the development of the sexual 'marketplace', ranging from prostitutes who catered for all tastes, to homosexual 'molly' houses, to a generalised fetishization of sexual characteristics. There are numerous references in the drama to homosexuality, sadomasochism, and voyeurism, as well as libertinism and prostitution.

However, on the other hand, there was widespread moral disapproval of these developments. Even a royal supporter like Pepys notes the King's 'horrid effeminacy' (enslavement to women) and 'the viciousness of the Court' and 'contempt the King brings himself into thereby'.[1] The King's promiscuity was often seen as a sign of political irresponsibility, as the arch-libertine Rochester himself noted: 'His sceptre and his prick are of a length, / And she may sway the one who plays with t'other / And make him little wiser than his brother.' When Rochester coined the designation 'merry Monarch' he was being sarcastic: Charles is 'A merry Monarch, scandalous and poor'. Charles, the poet ironically observes, is not such a fool as to strive, like the French king, to defend and extend his kingdom:

his only ambition is to conquer 'the best cunts in Christendom', regardless of religion and law:

> Whate'er religion and the laws say on't,
> He'll break through all to come at any cunt.[2]

Similarly, in Andrew Marvell's poem *Last Instructions to a Painter* the Kingdom appears to the recumbent Charles in allegorical female form and the King's response is to want to screw it, literally and figuratively.[3]

As we shall see in Chapter 2, the result was a contradictory attitude to sex in the drama. Masculinity, too, was thrown into crisis.[4] To this the dramatists also responded in a contradictory way. Dryden, for example, elevates the hero who 'weeps much, fights little, but is wondrous kind' in *All For Love*;[5] but denigrates male 'effeminacy' in *Troilus and Cressida*, the subject of Chapter 6. For women there were massive contradictions. Libertinism opened up a new freedom to assert sexual desire, but libertinism was itself a misogynistic philosophy, sanctioning desire for the male but not the female, and seeing women as prey. Women could for the first time become actresses and playwrights, a development of profound significance in the theatre, but they were often thought of as sexually available and morally compromised simply by their association with theatre and public exhibition. The actresses' changing room was open to the public. They were regarded as easy prey and it was hard for them to resist unwanted male attention.[6] The first professional woman playwright, Aphra Behn, was always hard up and never really respectable. Behn's attitude to libertinism varied between indulgence, caution and criticism, as we shall see in Chapter 3. 'Breeches' parts for actresses embodied the contradiction for women: on the one hand, women could dress and fight as men; on the other, we know from contemporary accounts that the audience saw such parts as a chance to revel in the titillating sight of the actresses' legs.

These contradictions of sex and gender must be seen within a context of political contradiction. Despite the triumphant rhetoric and ostentatious rejoicing which accompanied the reassertion of royal authority in 1660, the King soon came up against a crisis of authority. It was impossible to establish the ideological consensus, to obliterate memory of the interregnum, or to gloss over profound religious and political divisions in the nation. Charles faced criticism from the old cavaliers for being too lenient towards former supporters of Cromwell; but he also faced growing mistrust from parliamentarians such as Andrew Marvell for being soft on 'popery' and disposed towards 'arbitrary government' on the French model.[7] Europe was in political and religious turmoil, and the depth of English anxieties about the Protestant succession and the parliamentary freedoms thought to be associated with it was reflected in the overwhelming electoral victories and mass support of the opposition to the government in the late 1670s and early 1680s. The Exclusion Crisis of 1678–83 almost erupted into another civil war. At this time party political division emerged for the first time in England, as royalist and parliamentarian factions hardened into Tories and Whigs. I have written a book about the Exclusion Crisis and its effect on the drama, where I also discuss in detail the nature of Whiggism and Toryism and of the dramatic 'language of politics'. I suggest that this book, *Restoration Theatre and Crisis*, might provide useful background for the present study.[8] Ultimately these tensions were to explode in the revolution of 1688. The ejection of James II in 1688 was followed by significant reversals at the level of political ideology, law, constitution and foreign policy, and led to a changed culture.[9] The plays I have selected are all pre-1688, for the simple reason that the drama changed after the revolution, and cannot legitimately be termed Restoration drama, any more than this new era can reasonably be considered to fall within the Restoration period.

Charles II took a keen personal interest in the theatre, and personally inaugurated the new heroic genre which is the subject of Chapter 1. The assertion of royal control in the theatres also took the form of censorship and strict limits on theatrical outlets: only two theatres were licensed, though plays could also be performed at Court. Yet, as we shall see in Chapter 1, contradictions emerged in the drama's attitude towards royal authority, even during the early Restoration period of the ascendancy of the royalist heroic play. In Chapters 4 and 5 we shall see that in the Exclusion Crisis 'oppositional' tragedy develops and contradictions are evident even in plays in which dramatists were apparently straining every nerve to offer a royalist and Tory message. Censorship, while it may have worked to some extent to limit criticisms of the authorities in performance, did not stop publication. Even during the Exclusion Crisis play texts appeared in print uncensored, even when the play was banned from performance.[10]

[The fact there were only two licensed theatres in London meant that the Restoration audience was more dominated by royal and aristocratic tastes than the theatre of Shakespeare's time.]This is symbolized by the social composition of those immediately in front of the players: Shakespeare's 'groundlings' were replaced by an audience which contained many gentlemen and noblemen, seated on benches in the 'pit'. Yet the audience was by no means homogenous. Humbler people sat in the galleries above the front tier of boxes, and people of 'middle rank' sat in the pit or the galleries or even took boxes themselves.[11] Restoration theatres were grander than theatres earlier in the century. Stage design was more elaborate, with a proscenium arch, and realistic sets made of painted wings, borders and shutters. Scenes could be changed by sliding movable backdrops along grooves in the stage, shutters opened to stunning tableaux. Machines for enabling people to fly created exciting new possibilities, and there was increased use of music and spectacle. All these factors might be supposed to have created a more culturally dominating experience for the audience.

Yet there are contradictory aspects. In front of the proscenium arch a forestage extended right into the pit. Most acting took place here. The forestage also allowed intimate exchanges with the audience in prologues and epilogues, often spoken by actresses. The prologues and epilogues were spoken with an air of familiarity and were full of in-jokes. We know from Pepys's diary that he and others went to the theatre regularly, sometimes several times a week. They knew the actors and understood the theatre's conventions. Going to the theatre was a much more ordinary and everyday experience, and therefore less intimidating than it can be in our own time. Nor was the audience respectfully silent. The candles remained lit throughout the performance, permitting flirting, the sale of everything from oranges to sexual favours, a ribald exchange of witticisms, by no means always connected to the play, and sometimes fights. The audience, in other words, were a theatre in themselves. Theatres did not really rank as 'high culture' in the Restoration. Plays rarely ran for more than six days, and were seldom very profitable. Actors were so poorly paid that many had second jobs. Authors got box office receipts on the third night, since published texts were usually cheap and shoddy and yielded little profit.[12] Issues of cultural authority were just as complex in the theatres as in Restoration society.

The chapters which follow offer fresh readings of the plays in the contexts described above. I have also 'located' each play in the context of critical and scholarly debate. Criticism of Restoration drama has been uneven, large sections and whole genres having been neglected or misunderstood for centuries. The notes refer to the range of critical approaches to these plays, as well as to the latest thinking about them. An extensive bibliography points directions for further reading. This book is intended to appeal to different levels of scholarship, from beginning undergraduates to those embarking on more advanced study. The main text is largely kept free of complicating debate, offering close readings of the plays which are intended to be lucid and stimulating. The notes refer the reader to the critical and historical debates, as well as to other plays and to theatrical conditions. Sometimes I have referred to my own previous work. This is merely to avoid repeating myself and to point the reader in the direction of further relevant material. There is no obligation to pursue these pointers in order to understand the present volume. The reader who wants to read and follow up the notes will end up with a very thorough understanding of Restoration drama in all its various contexts. The reader who merely wants to dip into the drama can read the discussion of the plays and leave the notes alone.

The one chapter in which I have broken my own rule about keeping the debate to the notes is the chapter on Lee's *Lucius Junius Brutus*. At first I tried to write this chapter in the same detached vein as the others. However, a polemical note kept creeping in, since this is an area in which I have published work previously, and been challenged. In the end I thought it would be more honest to admit my critical partisanship. I hope it will be enlightening to show that Restoration drama is not a dead and remote field, but as much an area of lively scholarly debate as any other.

This book is not intended to compete with existing surveys of the drama.[13] By focusing on readings of specific plays, it aims to be appealing, accessible and introductory, rather than completely comprehensive. At the same time the book does a lot more than offering readings of individual plays. Each chapter traces the development of a genre and its relation to other genres, and locates a particular play in relation to other drama, as well as to theatrical, social and political developments. The book as a whole traces generic developments over the whole Restoration period, as well as following through the treatment of particular themes, and shifts in dramatic tone and 'mood'.

No selection of plays can be truly representative, but I have aimed for a good cross-section, exemplifying the range of genres. Dryden is so seminal that it was fairly easy to select his two-part *The Conquest of Granada* to exemplify heroic tragi-comedy in Chapter 1. In this chapter I discuss the development and progress of the genre, mentioning many other heroic plays by Orrery, the Howards, Lee, Crowne, Otway and others. The comedies in Chapters 2 and 3, Wycherley's *The Country Wife* and Behn's *The Rover*, were chosen as a pair, for their similarities and differences. I thought it was essential to include the most popular comedy by the first professional female dramatist, so *The Rover* was an easy choice. The other was more difficult, since there were many plays I could have chosen: Etherege's *The Man of Mode* is just one example. However, *The Country Wife* seemed a good choice, as it offers interesting insights into Restoration comic method, and stimulating comparisons with *The Rover*. In Chapters 2 and 3 I discuss also types of comedy other than sex comedy. The tragedies, *Lucius Junius Brutus* and *Venice Preserv'd*, were also chosen as a pair, being so similar in many ways, and typical of the new genre of political tragedy, yet also politically quite different. Popularity was also a factor in my choices: *The Country Wife* and *The Rover* have stood the test of time, and both are performed, as well as discussed by critics, today. If any Restoration tragedies may be said to be popular today, it is *Lucius Junius Brutus* and *Venice Preserv'd*, both included in David Womersley's recent Blackwells anthology. Of course Dryden's *All For Love* was also a contender, but Dryden is the subject of two other chapters, so I contented myself with discussing this play more briefly in Chapter 4, together with Lee's *The Rival Queens* and other outstanding examples of the genre. The adaptation of Shakespeare was the most difficult choice. *Troilus and Cressida* was chosen because it represents a different genre from the foregoing plays, and also because Dryden prefaces it with an important essay on Shakespeare and on dramatic method. Dryden himself considered this play to exemplify his concerns in adapting Shakespeare for the Restoration stage. I discuss many other Shakespeare adaptations in Chapter 6, including Dryden's own *All For Love*, Tate's *The History of King Lear* and *The Ingratitude of a Common-wealth* (*Coriolanus*), and Ravenscroft's *Titus Andronicus*. Where all else was equal, I chose plays which I liked and found most interesting. I hope to communicate my enthusiasm to others, especially to those approaching Restoration drama for the first time.

Notes

1   The Diary of Samuel Pepys, VII, 323–4, VIII, 288.

2   *The Earl of Rochester's Verses For Which He Was Banished* in John Wilmot, Earl of Rochester, *Complete Poems and Plays*, ed. Paddy Lyons, London, J. M. Dent (Everyman), 1993.

3   See Maximillian E. Novak, 'Libertinism and Sexuality' in the *Blackwell Companion to Restoration Drama*, ed. Owen; Turner, 'The Libertine Sublime' and 'The Properties of Libertinism'; Hammond, 'The King's Two Bodies'; Chernaik, *Sexual Freedom in Restoration Literature*; Braverman, *Plots and Counterplots: Sexual Politics and the Body Politic, 1660-1730*.

4 See Laura Rosenthal, 'Masculinity in Restoration Drama' in the *Blackwell Companion to Restoration Drama*, ed. Owen; and Straub, *Sexual Suspects*.

5 *The Works of John Dryden*, ed. E. Niles Hooker *et al.*, Berkeley, University of California Press, 1956–, vol. XIII, 20.

6 See Howe, *The First English Actresses*; Lowenthal: 'Sticks and Rags'; and Payne Fisk, 'The Restoration Actress' in the *Blackwell Companion to Restoration Drama*, ed. Owen.

7 Andrew Marvell, *An Account of the Growth of Popery and Arbitrary Government in England*, 'Amsterdam', 1677. See my 'The Lost Rhetoric of Liberty: Marvell and Restoration Drama'.

8 *Restoration Theatre and Crisis*, Oxford: Clarendon Press, 1996.

9 For the debate about how to interpret Restoration history and politics see my *Restoration Theatre and Crisis*, chapter 2. *Albion* 25:4 (1993) contains a fascinating debate between all the leading historians of this period. See also Scott, *England's Troubles*; and Harris, 'What's New About the Restoration'. For background reading see Hutton, *Charles II*; and Downie, *To Settle the Succession of the State: Literature and Politics, 1678–1750*, 187–222.

10 See Matthew J. Kinservik, 'Theatrical Regulation During the Restoration Period' in the *Blackwell Companion to Restoration Drama*, ed. Owen; Winton Calhoun, 'Dramatic Censorship' in *The London Theatre World, 1660–1800*, ed. Hume, 286–308; and Weber, *Paper Bullets*.

11 Love, 'Who Were the Restoration Audience?'; Scouten and Hume, 'Restoration Comedy' and its Audiences'; Botica, *Audience, Playhouse and Play in Restoration Theatre*.

12 See Edward A. Langhans, 'The Post-1660 Theatres as Performance Spaces' in the *Blackwell Companion to Restoration Drama*, ed. Owen and 'The Theatre' in *The Cambridge Companion to British Restoration Theatre*, ed. Payne Fisk, 1–18; Joseph Roach, 'The Performance' in *ibid.*, 19–39; Howe, *The First English Actresses*, 1–18. *Introduction to The London Stage*, ed. Van Lennep *et al.*, *The London Theatre World*, ed. Hume; Boswell, *The Restoration Court Stage*; Hume, 'The Nature of the Dorset Garden Theatre'; Holland, *The Ornament of Action*; Powell, *Restoration Theatre Production*; Styan, *Restoration Comedy in Performance*; Milhous and Hume, *Producible Interpretation*; Lewcock, 'Computer Analysis of Restoration Staging' I and II; O'Connor, 'Late Seventeenth-century Royal Portraiture and Restoration Staging'.

13 Hume, *The Development of English Drama in the Late Seventeenth Century*; Bevis, *English Drama: Restoration and Eighteenth Century, 1660–1789*; Hughes, *English Drama 1660–1700*.

Heroic tragi-comedy:
John Dryden's *The Conquest of Granada by the Spaniards*, Parts I and II

Perhaps it is a symptom of the uncertainties and contradictions of the Restoration period that the mixed genre of tragi-comedy is widespread. Indeed, tragi-comedy of various kinds can be said to have predominated after 1660.[1] Nancy Maguire in *Regicide and Restoration* argues that this is because there had been too much tragedy in the interregnum and too many betrayals, only the greatest of which was the beheading of Charles I and 'tragedy as formerly understood was impossible after 1660'.[2] The mood of the 1660s was publicly festive but privately jittery, outwardly united around the restoration of the monarchy, but fraught with the anxieties and insecurities which any major political reversal must generate. For reasons of expediency Charles II's policy was of forgiveness and reconciliation with many former supporters of Cromwell. Discontents were widespread, especially among former royalists who felt unrewarded while their erstwhile enemies flourished, but most were willing or felt obliged to be part of the mass effort of wishful thinking. For authors it was scarcely fashionable – or safe – to disrupt the cultural 'mood' of celebration. Tragi-comedy was a genre eminently suited to the early Restoration *Zeitgeist*. It was a form which enabled dramatists such as Edward and Robert Howard to explore serious themes without deadly consequences. Everything ends on a note of optimism in keeping with the spirit of the 1660s. As we shall see, heroic drama epitomizes this tragi-comic mode of outward celebration and covert contradiction. Tragedy, the subject of later chapters of this book, develops in the darker mood of the 1670s, as the optimism generated by the restoration of the monarchy diminishes. By the late 1670s tragi-comedy tends to be used deliberately to invoke the memory of early Restoration values: examples are Dryden's

The Spanish Fryar (1680), Behn's *The Young King* (1679), and Tate's
King Lear (1681). In each case the dramatist's adoption of the genre
enables something special to be articulated, which has to do with
redressing power and gender imbalance without violence, and with a
strong emphasis on political responsibility coupled with good humour,
forgiveness and reconciliation around the values of 1660.

Of the various kinds of Restoration tragi-comedy, heroic drama is the
most innovative and prominent. What kind of tragi-comedy is it? There is
a happy ending, but the heightened language, aristocratic characters and
'high' subject matter – noble loves, honour, exalted and beleaguered virtue,
warrior heroism – are typical of tragedy. Heroic drama was intended to be
larger than life. Dryden, the chief exponent of the genre, argued in his
essay *Of Heroique Playes* prefacing *The Conquest of Granada* that 'serious
Playes ought not to imitate Conversation too nearly';[3] and his heroic plays
are written accordingly in the heightened language of the rhyming couplet.
Among other sources, Dryden draws his inspiration from Davenant's *The
Siege of Rhodes*, a semi-opera of the 1650s celebrating love and valour.
However, there is an important difference between the two dramatists:
Davenant thought heroic poetry should imitate heroic drama in being
'dress'd in a more familiar and easy shape: more fitted to the common
actions and passions of humane life: and, in short, more like a glass of
Nature, showing us our selves in our ordinary habits'.[4] Dryden leaves
naturalistic representation to historians and thinks instead that heroic
drama should follow heroic poetry, and that 'an Heroick Poet is not ty'd to
a bare representation of what is true, or exceeding probable: but that he
may let himself loose to visionary objects, and to the representation of such
things, as depending not on sence, and therefore not to be comprehended
by knowledge, may give him a freer scope for imagination' (12).

This 'heightened', non-naturalistic quality has caused some difference of opinion about the nature of the genre. *The Revels History of Drama
in English* includes heroic drama in the chapter on tragedy, but calls it
'quasi-tragic drama'.[5] The Aristotelian notion of tragedy centres upon
flawed greatness: the protagonist brings about his own downfall through
some fatal weakness of character, arousing our pity and fear in the process.
Eugene Waith therefore distinguishes heroic drama from tragedy on the
grounds of its 'concern with potentiality rather than limitation – with
greatness rather than error'. Taking account of Dryden's sources, and of
what he says about the play in *Of Heroique Playes*, Waith also argues that
'The design of *The Conquest of Granada*, then, belongs squarely in a

tradition of heroic poem which has been importantly modified by romance'.[6] Robert Hume in *The Development of English Drama in the Late Seventeenth Century* concurs: 'the happy ending is a return to the epic-romance pattern'. Hume suggests that the play is 'closer to *comédie héroïque* than to tragedy'.[7] However, heroic comedy differs markedly from the kind of Restoration comedy we shall look at in the next chapter. Its elevated language is a far cry from the witty, ironic and satirical language of much Restoration comedy. As Nancy Maguire has shown in *Regicide and Restoration*, heroic drama is serious tragi-comedy, heavily influenced by the early Stuart court masque.

The generic indeterminacy of heroic drama is partly due to the fact that Dryden's sources are so wide-ranging. Critics have had much debate about the sources of heroic drama.[8] The sources which have been correctly identified include: French romances, particularly those of d'Urfé, the de Scudérys and La Calprenède, and Spanish romances such as Ginés Pérez de Hita's *Guerras Civiles de Granada*; epic, especially chivalric epics such as Tasso's *Gerusalemme Liberata* and Ariosto's *Orlando Furioso*; heroic poetry, particularly Homer's *Illiad*; the 'hero' plays of Marlowe, Shakespeare and Chapman; the tragi-comedies of Fletcher and other Caroline dramatists; the work of Sir John Suckling and Edmund Waller; the plays of Corneille; Caroline court masques; Italian opera, which also influenced Davenant's *The Siege of Rhodes*, itself a major source; a range of critical writing from Tasso's *Discourses on the Heroic Poem* to French neoclassical critical theory; the writings of Hobbes; and the religious literature of casuistry. Dryden also draws in *The Conquest of Granada* on Restoration precedent, including the work of Orrery (the pioneer of Restoration heroic drama) and Tuke, and of course his own earlier plays, *The Indian Queen* (with Sir Robert Howard), *The Indian Emperour* and *Tyrannick Love*. The result of this plethora of diverse sources is a mixed genre and a peculiar drama which, as we shall see, does contain tensions and contradictions which we cannot explain away but simply have to accept.

Heroic drama is a drama of splendid artifice. In *The Conquest of Granada* we find clashing armies giving battle on stage to the noise of drums and trumpets; superhuman bravery and extraordinary sacrifices for love; instant reversals of fortune and ghostly revelations. The scenery and spectacle was more than ordinarily magnificent: diarist John Evelyn describes set designer Robert Streeter's 'glorious scenes and perspectives'.[9] Here Dryden follows Davenant who, in a revival of *The Siege of Rhodes* in

1661, had introduced quick scene changes with sliding flats. Three erotic songs and the semi-operatic spectacle of a zambra dance also enliven the action of Dryden's play; and there is a 'breeches part', a favourite device for titillating the audience with the sight of an actress in men's clothes. Yet heroic drama is also highly intellectual and somewhat schematic: much of the dramatic tension is created through set-piece debates between the characters about rival philosophies, clashing courses of action or the competing claims of love and honour. It is vital to recognize that the truth in these debates, like the excitement, lies in the dialectic. Critics have gone astray through trying to attribute a privileged perspective to one party or another. Although we are sometimes encouraged to marvel at an example of extreme, larger-than-life villainy, more often the tension lies in the clash between viewpoints which are equally, or almost equally, compelling, and in the toll which this clash takes on the characters.

The Conquest of Granada consists of two parts of a full five acts each. It was performed by the King's Company at the Theatre Royal, Part I in December 1670, and Part II in January 1672. Both parts were published in 1672 with a Dedication to James, Duke of York, and the prefartory essay *Of Heroique Playes* in which Dryden responds to his critics and sets out his intentions. The conquest referred to in the title is actually a reconquest, as Ferdinand and Isabella restore rightful Christian rule to a kingdom torn apart by strife between the feuding Moorish factions, Zegrys and Abencerrages. The opening scene shows that the Moorish king, Boabdelin, is unable to quell the in-fighting. There are obvious allusions here to the state of England, torn apart by civil war and then redeemed by the providential restoration of Charles II in 1660. This is not to say that Dryden has written a political allegory, but that his work is animated by the concerns of his time. Dryden was to say in his preface to a later play, *Troilus and Cressida*, that the moral of *The Conquest of Granada*, drawn from Homer, was that 'Union preserves a Common-wealth, and discord destroys it'.[10]

The providentialist scheme emerges strongly at the end, but for much of the action is subordinate to the adventures of the larger-than-life hero, Almanzor. The first we hear of him, before anybody knows who he is, is in a bullfight: 'But what the stranger did was more than man' (Part I, I.i.48). This super-manliness is Almanzor's chief characteristic. Almanzor's name (though not his character) occurs in one of Dryden's sources, Georges de Scudéry's *Almahide*, and was a common one among Muslim princes, meaning 'victorious'; but the way in which the name was pronounced on stage would probably have been 'All man, sir'. This is strongly suggested by the title of a collections of tales published around the same time as the play, called *Al-Man-Sir or, Rhodomontados of the most Horrible Terrible and Invincible Captain Sr Frederick Fight-all*; and by the Duke of Buckingham's parody of the character in his satirical play *The Rehearsal* as 'Drawcansir', a reference to Almanzor's propensity for drawing his sword and fighting for whatever cause is current. We also learn that Almanzor is 'observ'd by all, himself observing none' (Part I, I.i.66). He is unreflective, a kind of elemental force to whom others react, but who himself defers to nobody. He is frequently described in imagery of storms and is 'like a Tempest that out rides the wind' (Part I, II.i.22). Appropriately enough, we later learn that he was born in a storm at sea. There is a duality about Almanzor. On the one hand, he is intensely physical and animalistic: his own 'bent forehead' as he confronts his enemies (Part I, II.i.53 and V.i.294) resembles that of the bull whom he slays in Act I (Part I, I.i.79); and he is also frequently likened to a lion. On the other hand, Almanzor is also almost supernatural: he is repeatedly associated with references to ghosts, perhaps suggesting that he transcends normal corporeal limits. He desires to 'come on equal terms to Heav'n' (Part II, III.i.216), and is referred to as 'Divine' (Part I, III.i.306) and 'a god' (Part II, V.iii.114).

Almanzor espouses the cause of the weaker side without understanding the reason for the conflict: 'I cannot stay to ask which cause is best; / But this is so to me because opprest' (Part I, I.i.127). This shows the combination of honourable decency and political naivety typical of the heroic hero. Almanzor is able to establish order where Boabdelin cannot because of his extraordinary courage and prowess in battle. It is important to recognize that these warrior qualities have positive aspects for Dryden. Almanzor has to learn lessons to change, but he arouses admiration right from the start:

> Vast is his Courage; boundless is his mind,
> Rough as a storm, and humorous as wind;[11]
> Honour's the onely Idol of his Eyes:
> The charms of Beauty like a pest he flies:
> And rais'd by Valour, from a birth unknown,
> Acknowledges no pow'r above his own. (Part I, I.i.253)

Dryden says in his essay *Of Heroique Playes* that he has modelled Almanzor on other 'men of great spirits' (p. 16) such as Homer's Achilles, Tasso's Rinaldo and Artaban in La Calprenède's *Cléopatre*. Critics have also traced antecedents in English Renaissance drama, for example Marlowe's

Tamburlaine, Shakespeare's Antony and Coriolanus, and Chapman's Bussy D'Ambois. None of these offers an exact parallel, though Bussy comes closest.[12] Tamburlaine is not in fact a good analogy, as another character in the play, the villain Lyndaraxa, is explicitly likened to him.[13] As we shall see, there are similarities but important fine distinctions between the heroic hero and the heroic villain. Almanzor is manly, but lacking in emotional subtly or moral refinement; in need of civilizing, but able to bring to a corrupt society a primitive vigour and simplicity which can purge and re-energize it.

Almanzor is generous towards both friends and enemies, and much given to setting his captives free. He is contemptuous of politics and reasons of state, being himself open-hearted and incapable of political statesmanship or any other kind of deception:

> But I am yet to learn the Statesman's art.
> My kindness and my hate unmask'd I wear;
> For friends to trust, and Enemies to fear.
> My heart's so plain,
> That men on every passing thought may look,
> Like fishes gliding in a Chrystal brook:
> When troubled most, it does the bottom show,
> 'Tis weedless all above; and rockless all below. (Part I, IV.i.40)

Almanzor's clear stream image offers others the facility to see their own reflection. His primitive integrity serves, in effect, as a 'mirror' for those in power, through which they might know themselves better.[14]

Almanzor has certain royal qualities and possesses a natural sovereignty: 'Without a Realm a Royalty he gains' (Part II, I.ii.88). This is shown by the fact that he is constantly helping people who cannot help themselves and suffering from their ingratitude. 'Ingratitude' was the charge royalists made against those who had rebelled against Charles I in the Civil War and those who criticized or opposed Charles II. Almanzor, however, bears a closer resemblance initially to James, Charles II's brother and heir (to become James II in 1685). This likeness is stressed in Dryden's Dedication to James, in which James is praised for Almanzor's qualities of bravery, honour and heroic ardour, and for sharing with Almanzor 'a frank and open Nature: an easiness to forgive his enemies; and to protect them in distress; and above all, an inviolable faith in his affection' (pp. 6–7). Both men are praised for their heroic capacity for true friendship, a quality which transcends other allegiances.

Almanzor's qualities emerge in the first and one of the most important set-piece debates in the play, which takes place in Act I in an atmosphere of urgency and tension. Condemned to death for his presumption by King Boabdelin, Almanzor retorts in the play's most famous speech:

> But whence hast thou the right to give me death?
> Obey'd as soveraign by thy Subjects be,
> But know, that I alone am King of me.
> I am as free as Nature first made man
> 'Ere the base Laws of Servitude began
> When wild in woods the noble Savage ran. (Part I, I.i.204)

There then follows a argument which brings in a range of Restoration ideas about nature, law and sovereignty. As Louis Teeter explains:

Almanzor's ... speech is an expression of the traditional juristic state of nature. The original condition of mankind according to this conception was an 'unnatural' creation made necessary by man's fall from his original virtue. The Stoic ethics, with its fusion of the conception of self-sufficiency and the doctrine of following nature, implied that the thoroughly rational, that is to say, thoroughly 'natural' man had no need of an 'artificial government'; he was outside of the legal and political relationships binding on his fallen brethren.[15]

Boabdelin responds that, by the law of nature, Almanzor is 'a common foe' who 'shou'd be hunted like a Beast of Prey'. This draws on the ideas of Hobbes:

Because the major part hath by consenting voices declared a sovereigne; he that dissented must now consent with the rest; that is, be contented to avow all the actions he shall do, or else justly be destroyed by the rest ... And whether he be of the congregation or not, and whether his consent be asked, or not, he must either submit to their decrees, or be left in the condition of war he was in before; wherein he might without injustice be destroyed by any man whatso-ever.[16]

Hobbes argued that, once a king was in power, he should be obeyed even if his rule was flawed. Almanzor, in contrast, argues: 'My laws are made but only for my sake, / No King against himself a Law can make' (Part I, I.i.214). In other words, he sees himself as a natural sovereign who makes his own laws. In helping the weaker side, he is also the guardian of natural justice:

> I saw th' opprest, and thought it did belong
> To a King's office to redress the wrong:
> I brought that Succour which thou oughtst to bring,
> And so, *in Nature*, am thy Subjects King. (Part I, I.i.218, my emphasis)

Almanzor's commitment to natural justice is stressed by the King's brother Abdalla who says that, in Africa, Almanzor 'to the juster cause the Conquest brought' (Part I, I.i.248). John M. Wallace calls Almanzor 'a great creature of natural law.'[17] The autocratic Boabdelin, on the other hand, is a breaker of oaths and a violator of the law of contract (Part I, I.i.316–19).

We also learn from Abdalla that Almanzor has been the victim of royal ingratitude in Africa, leading him to change sides. This is to be a recurring theme, as Almanzor changes sides repeatedly in response to the ingratitude of rulers for the services he has rendered them. This is in keeping with his natural law position, as natural law arguments stressed the duties of kings to help subjects.[18] The Hobbists in the play are the usurper Boabdelin and the self-centred villain, Lyndaraxa. Almanzor is no Hobbist, even though he was called one by Richard Leigh in 1673.[19] Leigh's intention was to discredit Dryden by accusing him of glorifying Hobbes: Hobbes's pragmatic case for 'de facto' royalism, according to which the monarch should be obeyed for reasons of public order and safety, was anathema to majority opinion in the Restoration which saw the King's power as God-given. Critics have disagreed about both Almanzor's and Dryden's attitude to Hobbes;[20] but it is important to realize the differences between Dryden's hero and the play's Hobbists. Almanzor is cast not so much in the mould of the brutish primitives of Hobbes's *Leviathan*, as in that of the nobles savages of the humanist Montaigne's essay 'Of Cannibals' who fight only to prove their valour and not for gain.

What is Dryden's own position on sovereignty? The truth lies somewhere in the play's dialectic. The politics of heroic drama are clearly royalist. Indeed, the creation of heroic drama was almost an act of state: Charles II had encouraged the Earl of Orrery to write such dramas on the French model, and Dryden, Charles's Historiographer Royal and Poet Laureate, had followed suit.[21] Dryden's notion of sovereignty, accordingly, seems to be a strong one, as can be seen in a passage which encapsulates one of his recurring themes: that the pursuit of passion rather than reason always leads to disaster.[22] Reason and sovereignty are associated in an exchange in which Abdelmelech tries to persuade Abdalla not to allow his infatuation for Lyndaraxa to overcome him. Abdalla rejects this appeal to reason because his reason is a 'Captive King', forced to bow to 'Rebels', the passions (Part I, III.i.62). Abdelmelech retorts:

> If Reason on his Subjects Triumph wait,
> An easie King deserves no better Fate. (Part I, III.i.66)

The thrust of the argument here rests upon the natural law concept that sovereignty should be strenuous, rather than resting on its rights.

In keeping with the idea of strong kingship, the class values of the play are hierarchical. Dryden speaks of his play in the Dedication to the king's brother, James Stuart, as a type of heroic poetry which 'excites to vertue the greatest men' (p. 3) and suggests that it takes a great man, James, to appreciate it. 'Great' in this context means upper-class: royal or aristocratic, powerful and important. This attitude finds reflection also in Dryden's notion of himself as a great man in relation to his audience, over whose minds he wants 'an absolute dominion' (*Of Heroique Playes*, 14). The play's hero, similarly, though he may espouse natural justice, is no egalitarian. He is 'one great Soul / Whose single force can multitudes control' (Part I, I.i.286), and he dismisses the common people with all the haughtiness of a natural sovereign:

> Hence you unthinking Crowd –
> Empire, thou poor and despicable thing,
> When such as these unmake, or make a King! (Part I, I.i.284)[23]

In his epilogue to Part II Dryden attacks his Renaissance predecessors essentially in class terms: Jonson, for example, is condemned for 'Mechanique', meaning plebeian, humour (p. 201). In his *Defence of the Epilogue, or, an Essay on the Dramatic Poetry of the Last Age*, appended to the published text, Dryden argues that the Renaissance dramatists suffered from 'want of Education and Learning' (p. 207), and criticizes Shakespeare for 'low expressions' (p. 213) and Jonson for meanness of thought and expression (pp. 213, 215). For all their merits, 'their wit was not that of Gentlemen, there was ever somewhat that was ill-bred and Clownish in it' (p. 215). The wit, language and conversation of his own times are superior, says Dryden, because they are more courtly. The King's exile in France has led to a beneficial civilizing influence on the drama. Heroic drama, then, is royalist and courtly drama.

The various ideas about sovereignty which Dryden's characters canvass had a particular urgency in the aftermath of the Cromwellian period and the restoration of the monarchy in 1660. Boabdelin, hanging on to power despite the Christian Ferdinand's superior title, is a Cromwellian figure. In an sharp exchange with the Spanish ambassador, the Duke of Arcos, Boabdelin appears as a Machiavellian, arguing that his own power is based on force, and that 'might makes right'. This associates him with Cromwell and his co-thinkers.[24] However, some complexity arises when, in Part II, Act I, scene ii, Boabdelin becomes an advocate of strong sovereignty. What are we to make of the Cromwellian speaker offering a royalist message?

Let us look more closely at the passage in question. Dryden's stated intention in *The Conquest of Granada*, cited above, is to stress the royalist theme that discord destroys a commonwealth, posing the need for strong kingship to quell faction and rebellion. The elaboration of this theme at the beginning of Part II bears more relevance to the situation in England in 1670/71 than to the action of the play. Abdalla's faction has stirred up 'the mad Peoples rage' (Part II, I.ii.22) in order to undermine Boabdelin's rule. Boabdelin's response alludes to current events in England:

> See what the many-headed Beast demands.
> Curst is the King whose Honour's in their hands.
> In Senates, either they too slowly grant,
> Or saucily refuse to aid my want:
> And when their Thrift has ruin'd me in Warr,
> They call their Insolence my want of care. (Part II, I.ii.29)

The reference here is clearly to Charles II's struggles with Parliament over the financing and conduct of the Second Dutch War, which had taken on a new urgency in the context of preparations for the Third Dutch War. A courtier responds with a typical royalist of aspersion upon leaders of the political opposition such as the Duke of Buckingham and the Earl of Shaftesbury: 'Curst be their Leaders who the Rage foment; / And vail with publick good their discontent' (35). Boabdelin asserts the need for strong sovereignty:

> But Kings who rule with limited Command
> Have Players Scepters put into their Hand.
> Pow'r has no ballance, one side still weighs down;
> And either hoysts the Common-wealth or Crown.
> And those who think to set the Skale more right,
> By various turnings but disturb the weight. (Part II, I.ii.49)

The strong message of respect for sovereignty here is combined with one of quietism: subjects should not try to interfere with the balance of power.[25]

Nothing in Dryden is ever simple, and this includes his politics. The fact that the Cromwellian Boabdelin is the speaker here alerts us to a disparity between the message and its advocate. This may subtly allude to a disjunction between theory and practice in Dryden's own society. For Boabdelin's faults, although they may reflect adversely on Cromwellian usurpers, have some have some relevance also to Charles II. This especially applies to Boabdelin's ingratitude and his breaking his word to his loyal servants. Charles had been accused of ingratitude towards the old cavaliers and failure to reward them ever since 1660 when he had been forced to make accommodations with many of those who had flourished under Cromwell.[26] In the late 1660s Charles began to lose the political confidence of the nation, following plague, fire, soaring taxes, misconduct of the Second Dutch War and fraternization with the Catholic Louis XIV of France.[27] At the time when Dryden was praising Charles for his courtliness in the *Defence of the Epilogue*, Charles was pushing England into renewed war with Holland at Louis XIV's behest. The debate in Part II, I.ii appears to have a royalist moral: 'When People tugg for Freedom, Kings for Pow'r. / Both sink beneath some foreign Conquerour' (Part II, I.ii.55). However, the message is actually ambiguous. Charles might have argued that the parliamentary opposition was laying the nation open to the Dutch threat, but the opposition could counter with equal if not greater plausibility that the King was courting the French menace. As for Boabdelin's tendency to break his promises, the need for a monarch to keep faith with his subjects became a standard theme in opposition pamphlets and polemics, as Charles lost Parliament's trust with a Declaration of Indulgence, a concession to Catholics made following a secret agreement with Louis. So Boabdelin's faults are uncomfortably close to home. Dryden may be a royalist but he is by no means uncritical of his own monarch.

A different political complication arises from the character of Almanzor, who, as I have already noted, was explicitly likened by Dryden to the King's brother and heir James. Dedicating a play to James in 1672 was a bold move. By the summer of 1672 James's Catholicism was more or less common knowledge. In the context of European religious war and French Catholic expansionism, the Catholicism of the heir to the throne caused a furore culminating in the Exclusion Crisis, 1678–83, so-called because the Whig opposition tried to exclude James from the succession to the throne. Eventually, of course, it culminated in James's removal from the throne and the revolution of 1688.[28]

To make James a hero, then, is a bold, royalist move. However, Dryden does not present his patron uncritically. The faults which Almanzor and James share are only too glaring on stage: arrogance, impetuosity, self-centredness and a propensity for changing sides. In relation to the latter, James had fought with the Spanish against England in the interregnum, and his Catholicism aroused fears that he would side with Catholic France against his Protestant countrymen. Almanzor's complete lack of patriotism and acknowledgement only of the ties of heroic friendship thus has an unfortunate resonance in relation to fears that James would place the interests of his foreign Catholic friends before those of his country. Moreover, the spectacle of Almanzor refusing to obey the sovereign and resorting to arms in the interests of a rival cause raised the spectre of James's unreliability: Parliament discussed in the 1670s the possibility that James might resort to arms if provoked by opposition. A similar resonance arises from the fact that the outbreak of popular discontent at the beginning of Part II is actually instigated not by opposition leaders but by a character who, like James, is the present king's brother. Almanzor also shares the political naivety which made James so unpopular, especially after he came to the throne. We see this for example in Part I, Act III, when Almanzor almost causes the death of the virtuous Ozmyn, his prisoner, by giving him into the care of his arch-enemy. In the drama of the Exclusion Crisis, the depiction of royal faults similar to those of Charles and James was to acquire a significant oppositional resonance, as I have discussed fully in my *Restoration Theatre and Crisis*. *The Conquest of Granada* is a more optimistically royalist text which papers over the ideological cracks; but there is no denying that the cracks are there.

The contradictions in Almanzor, his generosity and self-centredness, energy and excess, emerge in contrast with two sets of characters, one set notable for outstanding and exemplary virtue, and the other for rampant ambition and vice. Dryden has two main sources for the exemplary characters Ozmyn and Benzayda: cavalier drama, and the French tradition of *préciosité*, a movement for refining literature and manners, based upon noble ideals of love and honour and expressed in the romances of such writers as d'Urfé, the de Scudérys and La Calprenède. Ozmyn and Benzayda are in some ways the precursors of the sentimental characters who predominate on the eighteenth-century stage; although it is important to remember that they are also 'heroic' characters operating in the public sphere, unlike their more domestic and sentimental eighteenth-century descendants. The tone of the scenes in which they appear is elevated and also full of pathos and sentimentality. Given into the custody of his enemy Selin, Ozmyn shows his noble qualities: 'But, when true Courage is of force bereft, / Patience, the noblest Fortitude is left' (Part I, III.i.292). This stoicism in the face of death leads Selin's daughter Benzayda to fall in love with him. It is a quality she associates with true manliness: 'His manly suffering my esteem did move; / That bred Compassion; and Compassion,

Love' (Part I, V.i.75). This definition of manliness is different to the rugged assertiveness and physical toughness associated with Almanzor's 'manly pride' (Part I, V.i.205). Once again, Dryden offers a dialectic between two competing ideas and gives his audience something to think about. The response of his audience varied. Mrs Evelyn, wife of the diarist John, said of the play: 'the most refined romance I ever read is not to compare with it: love is made so pure, and valor so nice, that one would imagine it designed for an Utopia rather then our stage'.[29] Dryden's opponent Buckingham was less impressed and parodied Dryden's double depiction of masculinity in *The Rehearsal*, portraying the rugged hero in the ludicrous Drawcansir and the sentimental hero in over-scrupulous Prince Prettyman. Dryden's own view in *Of Heroique Playes* was that he was 'more in love with' the rugged type than the French-style 'patterns of exact vertue' (16); though in the end, as we shall see, Almanzor does have to learn to temper the worst excesses of his ferocity.

Both lovers are exemplary, but Benzayda perhaps has slightly the moral edge. She is a natural Christian, commending herself to Providence rather than Fortune (Part I, V.i.168), and quick to seize the opportunity of conversion at the end (Part II, V.iii.302). Benzayda is sentimental, but she also shows an interesting toughness. Just as Ozmyn shows a tender and in some sense a feminized masculinity, the feminine Benzayda is capable of showing manly qualities: 'What though my Limbs a Womans weakness show? / I have a Soul as Masculine as you' (Part II, III.ii.121). In Part II, IV.i, she dresses as a man to defend Ozmyn from his own father's wrath, and wins the old man over: '*Benzayda*, 'twas your Vertue vanquish'd me: / That, could alone surmount my Cruelty' (Part II, IV.i.134). Female cross-dressing has many functions in the drama, arousing a range of responses from titillation to admiration to horror. Benzayda's case is a positive example of woman's ability to dress and act as well as, if not better than, any man.

Benzayda's 'noble pity' (Part I, IV.ii.254) in turn arouses Ozmyn's love for her. The lovers undergo cruel persecution at the hands of both their fathers. Their attitude to their fathers is that parental cruelty abrogates the duty of obedience, but they will try to show filial piety anyway. Thus Benzayda, ordered by her father to kill Ozmyn, exclaims:

> When Parents their Commands unjustly lay
> Children are priviledg'd to disobey.
> Yet from that breach of duty I am clear,
> Since I submit the penalty to bear.

> To dye or kill you is th'alternative;
> Rather than take your life, I will not live. (Part I, IV.ii.283).

In the next Act, Ozmyn expresses a similarly Lockean view of parental obligation: 'Nature that bids us Parents to obey, / Bids parents their commands by Reason weigh' (Part I, V.i.122). This sits a little oddly with the self-sacrificing nobility of the chivalric code, which Ozmyn neatly summarizes: My duty to my life I will prefer; / But life and duty must give place to her' (Part II, IV.i.68). The lovers outdo one another in self-sacrificing conduct, each frequently offering to die if it will help the other or even the other's cruel parent. Ultimately, their nobility, demonstrated in a series of melodramatic and implausible episodes, leads to first one father then the other being won over. The Ozmyn and Benzayda plot thus exemplifies in the realm of the family the moral which Dryden drew in relation to the state: discord destroys the commonwealth while union preserves it. The tension between Lockean notions of children's liberties and royalist and chivalric ideas of their obligations reflects in the family sphere the political contradicitions discussed above in relation to the play's politics;[30] but the lovers balance all their obligations and rise above contradictory pressures by a willingness to die which moves all beholders. In later tragedy, as we shall see, the self-annihilation of virtuous characters is powerless to persuade corrupt authority, engendering a sense of political darkness and complexity. Once again, we see heroic drama canvassing but containing political, sexual and ideological contradictions.

At the opposite pole to Ozmyn and Benzayda are Lyndaraxa and her brother Zulema. Lyndaraxa proclaims: 'Yes; I avow th'ambition of my Soul, / To be that one, to live without controul' (Part I, II.i.147). The noise of war excites her: 'Me thinks it is a noble, sprightly Sound' (Part I, III.i.252). She thinks killing is a 'noble sport' (Part I, III.i.271). She thinks she can master or stand in for Fortune (Part I, III.i.265). Thus far she seems similar to Almanzor. However, there are several important differences. First, Lyndaraxa is ambitious for absolute sovereignty. She is a tyrant to her 'suff'ring Subjects' (Part II, IV.ii.67), and also to her lovers, one of whom tells her as he falls under her spell, 'My Monarchy must end; and yours begin' (Part I, II.ii.84). Almanzor, in contrast, acknowledges his mistress's sovereignty: 'Thus I obey your absolute command' (Part II, III.i.142). More broadly, Almanzor's appetite is for honour and glory, not for power for himself. He despises worldly wealth and courtly goals of status and preferment, telling the King he has served, 'I think myself above reward' (Part I, V.i.255). The futility of Lyndaraxa's craving for rule emerges as she tries to domineer over Fate when she is dying: 'Tell her I am a Queen; – but 'tis too late; / Dying, I charge Rebellion on my fate' (Part II, V.iii.261). A second and associated difference concerns pride. Lyndaraxa is arrogant: 'For I am sure I'm never in the wrong' (Part I, IV.ii.200). Almanzor is not: 'If I am proud, 'tis onely to my Foes; / Rough but to such who Vertue would oppose' (Part II, III.iii.9).

Third, whereas Almanzor is incapable of deception, Lyndaraxa is a consummate politician, mistress of dissimulation in the pursuit of her ambition. She is rhetorically skilful and even manipulates the discourse of women's weakness to her own advantage: playing for time until she sees which way the wind blows, she tells her lover she cannot promise fidelity because:

> I know not what my future thoughts will be:
> Poor womens thoughts are all *Extempore*. (Part I, IV.ii.179)

Fourth, whereas Almanzor can fall in love and undergo its civilizing influence, Lyndaraxa keeps firm control of her passions. She calculatingly determines to give herself to which ever of her suitors can gain and hold on to the crown: 'I will be constant yet, if Fortune can; / I love the King: let her but name the Man' (Part I, IV.ii.7). She does, however, inspire destructive passion in others, leading Abdalla to rebel against his own brother and king to become her 'Scepter'd Slave' (Part I, IV.ii.151), and Abdelmelech gradually to degenerate. Quite early on, Abdelmelech's passion leads him away from loyalty: 'For if a Prince Courts her whom I adore, / He is my Rival, and a Prince no more' (Part I, III.i.136). He a good man, capable of heroic actions, drawn in against his better nature: 'I know you false, yet in your snares I fall' (Part I, IV.ii.104). The 'Enchantress' Lyndaraxa (Part II, II.ii.9) bewitches her lovers to their downfall, in sharp contrast to Almanzor who arouses admiration and has, in general, a good effect on people.

Fifth, whereas Almanzor makes use of natural law arguments, Lyndaraxa is both Hobbist and Machiavellian. She resembles Boabdelin in her aspirations to absolute sovereignty, and also in being 'ingrateful' for others' service (Part I, V.i.49, 67). Lyndaraxa betrays the defeated Abdalla, who has lost his crown because 'A King is he whom fortune still does bless: / He is a King, who does a Crown possess' (Part I, V.i.43). This resembles the ideas of Hobbes as contemporaries understood them. Hobbes does not actually say so, but logical conclusion of his views on strong government is that obedience is owed to whatever person or party is able to seize power, a view for which he was reviled, as it appears to justify usurpers

such as Cromwell. Lyndaraxa also resembles the Machiavellian villains of
Renaissance drama who believe that power is based on force. Her brother
Zulema is also a Machiavellian who argues that statesmen and lovers alike
have no use for virtue (Part I, II.i.212), and that the brave man 'makes his
fate according to his mind' and can conquer Fortune (Part I, II.i.231).
These are crude versions of Machiavelli's arguments in *The Prince* which
had been common on the Renaissance stage in the mouths of ambitious
villains.[31] When Lyndaraxa curses 'dull Religion' which 'teaches us con-
tent' (Part II, III.ii.32), Dryden might be explicitly recalling the prologue
to Marlowe's *The Jew of Malta*, spoken by Machiavelli and caricaturing
the argument of *The Prince*: 'I count religion but a childish toy'.[32]
Lyndaraxa here resembles impious characters such as Barabas in The *Jew
of Malta* or D'Amville in Tourneur's *The Atheist's Tragedy*.

   The heroine Almahide is as full of suffering sensitivity as Lyndaraxa is
lacking in it. The noise of battle excites Lyndaraxa, but for Almahide, 'The
noise, my Soul does through my Sences wound' (Part I, III.i.251). Yet, like
her brother Ozmyn, she also knows how to be strong when she feels
herself on firm moral ground. At the end of Part I Almahide is ordered to
marry Boabdelin to whom she is promised, and who has just ordered
Almanzor's execution, Almahide admits her love for Almanzor publicly,
and defies both father and King. Her defiance is expressed in a 'feminine'
way which is very different from the arrogance of Lyndaraxa:

> My soul is soft, which you may gently lay
> In your loose palm; but when 'tis prest to stay,
> Like water it deludes your grasp, and slips away (Part I, V.i.332).

She agrees to marry Boabdelin only to spare Almanzor's life. Like Ozmym
and Benzayda, Almahide frequently offers to die in order to resolve
conflicts between love and duty, and actually tries to commit suicide.

   However, Almahide's is a more conflicted nature than that of the
précieuse characters.[33] She is more psychologically complex: 'I scarcely
understand my own intent' (Part II, I.ii.224). Almahide strives for virtue
but her desires cannot be entirely repressed. The Zambra dance she has
prepared 'In hope soft pleasures may your minds unite' (Part I, I.i.362) is
preceded by an erotic song in which a lover dreams that his mistress grants
him with her eyes the sexual fulfilment she denies him with her words
(Part I, III.i.198). The fact that the admission of passion is non-verbal and
within a dream shows how deep within the subconscious it lies. In the realm
of everyday discourse, female passion must be repressed. A grotesque

echo of the song's theme of the woman secretly granting what her words deny occurs in Part II, II.ii, when Lyndaraxa confronts Abdelmelech, whom she has betrayed for Abdalla. Abdelmelech has captured her fort, but she persuades him that he has only taken what she wanted to grant all along:

> This force you us'd my Maiden blush will save;
> You seem'd to take what secretly I gave. (Part II, II.ii.51)

Such partial resemblances have led some critics to see Lyndaraxa as the virtuous Almahide's passionate alter-ego.[34] However, Dryden's is a drama of fine distinctions, and it is important to notice the differences. Lyndaraxa's equation of military manoeuvres in which her subjects have died to love-ploys is callous and grotesque. She shows the effrontery of super-villains such as Richard III, seduces her lovers in spite of their full knowledge of her perfidy and their own folly, and arouses astonishment in the audience.

Almahide arouses a very different response, both in her lover and in the audience. Once she has married Boabdelin, Almahide strains every nerve to act and to feel like a faithful wife: 'But know, that when my person I resign'd, / I was too noble not to give my mind' (Part II, I.ii.148). She desires Almanzor in private, but talks the language of love to her husband in public. Some critics have found this puzzling and even distasteful, but we have to judge Almahide by seventeenth-century standards. It would be anachronistic to suggest that she should be true to her passions rather than to her ideals. Similarly, Almahide's struggle between desire and duty is sometimes represented as a struggle between private and public roles; but it is important to recognize that the idea of a private sphere in which domestic desires take priority over public obligations is really an eighteenth-century one. It is a notion which we find in its infancy in the Restoration, beginning to emerge in Dryden's *Aureng-Zebe*, which followed *The Conquest of Granada*, and in domestic tragedies such as Otway's *The Orphan*. In seventeenth-century terms Almahide is praiseworthy when she says, 'My Heart's not mine; but all my actions are' (Part II, I.ii.210). Dryden depicts a woman engaged in a noble struggle between outward conformity to wifely duty and the inward temptations of an impossible love. Even Almanzor admires her stand of marital constancy at some level. Almahide's loyalty to her husband also mirrors in the family the play's royalism in politics, a point emphasized by the fact that her husband is literally the sovereign. Her non-resistance to Boabdelin's increasingly oppressive conduct reflects the quietism in the political sphere discussed above.

Yet the struggle for obedience is not without its cost. Almahide is no mere two-dimensional pattern-card of virtue. She is also human, and makes mistakes. In Part II she gives Almanzor her scarf as a reward for agreeing to defend Boabdelin against the Spaniards. Almost immediately she realizes that the gift will inflame Boabdelin's jealousy: 'I wish it were not done' (Part II, III.i. 7). Moreover, her determination to act the part of a loving wife, though noble, may be ill-advised. Boabdelin is not deceived: 'O goodness counterfeited to the life! / O the well acted vertue of a wife' (Part II, III.i.78). Though her motives are pure and he is twisted by jealousy, his words state no more than the plain truth. The moment at which Almahide tries to commit suicide offers a further instance of interesting psychological conflict. Unlike Ozmyn and Benzayda, who make rather facile offers to die whenever honour seems to demand it, Almahide's attempted suicide (prevented by Almanzor) represents a more tormented attempt to escape from the ravages of her own desires: 'You've mov'd my heart, so much, I can deny / No more; but know, *Almanzor*, I can dye' (Part II, IV.iii.265). She goes on to complicate matters further after the villains' plots cause doubts of her chastity and she is put on trial for her life. Vindicated by her champions in combat, and pronounced free, she tells Boabdelin she will not sleep with him any more because he has doubted her in spite of her 'Love so pure and true' (Part II, V.ii.151). This is not disingenuous: her love was pure and true, all the more so because it went against her inclinations. However, she also inflames Boabdelin's jealousy by telling Almanzor publicly that she needs a word with him in private. The jealousy is causeless because all she wants to do in private is to renounce Almanzor also. This all seems rather clumsy and tactless, though of course it could be argued that she is giving Boabdelin an opportunity to show his faith in her, and to make good his previous unjustified doubts.

Further tensions arise in the treatment of love in which Almanzor is a novice. The Spanish Queen Isabella propounds a philosophy of chivalric love on the model of the French romances:

> Love's a Heroique Passion which can find
> No room in any base degenerate mind:
> It kindles all the Soul with Honours Fire,
> To make the Lover worthy his desire. (Part II, I.i.143)

In the final battle between Moors and Spaniards at the end of Part II, Isabella and Ferdinand share a vision of warriors on both sides inspired by love, 'Each youth encourag'd by his Ladies sight' (Part II, V.iii.135). This perspective makes the royal couple particularly receptive to Ozmyn and Benzayda, and inclined to promote the interests of Almanzor and Almahide as a couple at the end. However, nothing in Dryden is ever quite so simple. The same attitude makes Ferdinand blind to Lyndaraxa's treachery. Because she is a woman, he praises her in chivalric terms and naively confers upon her the crown of Granada, a disastrous move, from the consequences of which he is rescued only by accident.

A similar duality emerges in relation to women's beauty. In Part I, Act III, the maid Esperanza tells Almahide to be 'heroic' in beauty:

> Madam, you must not to Despair give place;
> Heav'n never meant misfortune to that Face.
> Suppose there were no justice in your cause,
> Beauty's a Bribe that gives her Judges Laws.
> … Fate fears her Succor like an Alms to give:
> And would, you, God-like from your self should live. (Part I, III.i.296)

Here beauty, creating its own justice and its own fate, is on a par with Almanzor's heroic prowess in battle. Yet this is a dangerous philosophy, and not one which Almahide ever espouses. 'Heroic beauty' can be terribly destructive, as when Lyndaraxa subjugates Abdalla: 'I see I must become more absolute' (Part I, IV.ii.191). His subordination at this moment leads him to hand Lyndaraxa the keys of his castle, and so sets in motion a train of events which will culminate in his death. Lyndaraxa's other lover Abdelmelech explains the obsessive nature of this kind of love at the end, after he has stabbed and fatally wounded both Lyndaraxa and himself: 'Forgive a love, excus'd by its excess, / Which, had it not been cruel, had been less' (Part II, V.iii.250).

Almanzor's first experience of love at first seems equally destructive. Love seems to undermine and 'unman' him:

> Armes, and the dusty field I less admire;
> And soften strangely in some new desire.
> Honour burns in me, not so fiercely bright;
> But pale, as fires when master'd by the light. (Part I, III.i.330)

He is seized by a 'Lethargy of Love' (337). Dryden expresses the view in the preface to *Troilus and Cressida* that love is effeminizing and less conducive to virtue than friendship: 'Friendship is both a virtue, and a Passion essentially; love is a passion only in its nature, and is not a virtue but by Accident; good nature makes friendship; but effeminacy Love.'[35] As we shall see, in the play Paris is unequivocally condemned for putting love before his country, and the privileged perspective seems assertively masculinist and places heroic friendship before love. This strongly suggests that falling in love is to be viewed as an emasculation of Almanzor, and a diversion from his heroic purpose. We do indeed find the privileging of the male bond in *The Conquest of Granada*, for example when one of Lyndaraxa's lovers kills the other, then reviles *her* for her role in the dead man's destruction (Part II, IV.ii.65).

However, once again, Dryden sees both sides of the issue. In the end love is a beneficial and civilizing influence upon Almanzor. When he learns that Almahide is promised to Boabdelin, and begins, clumsily, to struggle with notions of right and wrong, Almanzor also begins to accept his own limits and to realize that he cannot control time or Fate (Part I, III.i.406). Almanzor's is 'an untaught first love. / Yet rude, unfashion'd truth it does express' (Part I, III.i.418). There is a crucial difference between Almanzor's love and the infatuation which grips Lyndaraxa's lovers against their better nature. Almanzor's love may fall outside social convention in that he loves another man's fiancée, but his good instincts draw him towards a virtuous woman. He later shows himself impervious to Lyndaraxa's charm. Moreover, whereas Lyndaraxa's lovers degenerate, love for Almahide brings out the best in Almanzor, spurring him on to greater and more self-denying heroism. We can see the difference between Almanzor's love and crude passion in an exchange he has with Zulema who also wants Almahide. Abdalla grants Almahide to Almanzor as a captive of war. He instantly sets her free: 'I dare be wretched not to make her so' (Part I, III.i.453). This chivalry is dismissed by Zulema as romantic:

> But, Sir, I love not your Romantique way.
> Dream on; enjoy her Soul; and set that free;
> I'me pleas'd her person should be left for me (Part I, III.i. 488)

This is one of many moments in the play when Dryden draws attention to a fine distinction, in this case between healthy and unhealthy desire.

Almanzor's natural goodness gives him an instinctive sense of the need for greater refinement; and he says also, in an image drawn from alchemy, that refinement will come from a natural progression from his present raging desire to a purer love: 'This raging fire which through the Mass does move, / Shall purge my dross and shall refine my Love' (Part I, III.i.423).

Almanzor's actions in Part II, as he defends his rival Boabdelin at Almahide's request, even though he knows she will not requite his love, prove Queen Isabella's maxim that love 'kindles all the Soul with Honours Fire, / To make the Lover worthy his desire' (Part II, I.i.143). When Lyndaraxa tries to attract him in Part II, III.iii, Almanzor underscores the difference between them by telling her, 'Your Love is not refin'd to that degree' (Part II, III.iii.123). Almanzor is tested by Lyndaraxa's attempted seduction and emerges triumphant: 'My Love's my Soul; and that from Fate is free; / 'Tis that unchang'd; and deathless part of me' (Part II, III.iii. 174). Another test comes when the villains' plots cause Almanzor to doubt Almahide's chastity. He vows to defend her in trial by combat 'Not now for Love; but for my Honour's sake' (Part II, V.i.10). His doubt of Almahide is a flaw, though a natural and human one in the circumstances, but the point is that his honour and heroism prompt him to do the right thing anyway.

An interesting twist to the shifting notions of manhood in the play occurs when, under the influence of love, Almanzor begins to get in touch with his feminine side: 'If I some fierceness from a Father drew, / A Mothers Milk gives me some softness too' (Part II, III.iii.11). However, it would be misleading to suggest that the play is structured around the idea of the manly man tamed by the love of a good woman, or that we simply see Almanzor progress towards the superior Almahide. It is also necessary for Almahide to make some changes, and to become more like a man. In the end there has to be a compromise between Almanzor's excessive vigour and spontaneity and Almahide's over-scrupulous and repressive virtue. Almahide's speech of despair at the end of Part I reveals (only half-intentionally, or perhaps sarcastically) the problems of each extreme:

> How blest was I before this fatal day!
> When all I knew of love, was to obey!
> 'Twas life becalm'd; without a gentle breath;
> Though Not so cold, yet motionless as death:
> A heavy quiet state: but love all strife,
> All rapid, is the Hurrican of life. (Part I, V.i.367)

Ultimately, firmness must be allied with softness in a state somewhere in between the tempest or hurricane and a dead calm. The truth is in the dialectic, not in any one character. Moreover, the characters' views change and no character should be judged on any one statement or answer. In Almanzor's encounters with Almahide Dryden's aim seems to be to create tense and poignant dramatic situations in which both lovers suffer. Critical interpretations of the play have ranged between two extremes: Almahide's superior virtue and/or Almanzor's male oppression of her; and Almahide's frigidity and folly and/or the bankruptcy of her Platonic code of love. However, in every scene in which they are together, both have a legitimate point of view. In Part II, V.iii, for example, Almanzor is right to say that he does not deserve to be banished from Almahide's vicinity, as he has done nothing wrong; but she is right to say that his continued presence will threaten her good name, especially since she has just renounced her husband's bed. The dramatic tensions arises precisely from the conflict of two legitimate points of view. Dryden is concerned here not to insist upon one privileged definition of virtue but to show that heroic ideals are problematic and hard to live up to, and to arouse admiration and pity for flawed and frail human beings who are nevertheless making the attempt.

Whereas many of the opposing ideas and philosophies in the play are simply left as oppositions with no attempt at resolution, the love dialectic is partially resolved, or at least worked through to some kind of new state of awareness. The lovers are brought together at the end, though only at the insistence of the *dea ex machina*, Queen Isabella; and only to the point of betrothal, as Almahide insists on mourning Boabdelin's death for a year before she and Almanzor can marry. There is therefore a provisionality about the ending which constitutes only partial closure. This is not the same, however, as no move towards closure at all. It is important to remember, moreover, that Almahide's demurral at the end is partly a matter of form: there was no acceptable discourse of desire for Restoration women. Her modest reluctance and insistence on observing the proprieties is an invitation to Almanzor's rhetorical conquest and to Queen Isabella's intervention.

Insight in *The Conquest of Granada*, then, is achieved through dialectic, and closure or truth is ever only partial. This is reflected in the fact that there is a tension between Providentialism and provisionality in the play. That there is a Providentialist schema is unquestionable. This is brought out using sensational devices and supernatural effects. First, Almanzor feels a natural affinity with the Spanish Duke of Arcos (later to be revealed as his father), and a sense of sadness and foreboding at being his foe (Part II, II.iii). Then in Part II, IV.iii, the ghost of Almanzor's mother appears to tell him that he was born a Christian and that the full secret of his birth will be revealed if he avoids 'Crimes of lawless Love' (Part II, IV.iii.132).[36] His response is defiant: 'He who dares love; and for that love must dy, / And, knowing this, dares yet love on, am I' (Part II,

IV.iii.157). This defiance sets in motion a potentially disastrous chain of events. Yet in his defence of Almahide's honour, despite his doubts of her chastity, he acts as the instrument of justice and of Providence. The first time the word 'Justice' appears thus capitalized is at the moment when Almahide becomes aware of the Christian God and commends herself to him: 'Let me thy godhead in thy succour see: / So shall thy Justice in my safety shine, / And all my dayes, which thou shalt add, be thine' (Part II, V.ii.18). Boabdelin reinforces the point: 'And may just Heav'n assist the juster side' (24). Of course Almanzor wins, though not before he and his partner Ozmyn are both wounded as a result of Lyndaraxa's treachery. The moral is pronounced by Abdelmelech: 'Heav'n thou art just!' (88). In the climactic battle between Moors and Spaniards, the ghost's 'sacred voice' (Part II, V.iii.204) stops Almanzor just in time from killing his father, the Duke of Arcos. Meanwhile, in a moment of pure melodrama, Arcos has recognized his son by a heart-shaped birthmark, and by a ruby cross which Almanzor has worn since birth, tied round his arm with his mother's bracelets. These two signs are of course symbolic of Almanzor's brave heart and his unconscious Christianity. It is now revealed that Almanzor is not only of Christian birth but royal;[37] and, moreover, the child of a heroic love: his father was exiled for secretly marrying the sister of the old king, Ferdinand's father. Thus we see the working out of a divine plan. The other aspect of Providentialism is poetic justice. We see this, for example, as Lyndaraxa meets her end and the onlookers moralize:

Selin.   She's dead and here her proud ambition ends.
Abenamar. Such fortune still, such black designs attends. (Part II, V.iii.266)

Conversely, Almahide recognizes that Heaven has vindicated her own just cause, and vows to become a Christian (Part II, V.iii.296).

The Providentialist schema in *The Conquest of Granada* represents a striking energy and optimism on Dryden's part in overcoming doubts and contradictions. We can see this in the way Lyndaraxa's treachery serves the ends of good. Lyndaraxa is only banished by Boabdelin, not imprisoned, so she is able to work further mischief by betraying Granada to the Spanish. She apostrophizes him: 'Thou shou'dst have punish'd more or not at all' (Part II, V.ii.101). In political terms, Boabdelin's fatal clemency recalls that of Charles II: according to royalists he had been much too merciful to parliamentarians and Cromwellians in 1660, with the result that a political opposition was growing up around figures such as the Earl of Shaftesbury. The notion of Charles's fatal mercy was to become central in royalist propaganda. It was a way of appearing to praise Charles, but also of encouraging him to be firmer with 'rebels'. In *The Conquest of Granada*, however, it is accepted and turned to good account, as it serves the ultimate purpose of Providence by ensuring a Christian victory. As I noted above, heroic drama's optimism papers over ideological cracks in a way which becomes impossible in later tragedies of the Exclusion Crisis period, such as Otway's *Venice Preserv'd* or Dryden's own bleak *Oedipus*, written with Nathaniel Lee in 1678.[38]

However, there are discordant notes.[39] One of these emerges, ironically, in the very statement of Christian victory with which Almanzor closes the play:

> The toyles of war shall help to wear each day;
> And dreams of love shall drive my nights away.
> Our Banners to th'*Alhambra*'s turrets bear;
> Then, wave our Conqu'ring Crosses in the Aire;
> And Cry, with showts of Triumph; Live and raign,
> Great *Ferdinand* and *Isabel* of *Spain*. (Part II, V.iii.343)

This seems to offer a satisfactory yoking of Almanzor's formerly clashing impulses to war and love, under the banner of a Christian purpose. However, the fact that he will spend the year of waiting for Almahide in pursuing and killing Moors on Ferdinand's behalf seems rather vindictive. These are his former countrymen. He has changed sides yet again. Moreover, Almanzor's religious views are undeveloped. Earlier in Part II he cursed the Gods: 'You sit in State; and make our pains your sport' (Part II,III.iii.188). Now he has embraced a Christian triumphalism which seems rather crude. Spiritual conversion is to be left to the women. Almanzor's injunction to wave 'Conqu'ring Crosses', addressed presumably to the fighting men present, underlines the extent to which, for the men in the play, Ferdinand's triumph is based on force rather than the Christian spirit.

A further discordant note concerns sex, and specifically the problematic resonances of libertinism.[40] As mentioned in the introduction, the libertinism of the Stuart brothers was a problem for many of their subjects. In Part II Almanzor speaks of the jealous husband Boabdelin in exactly the terms which libertines in comedies use in speaking of the wealthy husbands of young, pretty women whom they wish to seduce: 'Why is this Miser doom'd to all this store: / He who has all and yet believes he's poor?' / ... Dull husbands have no right to jealousie: / If that's allow'd, it must in Lovers be' (Part II, III.i.86, 104). In Part II, IV. iii Almanzor urges

Almahide to 'Live but to night' (231) and to subordinate virtue to pleasure: 'Praise is the play of Heav'n for doing good; / But Loves the best return for flesh and blood' (263). Here he seems to resemble Lyndaraxa when she tried unavailingly to seduce him:

> There's no such thing as Constancy you call:
> Faith ties not Hearts; 'tis Inclination all.
> Some Wit deform'd or Beauty much decay'd,
> First, constancy in Love, a Vertue made. (Part II, III.iii.162)

However, Almanzor cannot sustain his libertine posture in the face of Almahide's suicide attempt: 'Deny me; hate me; (both are just) but live! / Your Vertue I will ne'r disturb again' (271). I noted above the subtle but important difference between Almanzor in this scene and Zulema who tries to rape Almahide and joins his sister in slandering her reputation by accusing her of an affair with Abdelmelech, so that she is put on trial for her life. Almanzor is guilty of a resurgence of libertine behaviour later in the scene, when he clutches Almahide's hand and kisses it repeatedly by force. However, Zulema's attempted rape again serves as a point of contrast to stop us judging Almanzor too harshly.[41] Soon after the hand-kissing the jealous Boabdelin enters, intending to kill both Almanzor and Almahide. Almanzor's first thought is for Almahide's safety. This is quickly followed by news of the Spanish incursion, and by Almanzor's superhuman nobility of character, as he swears once again to defend his rival, and to obey Almahide's instruction: 'Now brave *Almanzor*, be a god again; / Above our Crimes, and your own passions reign' (Part II, V.iii.114). A libertine would not wish to regulate or be able to subdue his passions.

Dryden sustains the elevated language and high moral tone of his play's heroic exchanges in the face of a recognition of the ease with which appetitive libertinism can break through. Mrs Evelyn, quoted above, admired this effort: 'I do not quarrell with the poet, but admire one borne in the decline of morality should be able to feigne such exact virtue: and as poetick fiction has been instructive in former ages, I wish this the same event in ours.'[42] Others, as we shall see, were more scathing. Dryden's own prologues and epilogues, rather disconcertingly, draw ironic attention to the disparity between the lofty values of heroic drama and 'the decline of morality'. The tone of the prologues and epilogues is not elevated, but witty and bawdy. The prologue to Part I was probably spoken by Nell Gwyn, who played Almahide. This casting was in itself somewhat ironic: the actress who played the part of the ultra-virtuous heroine had had her first illegitimate child by Charles II in May 1670, only six months before the play opened, a fact referred to in the epilogue to Part I. A similar irony occurs in the casting of Dryden's own mistress, Anne Reeve, as Esperanza, who advises Almahide to convert to Christianity. The first prologue draws upon the debunking role of the comic actor to satirize French fashions and farce, and begins a series of sexual metaphors which run through the other prologues and epilogues. Comic actors are 'Like a young Girl, who better things has known, / Beneath their Poets Impotence they groan' (p. 19). The impotent poet also occurs in the epilogue to Part I, spoken ironically by the virile Charles Hart, who played Almanzor:

> But elder wits are like old Lovers curst;
> Who, when the vigor of their youth is spent,
> Still grow more fond as they grow impotent. (p. 99)

The prologue to Part II begins by likening the long-awaited continuation of the play to a masked woman in the pit who keeps the audience guessing about her identity and morals. In a metaphoric shift the poet then becomes the masked woman, tantalizing his public: 'So, our dull Poet keeps you on with Masquing' (p. 104). Perhaps in a bitter reference to his critics, Dryden taunts that the result (tonight's play) 'Will prove a Dowdy [i.e. ugly woman], with a Face to fright you' (p. 104). A sense of provisionality is engendered by the disparity between the loftiness of the play and the ironic sexiness of the prologues and epilogues, which also creates an uncertainty of tone. A sense of uncertainty or of the disruption of certainty also comes from disjunction between speaker and spoken in the prologues and epilogues, and the way in which gender identities are perpetually shifting through metaphor.

Heroic drama, then, is a genre in which harmony is established despite discordant notes; and 'greatness' is both asserted and qualified. It used to be the accepted view that this peculiar genre was an eccentric diversion, a freak dramatic episode or literary blind alley. This is false. The great heroic experiment had a significant effect on the future. The long-term influence of heroic drama, as James A. Winn has shown, lay in primarily in opera: 'the elaborate English semi-operas of the later seventeenth century, which began to flourish just as the rhymed heroic plays waned ... absorbed many of their most striking theatrical conventions'.[43] The immediate response to heroic drama was quite sharply polarized. Dryden's heroic plays, in particular, were both imitated and attacked. The imitations were by young dramatists at the start of their careers who were to become the major serious dramatists of the mid-Restoration period. John Crowne's *The History of Charles the Eighth of France* (1671) was extremely successful and was clearly modelled on *The Conquest of Granada*, as was Crowne's two-part *The Destruction of Jerusalem by Vespasian* (1677). However, Crowne, who was later to follow Dryden's lead in politicized adaptations of Shakespeare, showed some ambivalence towards the heroic mode pioneered by his mentor, apologizing in the epilogue to *Charles the Eighth* for 'the whining noise of a dull Rhiming play'.[44] Elkanah Settle in *The Empress of Morocco* (1673) brought the heroic play into disrepute through ineptitude rather than by design, and was attacked by Dryden for having produced 'a Rhapsody of non-sense'.[45] Dryden may have been smarting from the attacks on his own play; or he may have been stung by the patronage Settle received from powerful courtiers. Dryden accuses Settle, with some justice though unnecessary virulence, of the faults his own enemies falsely attributed to him: ignorance, bad grammar, dullness, plagiarism, flatness of characterization and ill-breeding. Meanwhile, other dramatists developed the genre in a different direction. Nathaniel Lee's *The Tragedy of Nero* (1674) and Thomas Otway's *Alcibiades* (1675) draw out the potantial for crimiality in the larger-than-life protagonist, and become what Robert Hume has called 'horror tragedy' or 'the couplet bloodbath'.[46] However, Lee in *Sophonisba, or Hannibal's Overthrow* (1675) reverts to the more conventional heroic mode. Paul Cannan has argued that 'large-scale epics, inheritors of the Carolean heroic tradition' continue to be staged alongside the tragedies of the late 1670s, and cites as examples Tate's *Brutus of Alba*, the Dryden–Lee *Oedipus* and Banks's *The Destruction of Troy* (all 1678).[47]

The attacks on *The Conquest of Granada* took various forms: poems, pamphlets and plays.[48] Of the poems, Rochester's 'An Allusion to Horace' was the most prominent; of the plays, *The Rehearsal*. Written by George Villiers, Second Duke of Buckingham, with the help of Martin Clifford, Thomas Sprat and Samuel Butler, this play was staged in December 1671 by Dryden's own King's Company, only eleven months after the première of Part II of *The Conquest of Granada*. Dryden is portrayed in *The Rehearsal* as a conceited but ingratiating playwright called Bayes who superintends a rehearsal of a heroic play to the mockery of an honest countryman, Frank Smith, and his friend Johnson. These men marvel at dramatists 'that scorn to imitate Nature; but are given altogether to elevate and surprise', meaning, in the result, merely 'Fighting, Loving, Sleeping, Rhyming, Dying, Dancing, Singing, Crying; and every thing, but thinking and Sence'.[49] They accuse Bayes/Dryden of making tragedy laughable, ridiculously seeking new theatrical effects and stealing from classical sources. The play which is being rehearsed has a an incomprehensible plot and is full of nonsensical, rhyming rant. One of the actors explains: 'the grand design upon the Stage is to keep the Auditors in suspence; for to guess presently at the plot, and the sence, tires 'em before the end of the first Act: now, here, every line surprises you, and brings in new matter' (I.i.153). This mocks the fast pace of the action of *The Conquest of Granada*, as well as Dryden's quest for novelty, and his revelling in keeping his audience in suspense in the prologue to Part II.

Dryden's Almanzor becomes Buckingham's huffing Drawcansir, 'a fierce *Hero*, that frights his Mistress, snubs up Kings, baffles Armies, and does what he will, without regard to numbers, good manners, or justice' (IV.i.102). Ozmyn becomes the over-scrupluous Prince Prettyman:

How strange a captive am I grown of late!
Shall I accuse my Love or curse my Fate?
My Love, I cannot; that is too Divine:
And, against Fate, what mortal dares repine? (II.iii.1)

Dryden's romantic setting becomes the humdrum Brentford. The two kings of Brentford who go hand in hand represent a mockery both of Dryden's exalted notions of male friendship and of his penchant for doubling: it is normal in the heroic plays for there to be two pairs of lovers where Renaissance drama would have one, and Dryden also, as we have seen, has two kings of Granada. Buckingham has two princes as well as two kings, whilst Lyndaraxa's two lovers in *The Conquest of Granada* become in *The Rehearsal* two usurpers who are both lovers of the same woman, Lardella. Dryden's liking for spectacular and supernatural effects is parodied, for example in IV.i with the entry of the goddess Pallas, an opening coffin, the discovery of a banquet and a dance, all ridiculously jumbled together; and the crowded action of Dryden's play is mocked by an over-full stage because, as Bayes puts it, 'your Heroic Verse never sounds well, but when the Stage is full' (IV.i.270). The struggle between love and honour is parodied in Prince Volscius's struggle to put on his boots:

My Legs, the Emblem of my various thought,
Shew to what sad distraction I am brought.
Sometimes with stubborn Honour, like this Boot,
My mind is guarded, and resolv'd: to do't:

> Sometimes, again, that very mind, by Love
> Disarmed, like this other Leg does prove.
> Shall I to Honour or to Love give way?
> Go on, cries Honour; tender Love saies, nay:
> Honour, aloud, commands, pluck both Boots on;
> But softer Love does whisper put on none …
> So does my Honour and my Love together
> Puzzle me so, I can resolve for neither.
>
> [*Goes out hopping with one Boot on, and the other off*] (III.v.88)

Buckingham also makes play with the gap between the lofty virtue of Dryden's heroines and the reality of the actresses' sex lives. In a blatant reference to the casting of Dryden's own mistress in *The Conquest of Granada*, Bayes says of the character Amarillis, 'I writ that Part only for her. You must know she is my Mistress' (I.i.179). He is rendered all the more ridiculous by an aspersion on his virility: he has not actually made love to her, but only talked bawdy.

Sex is also the medium for parody in *The Farce of Sodom or The Quintessence of Debauchery*, possibly by John Wilmot, Earl of Rochester.[50] *The Conquest of Granada* opens with a speech by King Boabdelin: 'Thus, in the Triumphs of soft Peace I reign; / And, from my Walls, defy the Powr's of *Spain*' (Part I, I.i.1). *Sodom* opens with a parody by the suggestively named King Bolloximian:

> Thus in the zenith of my lust I reign,
> I drink to swive, and swive to drink again.
> Let other monarchs who their sceptres bear,
> To keep their subjects less in love than fear,
> Be slaves to crowns – my nation shall be free.
> My pintle only shall my sceptre be.
> My laws shall act more pleasure than command,
> And with my prick I'll govern all the land.[51]

Bolloximian is also a caricature of the heroic hero, whose considerable energies find their outlet not in battle but in universal buggery. The two kings and male friendship themes are satirized in Bolloximian's relationship with King Tarsehole of Gomorrah, who sends him forty young boys to bugger. Bolloximian's unregenerate desires, like Lyndaraxa's, end in self-destruction, and he is equally unrepentant, as may be seen from his final speech, addressed to his chief pimp, which concludes the play:

> Let heaven descend, and set the world on fire –
> We to some darker cavern will retire.

There on thy buggered arse I will expire.
[*Leering all the while on* Pockenello] (V.i.82)

The women are no better. An idea of the play's attitude to female virtue
may be gained from a discussion in Act I between Queen Cuntigratia,
Officina the 'She-Pimp of Honour', and the Maids of Honour, Fuckadilla,
Cunticula and Clitoris. The topic is the heroic qualities of General
Buggeranthus:

Cunticula. His prick is as good mettle as his sword.
Officina. Truly I've heard it is both long and large.
Cuntigratia. Then with my open cunt I'll give him charge. (I.ii.56)

The ladies are so stimulated by this discussion that they have immediate
recourse to their dildoes; and this is swiftly followed by a scene in which
the young Prince Prickett loses his virginity to his sister.

It seems clear then that Dryden's contemporaries identified the heroic
hero with libertinism, even if Dryden intended a fine distinction betwen
the two. In part the motivation for such attacks on Dryden was political:
the royalism of the heroic play was countered by satire of the libertine who
recognizes no obstacle to his sexual desires, in plays such as Shadwell's
The Libertine and Lee's *The Princess of Cleve*. These plays have a politically oppositional character, as I have discussed in my *Restoration Theatre
and Crisis*. Buckingham, also, was associated with the Country Party opposition to Charles II's government and it is no accident that he mocks heroic
drama in *The Rehearsal* from the perspective of an honest countryman.

Possibly as a result of these attacks, Dryden himself began to lose
interest in heroic drama after *The Conquest of Granada*. *Aureng-Zebe*
(1675), his last rhymed serious play, has a more restrained hero. The more
rugged qualities of Almanzor are displaced on to the viallain Morat, and
even he is reclaimed before death by the love of a virtuous woman. The
play has a quality of domestic pathos which prefigures later tragedy. In the
meantime, however, Dryden had turned to witty comedy with *Marriage A-
la-Mode* (1672). It is to comedy that we must also now turn.

Notes

1 See the survey in Hughes, *English Drama*, chapters 2–5.

2 Maguire, *Regicide and Restoration*, 35. See also 35–7, 42, 59–62, 82–4.

3 *The Works of John Dryden*, vol. XI, 8.

4 *Of Heroique Playes*, *ibid.*, 11. Dryden paraphrases the views expressed in
   Davenant's preface to *Gondibert*.

5 *The Revels History of Drama in English*, Vol. V, 256.

6 Waith, *Ideas of Greatness*, 3, 217.

7 Hume, *The Development of English Drama*, 272–3.

8 For a discussion of the sources of heroic drama see, in addition to Dryden's own essay *Of Heroique Playes*, Waith, *The Herculean Hero* and *Ideas of Greatness, passim*; Altieri, *The Theatre of Praise,* chapter 1; Maguire, *Regicide and Restoration*, 54–9, 62–3, 89–90; *Revels History*, V, 256–7; Bevis, *English Drama: Restoration and Eighteenth Century*, 40–2, 46; Hume, *Development*, 242, 273; Sherwood, 'Dryden and the Critical Theories of Tasso'. For the sources of *The Conquest of Granada* specifically see in addition Dryden's *Works*, XI, 413–426 and Hughes, *Dryden's Heroic Plays*, 164–6. Prewar discussions are listed in Dryden's *Works*, 417, n. 38 and Waith, *Herculean Hero,* 216–17, notes 4 and 5.

9 Cited in Van Lennep *et al.* (eds), *The London Stage 1660–1800*, vol. I, lxxxiv.

10 Dryden, *Works*, XIII, 234.

11 'Humorous' here means moody and refers to the medieval notion of the four humours, blood, phlegm, choler and melancholy, the balance of which determined a person's personality.

12 The best account of these antecedents is still Waith's in *The Herculean Hero*.

13 Part II, V.iii.241 and see note on p. 456.

14 From medieval times onwards texts were published which claimed to be 'Mirrors' for princes, judges, magistrates and so on, by holding up to those in power the qualities expected of godly rulers. The best known example is *A Mirror for Magistrates*, which went through numerous editions in the sixteenth and early seventeenth centuries.

15 'The Dramatic Use of Hobbes's Political Ideas', 164. See also Winterbottom, 'The Place of Hobbesian Ideas in Dryden's Tragedies'; and Dryden, *Works*, 417, n. 39.

16 *The English Works of Thomas Hobbes*, vol. III, 162, cited Teeter, 'The Dramatic Use of Hobbes's Political Ideas', 166.

17 'Dryden and History: A Problem in Allegorical Reading', 287. On natural law arguments in Restoration drama see also Staves, *Players' Scepters*, chapter 5.

18 Fortescue, *De Natura Legis Naturae*, chapters 24 and 27. For widespread assumptions about the duties of kings see H. A. Lloyd, 'Constitutionalism' in *The Cambridge History of Political Thought, 1450–1700*, ed. Burns and Goldie, especially 258–64; and J. P. Somerville, 'Absolutism and Royalism' in *ibid.*, 347–73.

19 *The Censure of the Rota*, London, 1673, p. 3.

20 See e.g. *Revels History*, 256, 262 ; Jefferson, 'The Significance of Dryden's Heroic Plays'; Kirsch, *Dryden's Heroic Drama,* 41–2; King, *Dryden's Major Plays*, 64–78; Barbeau, *The Intellectual Design of John Dryden's Heroic Plays*, 25–40; Dryden, *Works*, XI, 417, 424–5; Staves, *Players' Scepters*, 199, 296–7; Hughes, *Dryden's Heroic Plays*, 81, 97; Haley, *Dryden and the Problem of Freedom*, 175–80, 198–9.

21 Braverman, *Plots and Counterplots*, 36-7, 114-34. For an account of the
    correspondence between heroic drama and the Restoration *Zeitgeist* see Bevis,
    English Drama: Restoration and Eighteenth Century, 40-2. For the politics of
    the heroic play see: Haley, *Dryden and the Problem of Freedom*, chapters 5 and
    6; Maguire, *Regicide and Restoration*, chapter 1 and 206-14; Brown, *English
    Dramatic Form*, chapter 1; Staves, *Players' Scepters*, 126-9; Dryden, *Works*,
    427. For closely historicized readings see McFadden, *Dryden the Public Writer,
    1660-1685*, 88-94; Thompson, 'Dryden's *Conquest of Granada* and the Dutch
    Wars'.

22 See also Hughes, *Dryden's Heroic Plays*, 24.

23 Almanzor's class values are feudal: anti-capitalist from a reactionary perspective.
    See his contemptuous references to usury, I.i.337-42. Dryden was to express
    such a perspective more explicitly after the 1688 revolution in *Amphitryon*.

24 Raab, *The English Face of Machiavelli*, chapters 2 and 3; Pocock, *The Machia-
    vellian Moment*, 376-80. See also John M. Wallace, *Destiny His Choice: The
    Loyalism of Andrew Marvell*, Cambridge, Cambridge University Press, 1968,
    chapters 2 and 3.

25 For the meaning and resonance of quietism see my *Restoration Theatre and
    Crisis*, sections indexed.

26 I discuss the dramatic repercussions of this in my *Restoration Theatre and
    Crisis*, 7, 111, 214, 219, 238, 308.

27 See Pincus, *Protestantism and Patriotism*, 343-440.

28 For an account of the importance of the Protestant succession at this time and
    the effect of this issue on literature see Downie, *To Settle the Succession of the
    State*, chapters 1 and 2.

29 Cited Dryden, *Works*, XI, 411.

30 For Locke's ideas on the family see the *Treatises on Government*, First Treatise,
    sections 87-93; Second Treatise, chapter 6. The political resonance of family
    themes in the play was enhanced by Locke's association with opposition
    politicians: see Haley, *The First Earl of Shaftesbury*, and Richard Ashcraft,
    Revolutionary Politics and Locke's Two Treatises of Government.

31 For the Machiavellian villain in Renaissance drama see Irving Ribner, 'Marlowe
    and Machiavelli'; N. W. Bawcutt, 'Some Elizabethan Allusions to Machiavelli',
    'Machiavelli and Marlowe's *The Jew of Malta*', and introduction to *The Jew of
    Malta*.

32 *The Jew of Malta*, p. 63, line 14.

33 For differing views of Almahide and of the play's sexual politics in general see
    Braverman, *Plots and Counterplots*, 117-20; Hughes, *Dryden's Heroic Plays*,
    103-114; Osborn, 'Heroical Love in Dryden's Heroic Drama'; Hagstrum, *Sex
    and Sensibility*, chapter 3; Evans, 'Private Greatness'; Coltharp, 'Pleasing
    Rape'. Especially useful is Quinsey, 'Almahide Still Lives'.

34 Hughes in particular offers a subtle discussion of 'the unconscious affinities that
    bind the heroine to the villainess': *Dryden's Heroic Plays*, 103.

35 Dryden, *Works*, XIII, 247.

36 On the role of the ghost see Armistead, 'The Higher Magic in Dryden's *Conquest of Granada*'.

37 He is not, however, the true king of Granada as Staves (60) and Braverman (125) allege.

38 For an analysis of *Oedipus* see my *Restoration Theatre and Crisis*, 204–8.

39 On unresolved contradictions in the play see Fisher, 'Daring to Be Absurd: The Paradoxes of *The Conquest of Granada*'; Braverman, *Plots and Counterplots*, 119, 125.

40 For a discussion of libertine elements in the play see Kirsch, 35–46; Turner, 'The Libertine Sublime'; and Coltharp, 'Pleasing Rape', *passim*. For a fuller discussion of Restoration libertinism in general see the next chapter.

41 Some readers may feel that Almanzor's 'sexual harassment' is as bad as attempted rape; but we should at least be aware that these are twentieth-century attitudes, unknown to Dryden and his contemporaries.

42 Dryden, *Works*, XI, 411.

43 'Heroic Song', 114.

44 First edition of 1672.

45 Dryden, *Works*, XVII, 83. See also Winn, *John Dryden and His World*, 255–61; and Novak, introduction to *The Empress of Morocco and its Critics*.

46 Hume, *Development*, 199. 200.

47 'New Directions in Serious Drama on the London Stage', 234.

48 See Winn, *John Dryden and His World*, 226–7, 229–31, 235–8; Dryden, *Works* 412–3, 429–32.

49 *The Rehearsal*, I.i.38, 46.

50 On the vexed question of authorship see Johnson, 'Did Lord Rochester Write *Sodom*?'; and Love, 'But Did Rochester *Really* Write *Sodom*?'

51 *Rochester: Complete Poems and Plays*, I.i.1–8.

Comedy I:
William Wycherley's *The Country Wife*

Both *The Country Wife* and *The Rover*, which is the subject of the next chapter, were reasonably successful in their own time, and both are popular today. *The Country Wife* remained in the repertory until 1753, and was revived in 1924 (although a revised version, *The Country Girl* by David Garrick, remained popular through the nineteenth century). Behn's reputation went into eclipse earlier in the eighteenth century than Wycherley's and the revival of interest in her work in the twentieth century had to wait longer; but this has been compensated for by the flourishing of her reputation in recent years. Both plays, then, have a claim on our attention because they have endured the test of time. Yet we must be careful about assuming that these two plays are 'typical' Restoration comedies. Both plays may be described as 'sex comedies', a sub-genre which enjoyed a vogue in the 1670s. No play conforms absolutely to 'type'; but we may say that the fashion begins with Dryden's *An Evening's Love* (1668) and Betterton's *The Amorous Widow* (1670?), and was at its height when *The Country Wife* was first performed, probably on 12 January 1675. Prior to that, comedy tended to be political and satirical; and this type of comedy was revived in the Exclusion Crisis, 1678–83, when sex comedy declined. So the heyday of sex comedy is a fairly brief period of about ten years – though it was revived in modified form in the work of Congreve and others after 1688, and bawdy comedies continued to be appreciated well into the eighteenth century.[1]

The sex comedies do not represent the clear break with previous Restoration drama that we might imagine. Elements of the heroic plays persist in the comedies, even though the two genres are very different. This continuity with the heroic genre is evident in two aspects: first, in the 'virtuous' characters, Alithea and Harcourt in *The Country Wife* and Florinda and Belville in *The Rover*. These pairs bear a distinct resemblance to Dryden's Ozmyn and Benzayda. Second, the rake-protagonist in the sex comedies has some of the extravagant qualities of the 'huffing' heroes of the heroic plays, including excess of words and deeds. The continuity may have been emphasized by the fact that Charles Hart, who played the rake Horner in *The Country Wife*, had also played Almanzor in *The Conquest of Granada*. The rake in comedy may not share the idealism of the heroic hero, but he has the same over-inflated ego and total commitment to personal and social autonomy. The sex comedies appear to be a diversion from the increasing political tensions of the 1670s, discussed in the previous chapter. However, there is also a degree of political continuity with heroic drama: most sex comedies also endorse the values of a particular 'cavalier' class, upholding the town-based, upper-class wits, at the expense of country dolts, upstart city gentry, tradesmen, the professional classes and other outsiders.

In recent times the sex comedies have attracted far more attention in both criticism and performance than either heroic plays or satirical and political comedies, and are more likely to be taught. In one sense this justifies our selection of these plays for consideration; but we must also be aware that the process of making such a selection perpetuates the undue prominence of sex comedy over other Restoration comic forms. Since the sex comedies have received so much more critical attention than the heroic plays, it might be helpful initially to 'map' the critical debate, and to highlight the central questions which have dominated it. First and foremost is the question of how 'sexy' sex comedy is. How far does it promote or endorse the rakes' libertine values and how far does it anatomize them or hold them up to critical scrutiny or satire? This issue dominated criticism of the play from the early twentieth century until the early 1980s, and continues to be of interest.[2] It is complicated by several factors. In the first place, libertinism itself is not simply a philosophy of 'anything goes', sexually speaking, but propounds freedoms for the aristocratic rake which are not extended to women or to men outside the charmed circle. So a play might endorse libertinism in the male elite but deride it in base imitators or women. Second, comedies may appear to endorse libertinism while actually depicting it with a satirical edge; or, more commonly perhaps, they may appear to condemn while actually titillating in the same way that violence against women may be ostensibly condemned but actually relished or fostered in Hollywood movies today. The matter is further complicated by the fact that what we know about the plays' reception tells us that a reaction of titillation and relish co-existed with moral disapproval, primarily from (some) women and from committed Christians. Again, the parallel with the USA today is striking.

The perspective taken on libertinism varies between dramatists. D'Urfey, for example, takes an indulgent view. Shadwell in *The Libertine* and Lee in *The Princess of Cleve* take a critical and satirical stance, associated with their political critique of the Court, whence libertine values chiefly emanated. Wycherley and Behn are somewhere in between. The actual number of comedies promoting libertinism is small, but their novelty and impact in their own time and subsequently is disproportionally great. So the significance of the 'new sexiness' should not be underestimated.

However, it must not be overestimated either. The sex comedies should not be seen as entirely separate generically from the drama which preceded and succeeded them. They bear some relation to Renaissance antecedents, including elements of Jonson's 'humours' comedy and Fletcher's comedy of love and wit, while sentimental and moral elements typical of cavalier drama and (later) of eighteenth-century comedy are starting to creep in.[3] The comedies of Wycherley and Behn owe more to the Fletcherian comedy of wit than to humours comedy, whose chief proponent was Shadwell, but 'humours' elements persist in characters such as Pinchwife, as we shall see.

'Sexual politics' and the role of women have come to the fore in criticism over the last twenty years or so. How do the comedies explore power relations between the sexes? How far do particular plays promote male dominance and male bonds, and contain female transgression? How far do they open up a space for women's desire and female agency? Some critics argue that the humour of *The Country Wife* is essentially at women's expense and that male control is firmly in place at the end.[4] Others see more sexual freedom for women.[5] There is broad agreement that marriage is a central theme, but how sceptically is the institution treated? Different plays take different perspectives on abuses and inequalities within marriage, on women's economic and legal position and on incompatibility between love and social restrictions, between freedom of choice and arranged marriage.[6] As we shall see, male and female playwrights treat issues of sex and gender somewhat differently, though we must beware of simplistic preconceptions. Critics are now aware that 'sexual politics' goes beyond the treatment of women to include issues of masculinity and male sexuality, and I shall have more to say about this below.[7]

A minority of critics, most notably Laura Brown and Douglas Canfield, have focused on an important political dimension to the sex comedies, which may not at first be apparent.[8] Both these critics see the *The Country Wife* as ultimately conservative, disagreeing about the satiric targets that the play aims at en route to affirmation of the status quo: the 'author's own class' (Brown, 49) or 'parvenus' (Canfield, 269). The issue of class in the plays is further complicated and politicized by the fact that libertine and cavalier values emanated from the King and Court, and the plays' treatment of such values reflects upon the monarch himself.[9] Any criticism of the rake has an oppositional potential, politically.

Let us now take a closer look at *The Country Wife*, bearing some of these issues in mind. The prologue to the play is spoken by the actor Charles Hart, who is to play Horner. Allusions to Hart's former role as the huffing hero Almanzor in *The Conquest of Granada* allow Wycherley to make play with ideas of masculinity. His prologue eschews the common effeminizing analogy of poet-prostitute in favour of the 'manly' image of the playwright as cudgelled bully (i.e. street ruffian) who 'huffs' back at his critics. The playwright is mocked as somewhat ridiculous in his unconciliatory posture. The actor affects to mediate between the 'huffing' author and his critics (rather as Almazor mediated between Boabdelin and his rebels):

> Well, let the vain rash fop, by huffing so,
> Think to obtain the better terms of you;
> But we, the actors, humbly will submit,
> Now, and at any time, to a full pit. (p. 7)

Yet this metaphorically transforms the actor into a prostitute. The prologue ends with a reference to the way in which the theatre is 'open' to the audience, who can 'penetrate' even backstage:

> We set no guards upon our tiring-room,
> But when with flying colours there you come,
> We patiently, you see, give up to you
> Our poets, virgins, nay, our matrons too. (p. 7)

Hart's persona thus shifts from huffing hero to effeminized quasi-cuckold, obliged to yield up his women and put a brave face on it. There is a slippage in notions of masculinity in the prologue, which also draws attention to the difficulty in sustaining manliness: the tough guy and the submissive conciliator are equally powerless and equally ridiculous. The way is paved for the manipulator, Horner, another type of man.

What type of man is Horner? Critics have taken every conceivable perspective. Judgements of Horner have ranged from champion of sexual freedom to monster; from privileged trickster and true wit who exposes and satirizes the vices and follies of others to psychologically damaged individual.[10] In terms of 'sexual politics', they have ranged from seeing him as a supremely successful deployer of phallic power, to a feminized object of women's desire and manipulation.[11] Horner's name has a threefold significance, suggesting a cuckold-maker (the traditional symbol of the cuckold being horns), a wild beast with animalistic sexuality and the horned devil. The play opens with what would have been a shocking and sensational ploy: Horner has employed Dr Quack to spread the rumour that a failed treatment for venereal disease has made him a eunuch. The tone is cynical, as Horner and the Quack recount all the sections of society who will be sure to spread the 'secret', ranging from midwives, orange wenches, old women and female servants to 'city husbands' and 'old fumbling keepers'. Quack wonders why Horner is not ashamed: 'I have been hired by young gallants to belie 'em t'other way, but you are the first would be thought a man unfit for women' (I.i.34–6). This sets up a standard of normal male behaviour and identity, as involving boasting of the sexual prowess upon which a man's pride depends. Such 'normal' men are mocked, the boasting being presented as often unfounded. It is therefore possible to see Horner as more truly a man in not caring about outward show: 'let vain rogues be contented only to be thought abler men than they are, generally 'tis all the pleasure they have; but mine lies another way' (I.i.37–9). Since his pretence makes him seem no threat to husbands and gives him access to wives, he can really enjoy the sexual pleasure that others merely boast of. Yet the question remains: in a society so much concerned with appearances, can he really be manly if he has lost the reputation of manhood?

A significant 'marker' of manliness is true wit: false wit is consistently derided. The witty cavalier has taken the place of the clever servant (a central figure in ancient and Renaissance comedy).[12] Horner is the trickster whose ploys both exploit and expose the vices and follies of others. For example, his imposture immediately exposes the folly of Sir Jasper Fidget, duped into forcing his womenfolk upon Horner in the belief that he is mocking the latter's impotence. Hypocrisy is also exposed, as Lady Fidget's very disgust at the idea of a eunuch reveals her hidden lust. As Horner is able to tell her under the guise of banter, 'your virtue is your greatest affectation, madam' (I.i.103). As he cynically tells the Quack, 'now I can be sure that she who shows an aversion to me loves the sport ... your women of honour, as you call 'em, are only chary of their reputations, not their persons, and 'tis scandal they would avoid, not men' (I.i.164–9). This combination of wit and daring outspokenness must have caused a sensation in the theatre.[13]

As a man adopting the most stigmatized and ridiculous role in his society, Horner himself is not exempt from the humour of the scene. Moreover, his plot is flawed from the start. Among the advantages of his imposture, Horner lists the ability to be rid of his creditors and his former mistresses, themselves creditors of a sort: 'of all old debts; love, when it comes to be so, is paid most unwillingly' (I.i.152–4). This marks the fact that Horner is chasing a futile and ever-vanishing goal: once won, women become a burden to be shed, an obligation to be evaded. Act I concludes with his cynical reference to jealousy and the pox as diseases inevitably bred by 'love and wenching' (I.i.505). So what becomes of his own devotion to the same? Yet the fact that no one is exempt from mockery does not mean that the tone is heavily satirical or scathing: rather the contrary. The ingenuity of Horner's device and the subsequent deception and badinage all create a light, comic effect. The good humour is shown by Wycherley's cheerfully including himself as a comic target.[14] It is important to remember that this society, in which the theatre is so prominent and acting so pervasive, is a society of which Wycherley himself is very much a part. He writes as an insider, and the mockery is an insider's joke.

In the exchange with his male friends in I.i Horner draws out his society's ideas of true and false manhood and of the nature and significance of both male–female relations and male friendship. There are various types of 'false men'. Horner has already mentioned city husbands and old fumbling keepers, his potential cuckolds, and we encounter an example in Sir Jasper Fidget. Dorilant extends this to old men in general, 'shadows of men' or 'Half-men' (I.i.199, 201) who run tame among the women because they have lost their sexual potency. Pinchwife is a different type: a potential cuckold but also an ex-rake, a tormented figure whose fear of being cuckolded brings about the dreaded event. Metaphorically linked to the cuckold is Sparkish, a blockhead who thinks he is a wit, but is despised by all the others for his ineptitude and self-deceiving pride: 'His company is as troublesome to us as a cuckold's when you have a mind to his wife's' (I.i.254–6). Pinchwife is knowing where Sir Jasper and Sparkish are credulous, but all are butts of the rakes' wit and trickery, and all in different ways procure their own sexual betrayal.

Yet the exchanges about true and false manhood in the play have a comic provisionality, for two reasons. First, the false men are not that different from the others: Sparkish exhibits many qualities of the wits and 'the short-sighted world' sees no difference between him and them (I.i.253). In a sense he manifests cavalier qualities taken to their logical extreme, being over-committed to the idea of wit and to male friendship. It could even be argued that he is more a cavalier than his companions: the way he trusts his friends with his lady's honour is more truly in keeping with heroic and chivalric codes than the sly behaviour of those friends themselves. It says something about this society that heroic values of friendship, trust and freedom from jealousy and suspicion become foolish.

In the second place, it is doubtful whether there are any 'true men'. All are to some extent mocked, including Horner himself. There is little inherent and certainly no moral difference between Pinchwife's scheme to ensure marital fidelity by marrying a simple wife and Horner's scheme to get close to wives and seduce them by pretending to be a eunuch. Horner is animalistic: his intimates frequently refer to him as 'beast' and 'toad'. Pinchwife, cuckolded, likens himself to 'a kind of a wild beast' (V.iv.308). Harcourt comes closest in the play to conforming to a heroic standard, especially at the end when he stands by the woman he loves even though her reputation is compromised. His surname suggests courtliness in the best sense and his first name 'Frank' suggests sincerity. Yet he is not the milky character sometimes paired with the rake in comedies: his wooing Alithea under the nose of his rival is as bold and funny as Horner's seduction ploys, and pretending to be his own brother in holy orders to carry out an invalid marriage shows his ingenuity.

However, this points towards the problem with Harcourt as offering a standard: he is not all that different from the other men. The name 'Frank' has a less simple resonance than might at first appear. Sparkish uses it to mean excessive openness and amorality: 'I love to be envied, and would not marry a wife that I alone could love. Loving alone is as dull as eating alone. Is it not a frank age? And I am a frank person' (III.ii.372-4). The context – and the comedy – of these remarks is Harcourt's perfidy as a friend and boldness as a lover. Harcourt aids Horner in tormenting Pinchwife in III.ii, and physically restrains Margery's would-be protectors as Horner leads her off. He seems to have a libertine reputation (II.i.134, 175), and in the opening scene he comes off the worst in an exchange in which he disreputably proclaims what might be called cavalier attitudes to women:

Harcourt. No, mistresses are like books; if you pore upon then too much they may doze you and make you unfit for company, but if used discreetly you are the fitter for conversation by 'em.

Dorilant. A mistress should be like a little country retreat near the town; not to dwell in constantly, but only for a night and away, to taste the town the better when a man returns. (I.i.214–21)

Harcourt has, however grown emotionally by the end of the play, which is more than can be said for Horner.

The exchange between Harcourt and Dorilant raises the question also of what attitude Wycherley is taking to issues of love and friendship. It is hard to be sure, since the emphasis is on wit. Harcourt here describes heterosexual pleasures as 'effeminate' in the Restoration sense of over-focused on women (I.i.212), but his subsequent behaviour shows a different, more noble attitude to love. Dorilant, on the other hand, affects to be converted by Horner's misogynist railing. Horner reduces what we might term the homosocial perspective to its *reductio ad absurdum*, proclaiming ironically that 'Good fellowship and friendship are lasting, rational, and manly pleasures' (I.i.209–10) and that 'it is as hard to be a good fellow, a good friend, and a lover of women, as 'tis to be a good fellow, a good friend, and a lover of money' (I.i.222–4). In a sense this is disingenuous, as Horner does not value male friendship; but in another sense Horner states the truth but merely inverts his own relationship to it. Love will certainly exclude friendship: he has already told the Quack that he intends to shun former acquaintances, and to place pursuit of women before all else; and he even lets his supposed best friend Harcourt believe the eunuch pretence. Again, the discussion has a comic relativism in that all perspectives interrogate one another. Both love and friendship – and the pursuit of them – are treated ironically. The previously heroic tension between love and friendship (which later receives tragic treatment in Otway's *Venice Preserv'd*) is here itself mocked. Wycherley is poking fun at his society, and also at the heroes in the plays of his contemporaries: his play is full of in-jokes and references to other plays and characters in them. Yet he does not distance himself from them to the extent of suggesting that there is any alternative or privileged perspective.

Men enjoy their power-play up to a point, even if, like Sparkish, they are on the receiving end: it shows they are part of the gang. Male bonds seem strong in spite – or because – of the fact that relations between men are power relations. Moreover, humour greases the wheels of friendship, and wit excuses much. Even Horner, supposedly shunning friends and laying aside his claim to manhood in the pursuit of sex, still enjoys the friendship of Dorilant and Harcourt just as before: the wits continue to include him as one of themselves. Yet wit excuses much that seems quite cruel, and no friendship is entirely innocent or wholesome. Horner's baiting of his friends in I.i mocks the way men talk, building upon one another's conceits, quick to follow a lead and to outdo one another in praising wine, and criticizing women or fools. Horner is able to lead his friends on to adopt ridiculous and extreme positions. Far from exalting male bonds over heterosexual ones, Wycherley shows men's pleasure in making fools of one another. Sir Jasper thinks he is rubbing salt in the wounds of the eunuch; whilst Horner feigns friendship to Sir Jasper in order to cuckold him, but later finds that the burden of the loathsome friendship outweighs the rewards: 'the hardest duty a married woman imposes on a lover is keeping her husband company always ... keeping a cuckold company after you have had his wife is as tiresome as the company of a country squire to a witty fellow of the town, when he has got all his money' (V.i.7, 11). Horner is devious even in his friendships with other wits: he enjoys drawing out his friends' views and secretly deriding them. The so-called friends delight in abusing and secretly mocking Sparkish, who thinks he is one of them. They torment the already paranoid Pinchwife, revelling in playing upon his fear and jealousy. Indeed, one characteristic all the men in the play have in common is their delight in deriding and scoring points off one another. Such male friendship as exists has no future: the world of the play, in common with most Restoration comedies, is a world of young men. The young enjoy a barbed friendship, but the old have no chance. Old men are fools and cuckolds, and Pinchwife, at forty-nine, illustrates the problem of the man becoming old, attempting to emancipate himself from the society of rakes and settle down.

Are relations between the sexes privileged over male friendship, a site of greater truth and communication? Or are they also reducible to power-play? This is not an easy question to answer. Power-play definitely comes into Horner's plots. Yet it is possible to see Horner as a man sensitive to women's needs, and Wycherley by implication as critical of his society's notions of sex and gender roles. Horner values wit in women, not just sexual availability: 'methinks wit is more necessary than beauty; and I think no young woman ugly that has it, and no handsome woman agreeable without it' (I.i.425–7). This does not prevent him seducing the witless Margery. Yet even this can be seen as a service to Margery, an awakening. Horner seems to have women's sexual interests at heart: 'women ... are like soldiers, made constant and loyal by good pay rather than by oaths and covenants' (I.i.464–6).

Yet to see Horner as the agent of women's sexual liberation, and to take his remarks about female sexuality as pro-women, would be to postulate a neutral or even positive attitude in the Restoration to female sexual appetite, and to ignore the satirical edge to the depiction of women as 'longing for it'. In fact even libertine discourse had problems with female desire, and it is unlikely that Wycherley intended no barbed wit at women's expense. If he was simply pro-women or pro-sex, lines such as Horner's to Lady Fidget, 'your virtue is your greatest affectation, madam' (I.i.103), would lose their comic force. Women in charge would be neither comic nor grotesque. If it were possible to be simply pro-sex in Wycherley's society, the obsession with a reputation for chastity which drives women in the play would be meaningless.

In the play itself judgements of Horner's behaviour towards women vary. Pinchwife the ex-whoremaster has some right on his side when he says to his wife: 'he would ruin you, as he has done hundreds. He has no other love for women but that; such as he look upon women like basilisks, but to destroy 'em' (II.ii.120–3). It is only good nature and civility which prevent the ruin of several female reputations at the end of the play. However, Lady Fidget's opposite view also carries some credence. She thinks the eunuch pretence entirely admirable and beneficial for women:

But, poor gentleman, could you be so generous, so truly a man of honour, as for the sakes of us women of honour, to cause yourself to be reported no man? No man! And to suffer yourself the greatest shame that could fall upon a man, that none may fall upon us women by your conversation? (II.i.555–60)

What she does here is to co-opt his manoeuvre and turn it to her own advantage. What began as a way for Horner to seduce women and score over their husbands becomes a device for women's benefit, and this is borne out as Horner becomes by the end the property of Lady Fidget and her 'virtuous gang, as they call themselves' (V.i.96).

What does this say about Wycherley's treatment of women in the play? Lady Fidget, Dainty Fidget and Mrs Squeamish may be circumscribed by social convention but they are certainly not powerless. They are somewhat grotesque as they prattle of honour while objecting to the fact that men of quality pursue actresses in preference to themselves (II.i.354–411). It is very hard to see how such hypocrisy could be presented as at all attractive, and their names suggest a ridiculous fastidiousness. But they are winners in the sexual game as they manipulate oppressive social codes for their own advantage and make the best of a bad world.

To come to a better understanding of the play's 'sexual politics' it is useful to look at the china scene, IV.iii. Wycherley invites us to observe, not merely to delight in the scene, through the device of Horner inviting the Quack to watch his sexual manoeuvres from behind a screen. The Quack's comments seem to confirm Horner's daring: 'This indeed I could not have believed from him, nor any but my own eyes' (IV.iii.138). This watcher observes another, as Sir Jasper uncomprehendingly views the seduction of his wife under his very nose. This alerts us to the need to look carefully at appearances in the scene. What a careful look reveals, I think, is that Horner's power over women is open to question. In the opening lines, the word-play on 'honour' seems to Lady Fidget's detriment: she values 'my dear honour' in the sense of the sham of an undeserved reputation for chastity. Horner will show his 'honour' by keeping his word to service her sexually, and also in the sense of heroic (sexual) prowess. It is also no accident that the word sounds like his own name, which is an ironic reflection of the way values collapse into their opposites in this world. Horner's daring in the scene is breathtaking. He counters Lady Fidget's request to keep the 'dear secret' (IV.iii.65) of his potency from other women, for fear they will suspect her affair with him, by announcing his intention to sleep with them all: 'Nay, madam, rather than they shall prejudice your honour, I'll prejudice theirs; and to serve you, I'll lie with 'em all, make the secret their own, and then they'll keep it: I am a Machiavel in love, madam' (IV.iii.669). The whole exchange appears to show Horner's power as he plays with his conquest. Yet the conversation also reveals the less obvious reality that it is women who have secret knowledge, as well as the power to destroy reputations.

Of course the most titillatingly outrageous example of Horner's chutzpah (or of any rake's in Restoration comedy) is his seduction of Lady Fidget in his china closet while her husband watches and comments from the next room with unwitting encouragement and unconscious double entendre: 'Wife! He is coming into you the back way!' (IV.iii.132). Yet the initiative is not wholly Horner's, and the idea of 'looking for china' in Horner's closet is Lady Fidget's. Moreover, the presence of other women alters the sexual balance of power. In the first place they understand the secret language of 'china' where Sir Jasper does not, a further instance of women's privileged relationship to language and communication in the play. And in the second place they immediately assume that if 'china' is on offer, they can all have some:

Mrs Squeamish. O Lord, I'll have some china too. Good Master Horner,
    don't think to give other people china, and me none.
    Come in with me too. (IV.iii.190–2)

Horner becomes a purveyor of satisfaction for female consumers, a 'sex object'. It is a commonplace for the sex act to be described in terms of men stealing a woman's jewel. The dominant metaphor in the scene inverts this: the woman has stolen the man's china. As Horner says, 'Nay, she has been too hard for me, do what I could' (IV.iii.189). He, on the other hand, is no longer 'hard', no longer supremely potent, but depleted: 'Upon my honour I have none left now' (IV.iii.193). Lady Fidget, on the other hand, is still voracious: 'What, d'ye think is he had any left, I would not have had it too? For we women of quality never think we have china enough' (IV.iii.200). The remainder of the scene is taken up with Pinchwife's unwitting delivery of his wife's Margery's love letter to the astonished Horner, a further instance of women's ingenuity and sexual initiative.

In V.iv we see the 'virtuous gang' triumphant in their possession of Horner. In the conventional cuckolding paradigm the woman is a pawn in a power-play between men. Here the women affirm their power to drink and make a noise, assert their sexual needs, and order Horner to tell them the secrets of men's sexual behaviour. Horner has really become the women's plaything that he earlier pretended to be (to Sir Jasper's amusement and his own feigned disgust). His eunuch pretence has shifted from empowering ploy to a trap which places him in the power of the women who know the truth. The women resolve to become 'sister sharers' in Horner's services on their own terms (V.iv.169). Horner becomes 'Harry Common' (V.iv.177). That this is a move in a gender battle, reversing normal power relations, is suggested by the previous discussion of men's delight in sharing common women. In terms of female power, it should also be noted that Horner's cuckolding of Pinchwife eventually comes about through the contrivance of Lucy, who suggests that Margery disguise herself as Alithea, a drastic measure which also has the benefit of showing Alithea Sparkish's true character. Horner has tried to employ Sparkish to disengage Margery from her husband, a singularly ineffective stratagem.

This does not mean that the play is a statement in favour of women's liberation: all characters in the play are subjected to comic mockery. The women are both hypocritical and sexually voracious – just like the men.

Yet they are presented quite sympathetically, and are certainly not monsters. Pinchwife's misogynistic remarks clearly result from stress and are not endorsed. His outburst that women 'have more desires, more soliciting passions, more lust, and more of the devil' than men (IV.ii.62–4) is presented humorously and conflicts in any case with his obsessive mistrust of younger men as the primary agents of his wife's downfall. Pinchwife's abuse and oppression of Margery are presented unfavourably, and his preoccupation with controlling women is presented as neurotic and futile: 'I could never keep a whore to myself' (I.i.461–2). In attempting, like Molière's Alceste,[15] to create a young woman as *tabula rasa* for him to write upon, he abolishes the safeguards which enable a woman of the world like Alithea to safeguard her virtue: an irony which reaches its height when, teaching Margery to write letters in IV.ii, he fosters her dawning sense of agency.

There is considerable sympathy for Margery. She seems at first totally different from Lady Fidget and the others, and much nicer, though she does not have the stature or the subjectivity of a heroine. She is often seen as an innocent who catches 'the London disease they call love' (IV.iv.1). Margery seems genuinely affectionate towards her unkind husband and Alithea calls her a 'poor tender creature' (II.i.37). Yet she is also somewhat ludicrous in her naivety, something of a grotesque. As the play proceeds she becomes obstinate and self-willed and Pinchwife is even to be pitied in III.ii as he struggles to fend off the gallants and control his wayward wife. His cruelty in IV.ii, as he threatens to write 'whore' on her face with his penknife and stab out her eyes, nips our sympathy in the bud. Yet credence is given to Pinchwife's fears by Margery's natural sexual appetite and therefore potential for seduction. She is already fancying actors when we meet her in II.i, without knowing what her attraction signifies. Rather than being utterly distinct from the 'virtuous gang' she is simply on the other end of a continuum.

Margery is naive at the start but very quickly becomes socially adept, quickly mastering letter-writing and other social skills and turning them to her own advantage. Her husband's efforts at control are futile: Pinchwife's drawing his penknife upon her in IV.ii and his sword in IV.iv are comic episodes of impotent fury which mark the failure of the phallic power. In case we should miss this obvious point, it is underscored by Sparkish, who compares the drawn sword to activities in the marriage bed (IV.iv.48). Pinchwife continues to make futile recourse to his sword in V.iv, as his discomfiture is completed. That wider issues of gender are at stake is also clear from his own generalizing remarks about women as a sex and the trials of husbands in general. Yet again we see masculinity in crisis.

Margery plays a role in revealing this crisis. It would, however, be wrong to see her as the repository of natural qualities or true values in a corrupt society. Margery exists to some extent as a comic device: her simple country innocence is a counterpoint to Alithea's social knowledge, mirroring the pairing of the knowing Pinchwife and the gullible Sparkish. Margery is also a foil for Pinchwife's self-defeating behaviour, a comic device to show how a jealous man undoes himself by engaging in evasions and subterfuges which only increase both his wife's hankering after social and sexual knowledge and the rakes' desire to pursue her. That both Margery and Alithea flounder in society equally, and that the knowing Alithea comes closer to being undone than the gullible Margery, are comments upon society.

Alithea may be the best candidate for heroine, and some critics have tried to place her in this role; though, as with Horner, there is a plethora of perspectives on Alithea and Harcourt, ranging from 'exemplary' couple, to little better than the rest, to irrelevance.[16] Alithea's name suggests a morally privileged role, deriving from the Greek word for truth. Yet the fact that Alithea's name means 'truth' does not in the end help us much, as it could work either to ensure her privileged status or to show truth as debased in a corrupt society. And is the fact that her truth is compromised an indictment of her or of society? In her first exchange with Harcourt Alithea defends Sparkish against Harcourt's perception that his lack of jealousy springs from absence of love: 'Love proceeds from esteem; he cannot distrust my virtue. Besides he loves me, or he would not marry me' (II.i.233–4). From one perspective she is the champion of true values ignored in a corrupt society, merely misapplying them to the wrong man: Harcourt will show true faith in her virtue and real love based on esteem at the end when her reputation is compromised. Yet Alithea also emerges here as oddly similar to Margery, her supposed opposite. She is gullible in her belief in Sparkish, and foolish, if honourable, in her refusal to break with him. Her exchange with the servant Lucy in IV.i raises doubts even of the honour of her course, as Lucy asks, 'Can there be a greater cheat or wrong done to a man than to give him your person without you heart?' (IV.i.19–20). Alithea is good-hearted, but misguided.

Lady Fidget is hypocritical when she speaks of 'my dear, dear honour' (II.i.411), or rather, she has redefined honour as social reputation, regardless of actual virtue. Yet Lucy is equally critical of Alithea's 'rigid honour'

(IV.i.31) which goes against good sense: 'But what a devil is this honour? 'Tis sure a disease in the head, like the megrim or falling sickness, that always hurries people away to do themselves mischief. Men lose their lives by it; women what's dearer to 'em, their love, the life of life' (IV.i.31–6). To be sure, Wycherley has something to say here about the state of a society in which heroic values such as honour have little place. However, Alithea needs to acquire some of the pragmatism which Lady Fidget's so-called 'virtuous gang' have in over-abundance. Alithea is to learn that merely toeing the moral line is no protection from social damnation in a society concerned primarily with appearances. Her town knowledge does not stop her being almost undone. It is a fine irony that she is suspected of being Horner's lover when she is in fact the one woman who has no such aspiration.

Moreover, just as Alithea is opposite but also similar to Margery, so there is in another sense only a fine line between her and the virtuous gang. Like them, she is worldly and concerned with her reputation. One of her chief reasons for sticking to Sparkish is that 'I must marry him; my reputation would suffer in the world else' (II.i.242–3). Alithea takes what she calls 'the innocent liberty of the town' (II.i.44), about which her brother Pinchwife is with some justice more scathing. She engages in 'civility' with men 'in a box at the plays, in the drawing room at Whitehall, in St. James's Park, Mulberry Garden ...' (II.i.53–5). But Horner has already said that 'Women of quality are so civil, you can hardly distinguish love from good breeding' (I.i.162–4), and Sparkish confirms the difficulty in distinguishing: 'a man can't speak civilly to a woman now but presently she says he makes love to her!' (III.ii.304–5). By III.ii 'civil' has acquired a double entendre (cf. V.ii.40, 42, 61). Sir Jasper thinks by using the phrase 'civil women' (579) he is describes his wife and her friends as respectable, but his audience understands the term to mean sexually obliging. It is Alithea's 'civility' and worldliness which cause her to be suspected of immorality.

If it is wrong to claim a heroic role for Alithea, it may also be wrong to isolate any of the characters or to claim a privileged status for anyone. Wycherley seems primarily interested not in character but in opportunities for comic situations, and for a display of qualities through bringing together different types. He shares the Restoration predilection for doubling and opposites, and has fun with the pairing of a gullible woman accidentally inducted into social knowledge by her jealous husband, and a socially adept woman steadfast in her adherence to a fool and refusal to listen to a man of sense. In the same way he pairs Sir Jasper, forcing his wife upon Horner in the belief the latter is a eunuch, and Pinchwife, trying to hold his wife apart from Horner, in the belief the latter is a rake. By such contrasts and similitudes, Wycherley is anatomizing his society for comic effect.

Shifting power relations in society may be illustrated by reference to drink. In I.i Horner ironically expresses a preference for wine which is typical of cavaliers in comedies: 'Wine gives you liberty, love takes it away ... Wine gives you joy; love, grief and tortures, besides the surgeon's.'[7] Wine makes us witty; love only sots. Wine makes us sleep; love breaks it ... for my part, I will have only those glorious, manly pleasures of being very drunk and very slovenly' (I.i.225-6, 228-10, 238-9). Wine is usually seen as an aid to love rather than an alternative to it. Wycherley exalts drink, the marker of manliness, against love, as a prelude to other exchanges in which the meaning of the signifier is to shift. In III.ii. the significance of drink shifts in the course of a witty exchange between Horner and his friends. At first drink enters the conversation simply as a jocular comparison, a reason for dining with rich fools, just as the supposed eunuch Horner needs a reason for frequenting the ladies. Harcourt then interrupts the repartee with a blunt question, 'But do the ladies drink?' (III.ii.30-1). Drink now becomes the subject of the conversation. Horner claims he will drink with the women because 'I shall have the pleasure at least of laying 'em flat with the bottle, and bring as much scandal that way upon 'em as formerly t'other' (32-4). Harcourt prophetically suggests 'you may prove as weak a brother amongst 'em that way as t'other' (35-6). Horner's friends are disgusted by the idea of his drinking with women, claiming that drinking with women is unnatural, that drink quenches love, and that 'Wine and women, good apart, together [are] as nauseous as sack and sugar' (49-50). Drink is supposedly a sign of manliness and a social adhesive of male bonding. The fact that women drink at all is a surprise to all but Horner:

Quack. But do civil persons and women of honour drink and sing bawdy songs?
Horner. Oh, amongst friends, amongst friends. (IV.iii.21-2).

Horner's knowledge of women's secret drinking seems at first to empower him, enabling him to expose their hypocrisy. However, drink is a marker of manhood which women in this society assume for themselves. Far from being laid flat with the bottle, the women bring their own bottles to Horner's lodging, reveal that they are used to drinking two bottles each,

and that they, like the men, equate drinking with 'honesty' (V.iv.19). They
then carouse in a ritual which affirms both their power over Horner and
their barbed and provisional union with one another, in an exact mirror-
image of the men's relationships. Yet in a sense Horner and the whole
sexual game come second to the drink itself, as in Lady Fidget's extraordinary drinking song:

> Why should our damned tyrants oblige us to live
> On the pittance of pleasure which they only give?
>   We must not rejoice
>   With wine and with noise.
> In vain we must wake in a dull bed alone,
> Whilst to our warm rival, the bottle, they're gone.
>   Then lay aside charms
>   And take up these arms.
>
> 'Tis wine only gives 'em their courage and wit
> Because we live sober, to men we submit.
>   If for beauties you'd pass
>   Take a lick of the glass:
> 'Twill mend your complexions, and when they are gone
> The best red we have is the red of the grape.
>   Then, sister, lay't on,
>   And damn a good shape. (V.iv.26)

Drink is a rival for their husbands' affections, but instead of competing
with it they will possess it for themselves, a far more empowering paradigm
than anything available in the sexual game. Drink is the agent of women's
emancipation and self-expression. To describe taking up glasses as taking
up arms locates drink explicitly within a gender battle. The word 'sister'
reinforces this, as does the disdain for dieting and preserving the complexion. The other women affirm this: 'Dear brimmer', 'Lovely brimmer'
(V.iv.42, 45). Horner's knowledge of women's secret drinking, earlier a
sign of his power, shifts to an awareness of his and all men's ultimate
marginality. It is typical of the ironic social reflexiveness of this play that
drink actually plays a central role. It is both literally and metaphorically the
key to understanding how the play's society is to be understood.[18]

     There is a disjunction between sign and substance in the play, appro-
priate for a world based upon false appearances. Pretence is universal:
almost everyone is pretending to be something they are not, or coming to
grief through failing to do so. Appearances or 'signs' are, in a sense, what
the play is about. Even the words 'title' (or name) and 'sign' are played

upon. Sparkish, punning on the idea of a nobleman's title, says: 'a wit to me is the greatest title in the world' (I.i.328). Horner, punning on the idea of property and title deeds, says Sparkish is 'a cracked title' (I.i.370), meaning a 'bad buy' as a husband. Sparkish calls Horner 'a sign of a man' (I.i.316), implying there is no substance (since he is a eunuch). Horner replies: 'But the devil take me, if thine be the sign of a jest' (I.i.318). In III.ii Margery comments on tradesmen's or tavern signs: 'Lord, what a power of brave signs are here! Stay – the Bull's Head, the Ram's Head, and the Stag's Head!' (III.ii.202–3). These horned heads remind Pinchwife of the sign of a cuckold: 'Nay, if every husband's proper sign here were visible, they would be all alike' (205–6). But the signs stand also as a marker of animalistic sexuality representing the predatory gallants who are on the prowl in the scene, with Margery as their target. The signs thus slip from their supposed signification.

However, this is not to say that the signs become completely arbitrary: in the exchange between Pinchwife and Margery, quoted above, their symbolic function is clear enough. Word play seems to render everything fluid, but there is meaning, even symbolism, not complete arbitrariness. When in III.ii Horner gives Margery oranges and dried fruit, the symbolic significance is clear. The fruit is suggestive of flesh and fecundity, of sexually available orange wenches in the playhouse. Pinchwife responds aside, 'You have only squeezed my orange, I suppose, and given it me again' (III.ii.560–1). The bawdy associations of oranges and china are linked by Margery's references to them in IV.ii as 'China oranges' (IV.ii.13). Similarly, in the china scene china is not an arbitrary signifier.[19] On the contrary, china, a booming luxury import in the Restoration and a sign of fashionable taste, is a marker of self-indulgence and the new consumerism and therefore an appropriate symbol or objective correlative for 'consumerism' in sexual relations. China is also a far from arbitrary signifier in the sense that it is a code, part of a secret language which Horner and the women understand.

The play's fluidity of meaning had led to various attempts to 'fix' upon supposedly central themes: friendship, jealousy, selfishness, lust, materialism, the problem of communication, wit versus folly, honour versus hypocrisy (general or specifically female) and madness and theatricality. Yet *The Country Wife*, like its central character Horner, has proved notoriously difficult to 'pin down' and interpret. Consider the following statements, and note the use of the first person plural in both:

Both [Horner and Molière's Tartuffe] are grim, nightmare figures, dominating the helpless, hopeless apes who call themselves civilized men. Again, the
absolute. Again we feel that no mean is possible, because no mean can exist for
figures which seem automata animated by devils that drive them irresistably to
an extreme – and leave them there to laugh fiendishly. Is it a comedy at all? Not
in the ordinary sense. The clever, cynical dialogue, the scathing irony, the
remorseless stripping of all grace from man, are too overpowering.[20]

The hidden *Playboy* reader in all of us is bound to identify with [Horner's]
triumphs.[21]

These opposite judgements of the play obviously say as much about the
critics as about the play itself – if not more.

There are two ways of looking at the play's 'problem of meaning'. The
first, the view of Robert Hume and Judith Milhous, is that there is no
reason why the play should be considered as making any kind of statement. It can be performed as a 'perfect farce', as John Palmer labelled it as
long ago as 1913. Moreover, *The Country Wife* was written to be performed,
and 'the play can be made to mean pretty much what the director wants it
to mean'.[22] To this we might add that the comedies were considered
'popular culture' rather as films are today, so they were not necessarily
expected to do more than entertain. We do not need to look for a message
and can simply enjoy.

It is equally possible to speculate, however, about what the play's
'meaninglessness' might 'mean', paradoxical as this might sound. Several
critical works concentrate upon the very fact of the play's fluidity of
interpretative possibilities, stressing the slipperiness of signs in the play,
though they disagree about the extent and effect of the slippage between
words (or gestures or other 'signs') and meaning.[23] The instability of
meaning can be linked to a new Restoration world-view, whether the focus
is upon a revolution in language, a questioning of the dominant culture of
'wit', pragmatism in philosophy, secularism in a formerly religious climate,
capitalism undermining previous economic certainties, or new config-
urations of the gender battle. The instability of meaning thus becomes
'meaningfully' reflective of instability in the world beyond the play.

Yet we should beware of over-reading the play's 'meaningful
meaninglessness'. It is doubtful that there is any strong social critique.
One of the interpretative possibilities mentioned above may serve as an
example of Wycherley's determined indeterminacy: the rise of capitalism
and the perceived loss of idealized, heroic, feudal values. In the previous
chapter I argued that heroic drama papered over ideological cracks. *The*

Country Wife may expose these cracks, but not with any corrective purpose. It is perfectly possible to see the china scene as indicative of a new consumerism which seems to be satirized by Wycherley.[24] In a critique of materialism and mercantile or 'capitalist' values, Horner may be seen as a sexual 'capitalist', scheming and 'projecting', 'investing' in a plan to reap sexual dividends;[25] and the Quack mocks this when he says, 'Well, sir, how fadges the new design? Have you not the luck of all your brother projectors, to deceive only yourself at last?' (IV.ii.1–3). Yet it is equally possible to see the energy and exuberance of the bartering mentality in Horner and the female libertines, whereas the virtuous Alithea and Harcourt, embodying traditional aristocratic values of chivalry and trust, can seem somewhat static. Wycherley is not 'making a point'.

Whereas heroic drama seemed to 'contain' contradictions, sex comedy seems to collapse into them. In the end Wycherley is quite scathing (in a witty way) about his society, but too much of an insider to suggest any alternatives. The ending of the play seems to confirm not that truth will prevail but that society values appearances. This is only realistic. For Horner, being jealous and afraid of being a cuckold is 'all one' with actually being a cuckold (I.i.435). For Alithea at the end, seeming compromised is as bad as being compromised. Preservation of appearances matters more than revelation of the truth. The cuckolds realize their fate, but conspire with the others to reinstate Horner's eunuch pretence, on which everyone's 'honour' depends. The play ends with a dance of cuckolds, and Horner's moral: 'he who aims by women to be prized, / First by the men, you see, must be despised' (V.iv.432). Whereas the virtuous gang have become sister-sharers in their new lover, and Margery has moved from social marginality to initiation, all the men seem isolated: Pinchwife and Sir Jasper by their humiliation as cuckolds, and lack of fulfilment in marriage itself; Sparkish by the pursuit of male friendship which cuts him off from a loving bond with a woman while bringing only ridicule from the men. Dorilant is also resolved never to marry. Harcourt lets go of what the world thinks in standing by Alithea, and in doing so is rewarded with a loving union. If he is true to it, he will have to distance himself from his fellow-wits and their standards. Horner, of course, is cut off from other men by his pretence.

The preservation of appearances is in stark contrast to Renaissance antecedents such as Jonson's *Volpone*. Since there is no exposure, there can be no change or moral progress. Unlike Jonson's tricksters, Horner's pranks serve no corrective function and do not transform or purge society. We have witnessed a great performance, a masterpiece of acting and pretence. Horner continues to enjoy 'performance' in the other, sexual sense. It seems significant that, as Horner's energies continue to be dissipated in casual sex, the epilogue, spoken by the actress who played Lady Fidget, concludes the play by teasing men for failing to satisfy women sexually. The moral seems to be that we can enjoy the performance, but should not expect a climax.

Notes

1 Hume, *The Development of English Drama*, chapters 2, 3 and 7; and 'The Change in Comedy'.

2 An insight into issues in this debate may be gained from *Studies in the Literary Imagination* 10 (1977) which contains several essays on *The Country Wife*. See especially Novak, 'Margery Pinchwife's "London Disease"'; and Hume, 'The Myth of the Rake in Restoration Comedy'. On libertinism see also Underwood, *Etherege and the Seventeenth-century Comedy of Manners*; Traugott, 'The Rake's Progress'; Weber, *The Restoration Rake-hero*; and Chernaik, *Sexual Freedom in Restoration Literature*.

3 Following Hume (see note 1), the best recent discussions of generic issues are, in my view, Corman, *Genre and Generic Change in English Comedy*; and Hughes, *English Drama*, chapters 4, 6, 9 and 11.

4 See e.g. Sedgwick, *Between Men*, chapter 3; and Gill, *Interpreting Ladies*, who calls *The Country Wife* 'a nasty, gleeful misogynistic exploration of abasement' (73).

5 See e.g. Burke, 'Wycherley's "Tendentious Joke"'; Bacon, 'Wives, Widows, and Writings in Restoration Comedy'; and Young, *The Feminist Voices in Restoration Comedy*. Ogden in his introduction sees *The Country Wife* as critical of those who see women as objects (xxiii).

6 See Alleman, *Matrimonial Law and the Materials of Restoration Comedy*; Vernon, 'Marriage of Convenience and the Moral Code of Restoration Comedy'; Hume, 'Marital Discord in English Comedy From Dryden to Fielding' repr. in *The Rakish Stage*; Burke, 'Wycherley's "Tendentious Joke"'; Wheatley, 'Romantic Love and Social Necessities'; Cordner, introduction to *Four Restoration Marriage Plays*.

7 See Weber, *Restoration Rake-hero*, 53–69, and 'Horner and his "Women of Honour": The Dinner Party in *The Country Wife*'; Vieth, 'Wycherley's *The Country Wife*: An Anatomy of Masculinity'; and Freedman, 'Impotence and Self-Destruction in *The Country Wife*'; and Cohen, '*The Country Wife* and Social Danger'.

8 See Brown, *English Dramatic Form*, chapter 2; and Canfield, *Tricksters and Estates*, 126–30.

9 Neill, 'Heroic Heads and Humble Tails'; Braverman, 'The Rake's Progress Revisited'. Novak in 'Margery Pinchwife's "London Disease"' suggests that the impetus for libertine comedy in the 1670s came from the Court itself.

10 Criticism has canvassed every shade and nuance. At one extreme are views of him as negative and destructive: e.g. Dobrée, *Restoration Comedy*; Holland, *The First Modern Comedies*; Righter, 'William Wycherley'. Conversely, Birdsall in *Wild Civility* views him as a wholly positive and creative comic hero. For other positive views see: Fujimura, *The Restoration Comedy of Wit*; and Cecil, 'Libertine and *Précieux* Elements in Restoration Comedy'. Laura Brown tries to marry positive and negative judgements, arguing that moral and aesthetic judgements remain separate as we applaud his ingenuity but deplore his actions: *English Dramatic Form*, 49–55. Horner is seen as the instrument of social satire by Craik, 'Some Aspects of Satire in Wycherley's Plays'; and Chadwick, *The Four Plays of William Wycherley*; and as a tainted or satirized satirist by Zimbardo, *Wycherley's Drama*, 147–65; and Markley, *Two Edg'd Weapons*, 159–78. He is seen as neurotic or deranged by Kaufman, 'Wycherley's *The Country Wife* and the Don Juan Character'; and Marshall, 'Wycherley's "Great Stage of Fools"'.

11 Critics disagree about whether he expresses sexual hostility and aggression towards women: see e.g. Kaufman, 'Wycherley's *The Country Wife* and the Don Juan Character', 216; or whether he recognizes women's frustrations, appreciates their needs and ultimately recognizes his kinship with them: see e.g. Weber, *Rake-hero*, 62–5 and 'Horner and his "Women of Honour"'. Some see him as a successful male predator: e.g. Sedgwick, *Between Men*, chapter 3; others as an ultimately disempowered object of female desire and agency: e.g. Burke, 'Wycherley's "Tendentious Joke"'. Michael Neill sees both possibilities present, as 'dichotomies collapse into semiotic perplexity': 'Horned Beasts and China Oranges', 14.

12 Of course the play does contain a clever servant, Lucy, but she does not begin to make her presence felt until Act IV.

13 Wycherley includes a scandalized discussion of *The Country Wife* in his next play, *The Plain Dealer*, which gives some idea (albeit playfully exaggerated) of the play's reception.

14 Wycherley mocks himself as well as his critics in his prologue, and in various references to poets (e.g. I.i.188; III.ii.92–142), and to 'little inconsiderable fellows' granted sexual favours by great ladies, as he himself was favoured by Lady Castlemaine, the King's mistress (II.i.393). The tone of the mockery is always good-humoured and urbane.

15 Molière's *L'Ecole des Femmes* and *L'Ecole des Maris* are important sources or analogues for Wycherley's play, along with Terence's *The Eunuch* and Jonson's *Volpone*.

16 On Alithea and Harcourt as morally and socially normative see e.g. Holland, *The First Modern Comedies*, 83–4. For positive views see also Righter, 'William Wycherley'; Zimbardo, *Wycherley's Drama*; Rogers, *William Wycherley*, chapter 3; Muir, *The Comedy of Manners*, 78–9; Verdumen, 'Grasping for Permanence'; Thompson, *Language in Wycherley's Plays*, 71–91; Marshall, 'Wycherley's "Great Stage of Fools"', 424–6. The couple are seen as morally compromised by Markley, *Two Edg'd Weapons*, 175–7, and Gill, *Interpreting Ladies*, 66–70. Hume says, 'If Harcourt and Alithea are supposed to represent a high moral

norm in the play and to make us view Horner with disapprobation, then Wycherley made a mess of things': *Development*, 101. See also Milhous and Hume, *Producible Interpretation*, 91–4. For the idea that the couple are an irrelevance see Sedgwick's bizarre argument (in an otherwise stimulating and seminal essay) that their love (which does not fit into her homosocial schema) 'is one of those cul-de-sacs in Wycherley's drama, a self-enclosed bubble that seems to have floated in from another genre' (60). In fact, the virtuous couple is common in sex comedy: there is an example in *The Rover*, discussed in the next chapter. Ogden in his introduction to the play argues more plausibly against a central role for the couple on the basis of casting decisions in the original production (xxxii).

17 'besides the surgeon's': i.e. in treatment for venereal disease.

18 For a broader discussion see my 'The Politics of Drink in Restoration Drama'.

19 See Neill, 'Horned Beasts and China Oranges', 9.

20 Dobrée, *Restoration Comedy*, 94.

21 Weales, Introduction to *The Complete Plays of William Wycherley*, xii.

22 Milhous and Hume, *Producible Interpretation*, 74.

23 See e.g. Holland, *The Ornament of Action*, 195; Payne, 'Reading the Signs in *The Country Wife*'; Hughes, 'Naming and Entitlement in Wycherley, Etherege and Dryden'; Neill, 'Horned Beasts and China Oranges'; Thompson, *Language in Wycherley's Plays*, chapter 5; Markley, *Two Edg'd Weapons*, 159–78; Burke, 'Wycherley's "Tendentious Joke"'; Gill, *Interpreting Ladies*, 54–74; and Hynes, 'Against Theory?'.

24 For a discussion of consumerism and class issues in the play see Hinnant, 'Pleasure and the Political Economy of Consumption in Restoration Comedy'.

25 Neill speaks of 'the triumphant enterprise of the monopolist proprietor of this sexual exchange, the phallic projector, Mr. Horner': 'Horned Beasts and China Oranges', 8.

Comedy II:
Aphra Behn's *The Rover; or,*
The Banish't Cavaliers

*T*he Rover was first acted on or before 24 March 1677 with Charles II in attendance. The play was performed at Court in February 1680 and October 1685, and continued to be popular in the theatres well into the eighteenth century, albeit in toned-down versions.[1] The play then fell out of the repertoire until the late twentieth century, when there were several revivals, though at first only in adapted versions.[2] The play was first produced and published anonymously with pronouns in the prologue referring to the author as male, but Behn's name appears on the title page of the third issue in 1677, and there is a reference in postscript to her sex. Behn's *The Rover* is an adaptation of Thomas Killigrew's *Thomaso*, written in cavalier exile during the interregnum and not known to have been performed.[3] Behn makes significant alterations, making the action much faster paced and the speeches much shorter. The tone of Behn's play is in general lighter, though the fate of the prostitute Angellica Bianca, who gives her heart to Willmore and is rejected, brings in a darker note. The setting is changed from Madrid under the Inquisition to Naples during carnival time. This makes a fitting background for the heroines' adoption of disguises in order to scheme to avoid the fates of forced marriage and encloistering as a nun, as well as for the men's sexual predatoriness.[4] As for the characters, Behn splits Killigrew's romantic heroine into two sisters, the virtuous Florinda and the witty Hellena, and adds a cousin, Valeria; and she splits his complex Thomaso into the virtuous Belvile and the rake Willmore who is the 'rover' of the title. The fool Edwardo becomes Blunt, 'an English country gentleman', the word 'country' signifying literal gullibility (that is, worthiness to be gulled); but Edwardo also gives some characteristics as well as some actions, such as attempted rape of one of the heroines, to Willmore himself. This alerts us to Behn's indulgent mockery of male characters including her hero. Meanwhile, there is a greater focus on the female characters. The women are active agents in the plot, Willmore seeming at times comparatively passive as the women compete over him. There is a general preoccupation with the double standards, dilemmas and difficulties women face, which has led to debate about how far Behn may be described as a 'feminist' writer.[5] What is clear is that Behn is a consummate professional, and that her focus on women's difficulties and desires occurs within the parameters of writing for the stage and for 'box office' success.

Behn's play opens with a discussion between the women whereas *Thomaso* begins with men's talk. Behn flouts dramatic convention, in that it is a norm for Restoration comedies to begin with discussion between male friends. Wycherley played with this convention by opening *The Country Wife* with a discussion between Horner and the Quack, then a passage with his prospective cuckold before the male friends enter. This emphasizes Horner's 'off-centre' relation to homosocial norms and structures. Behn's opening likewise shows a significant shift of emphasis. The action is 'framed' by the women's perspective. The sisters Florinda and Hellena are presented as appealing characters and the exchange between them is lively and funny, so the audience is immediately involved with them. Although no character in Restoration comedy has the highly developed interiority of a character in a novel, Behn's women have a far more developed subjectivity than Wycherley's women. Moreover, the subject of the discussion is how to evade an oppressive female destiny. Florinda is destined for forced marriage twice over, by her father and brother who favour different but equally loathed husbands. Hellena is intended for a convent. The dramatic tension, the dynamics of the comedy and the manipulation of our sympathies all work to support the women. Our response to Horner's plots at the start of *The Country Wife* might be contradictory, moral disapproval vying with titillation and admiration of boldness. Behn makes these aspects work together: moral outrage (English Protestant disapproval of continental Catholic norms or simply revulsion at domestic tyranny) prompts the same 'direction' of response as the 'love interest' or titillation (we want Florinda and her lover to get together; we want to see whom Hellena will find as a lover).

Hellena's wit is immediately both sexy and endearing, but as in *The Country Wife* we are not meant to value one character above another. Rather, it is the 'double act' of virtue and wit which appeals.[6] The intertwining of the two different 'women's stories' represents different paradigms of female experience. Florinda resembles a heroine of French romance or cavalier drama (such as Serulina in *Thomaso*). She is moved by her Belvile's virtue more than by passion: 'I had a 1000 Charms to meet my Eyes and Ears, e're I cou'd yield, and 'twas the knowledge of *Belvile's* merit, not the surprizing Person took my Soul' (III.I.49–51). She is somewhat passive, waiting to be rescued. It is her cousin Valeria who engineers her escape from her brother's house in IV.iii and frees her from danger in V.i. Yet Florinda is no mere cipher: 'and how near soever my Father thinks I am to marrying that hated Object, I shall let him see, I understand better, what's due to my Beauty, Birth and Fortune, and more to my Soul, than to obey those unjust Commands' (I.i.18–22). Florinda here lays claim not to liberation for women but to the privileges due to her as a woman of the upper class. Florinda may be said to espouse a form of patriarchal ideology, but modified to give her what she wants. This is the best course for her. Within the parameters of her class perspective and strong moral sense she is extremely assertive: 'I wou'd not have a man so dear to me as my Brother, follow the ill Customes of our Countrey, and make a slave of his Sister' (I.i.59–61). Imagery of women as slaves recurs throughout the play.   *upper C = strong.*

Hellena is a new and more contemporary character,[7] full of mockery and a self-professed love of mischief:

'Tis true I never was a Lover yet – but I begin to have a shrew'd guess, what 'tis to be so, and fancy it very pretty to sigh, and sing, and blush, and wish, and dream and wish, and long and wish, to see the Man; and when I do look pale and tremble; just as you did when my Brother brought home the fine English Colonel to see you. (I.i.9–13)

This kind of mocking spirit will stand her in good stead, for, while she will hazard much to get a lover, she is able to remain detached from her own desire in a empowering way. Hellena's wit also enables her to get away with a lively assertiveness quite at odds with feminine propriety:

I'm resolved to provide myself this Carnival, if there be ere a handsome proper fellow of my humour above ground, tho I ask first. (I.i.33–4)

I don't intend every he that likes me shall have me, but he that I like. (III.i.37–8)

Florinda's expostulations make us aware how unconventional this is. Yet, although Hellena may seem more 'liberated' than her older sister, in fact she also espouses a male ideology, modified to give her what she wants. In her case it is the witty, cavalier ideology of the dispossessed royalists, younger sons and rake heroes. The sisters make different negotiations and accommodations with their world. In the process Behn helps us explore this world from women's perspective. We should beware of unconsciously positing some feminist norm from which Behn's women or Behn herself may be said to depart.

The pair of heroines is matched by a pair of heroes. Behn is following the Restoration fashion for 'doubling'. Again, it is a question not of valuing one above the other but of exploring through counterpoint different masculine 'narratives'. Belvile is the romance hero. I.ii establishes the other men's half-mocking respect for Belvile's superiority in his commit-ment to a virtuous but unattainable love. He and Florinda resemble the heroes and heroines of French heroic romance and English heroic drama. They are truer advocates of upper-class honour codes than Florinda's father whose mercenary arguments for arranged marriage are ventriloquized by her brother Pedro (who has a secret agenda) in the opening scene. We learn that Belvile has saved Florinda from 'the Licens'd Lust of common Souldiers' (I.i.67) at the siege of Pamplona, as well as protecting her father from insult, creating a debt of honour and gratitude. As we shall see in Chapter 5, Otway recapitulates this theme of earlier rescue and paternal ingratitude in *Venice Preserv'd*.

Yet Belvile's class position is anomalous as a cavalier in exile. He would have been at the siege of Pamplona as a mercenary in the French army, an illustration of the impossibility of remaining high-mindedly untainted by financial motives.[8] Though often shrewd in his comments on society, Belvile is remarkably undiscerning in love, repeatedly failing to recognize Florinda in disguise. When Florinda is threatened with rape later in the play, Belvile fails to protect her. It would be easy to see this as mere ineptitude. However, the problem goes deeper, to the heart of male–female relations: Belvile ironically prefigures the rape scenes by making Florinda's letter public property among his friends in I.ii. That the woman put at risk of rape by her lover's ideas about male friendship is a potentially tragic theme is shown by Otway's tragic reworking of it in *Venice Preserv'd*. I discuss the rape scenes further below, but am here concerned to point out Belvile's role in them and to make the point that we should beware of seeing Belvile as the virtuous foil for the rakish Willmore. Masculine roles and identities in this world are more complex and more compromised.

Willmore is the 'rover' of the title in two senses, as a wandering exiled cavalier and sexually. He bears a resemblance to the libertine Earl of

Rochester, to Behn's own lover John Hoyle, to Charles II and to Charles's brother James.[9] Willmore is intensely desirable, but the presentation of his character is not entirely positive.[10] As I noted above, he takes qualities from Killigrew's hero Thomaso but also from his fool Edwardo. He even sounds like Shakespeare's Bottom when he proclaims, 'Thou know'st I am no tame sigher, but a Rampant Lion of the Forrest' (I.ii.99–100). Like Horner, Willmore is an ambiguous figure, sexy and witty, but always in danger of becoming the mocked rather than the mocker, and the disempowered object of desire rather than the active and powerful subject. 'Love and Mirth! are my bus'ness in Naples' says Willmore, and he pursues both almost obsessively (I.ii.71). Both he and Hellena are frequently referred to as 'mad'. 'Love' for Willmore means sex, to which he is addicted: 'there's but one way for a Woman to oblige me' (I.ii.243–4). Willmore enjoys the game of sexual conquest almost as much as the act itself and is averse to commitment: 'I am parlously afraid of being in Love' (V.i.393–4). Yet at times he seems as eager in pursuit of the bottle as of women.

Willmore would scorn to be likened to Blunt, a comic butt among the other men who speaks in a crude and old-fashioned country style. Yet Willmore shares with Blunt a preference for women of easy virtue and a predisposition to rape. Behn is often critical of mercenary motives, and Blunt, an elder brother, is resented by the dispossessed and impoverished cavaliers for his wealth. Yet Willmore, supposedly generous, is actually quite mercenary: his first words to Hellena concern his unwillingness to part with what little money he has, and he is happy to spend Blunt's money and Angellica's. The difference between Willmore and Blunt is political: Blunt's estate has not been sequestered by the parliamentarians, and indeed an exchange in I.ii suggests he is actually a supporter of the Commonwealth (44–53). For the Tory Behn this may be enough to justify the total humiliation which is his fate, as he is tricked by the whore Lucetta, stripped and cast into the sewer.[11] In other plays by Tories revenge takes the form of cuckolding the Whig (or parliamentarian); here politico-sexual 'emasculation' takes a different form. Blunt then vows revenge on women and initiates an attempted gang-rape of Florinda which is foiled only at the last moment. Behn characteristically equates parliamentarian sympathies with nastiness towards women.

Lucetta, who dupes Blunt, seems a typical cheating whore. Yet the play resists denigrating her as a prostitute. The audience is invited to enjoy Lucetta's humiliation of Blunt. Indeed her mistreatment of him is gleefully anticipated by the other men in the play. The prostitute is less of an enemy than the English parliamentarian, a theme to which Behn returned in *The Revenge*.[12] Behn goes further in *The Rover*, questioning the facile categorizing of women and destabilizing gender categories. As we shall see, the prostitute Angellica refuses to stay in the 'whore' category, and Hellena, similarly, refuses to behave like a 'lady of quality'. Hellena and Florinda go to the carnival disguised as gypsies, and Willmore refers to Hellena subsequently as his 'little gypsy'. The gypsy persona locates her outside conventional social norms.

Hellena and Willmore are very similar. But she exposes his double standards:

Willmore. Oh, I long to come first to the Banquet of Love! And such a swinging Appetite I bring – Oh I'm impatient. – thy Lodging sweetheart, thy Lodging! Or I'm a dead Man!
Hellena. Why must we be either guilty of Fornication or Murder if we converse with you Men – and is there no difference between leave to love me, and leave to lye with me? (I.ii.183–9)

Hellena's wit makes Willmore seem ridiculous here. She mocks the familiar libertine motif that the man will die if the woman doesn't relieve his desire, and exposes the rake's discourse of love as crude sexual appetite. Later she exposes the double standard within Willmore's ideology of sexual freedom: 'what shall I get? A cradle full of noise and mischief, with a pack of repentance at my back?' (V.i.430–1). Sometimes her wit takes the form of verbal cleverness; sometimes, when flowery rhetoric might be expected, she gives extremely plain speaking:

Willmore. I can teach thee to Weave a true loves knot better.
Hellena. So can my dog. (V.i.433)

Hellena is mistress of the unexpected. She is desirable as a wealthy, well-born virgin who nevertheless acts on her desire and advertises her charms.[13] Where she differs from the prostitute characters, ironically, is in her self-possession. Economically the prostitute 'possesses' herself and can repeatedly sell herself, while Hellena is possessed by her father and brother. Yet Hellena is self-possessed in character. She has freedom to manoeuvre because she is able to keep a distance from her passions, rather than being subsumed by them. There is often an edge of self-mockery: 'hey ho, I'm as sad as a Lover's Lute' (III.i.5). She is a 'gay' character in the old sense of the word, entirely free from self-dramatization and self-pity. We like her because she makes us laugh, and it is the same for Willmore: Hellena's 'playing hard to get' tantalizes him, but it is her wit, primarily, which attracts him: 'A Pox on't, I cannot get her out of my Head: Pray Heaven, if ever I do see her again, she prove damnably ugly, that I may fortifie my self against her Tongue' (II.i.7–9).

Hellena is empowered at least verbally through wit, and it is wit which allows her to express desire. Her battle of wits with Willmore appears at times as a kind of extended foreplay. Wit enables her to avoid some of the familiar traps of desire, such as premature surrender and unwanted pregnancy. Yet there is a more subtle trap awaiting her precisely because of her association of wit and desire, which leads her to desire the witty man. Hellena desires Willmore because of his inconstancy rather than in spite of it: 'how this unconstant humour makes me love him!' (IV.ii.281). She relishes his effrontery: 'I can't be angry with him he dissembles so heartily' (III.i.136–7). This scene, in which she pursues Willmore and flirts with him despite knowing he has just come from Angellica's bed, is extraordinary from any perspective, seventeenth- or twentieth-century. Hellena, of course, claims equality with Willmore in inconstancy: 'I am as inconstant as you … I profess my self the gay, the kind, the Inconstant – the Devil's in't if this won't please you' (III.i.167, 173–4). However, we must always be aware of the undercurrent of irony in her speech. She may be affecting inconstancy herself only in order to tantalize him. Wit is paramount, and we will misinterpret the play if we take 'straight' everything said wittily.

The freedom of manoeuvre Hellena's wit gives her is limited. Critics disagree about whether Hellena is a more autonomous female subject and provides a liberated alternative to the conventional Florinda and the socially excluded prostitutes.[14] It may be a sign of empowerment that Hellena adopts male disguise as well as gypsy disguise. Often in Behn's plays male dress shows women's ability to act as men, though a major motive for cross-dressing in the Restoration theatre was to offer the audience the titillating sight of an actress's legs.[15] By dressing as a man Hellena is able to poke fun at Willmore and cause trouble between him and Angellica. It is a 'lark' or a 'wind up' rather than an act of assertion as such. It works for a while, then Willmore recognizes her and turns the tables and teases her back.

Hellena's teasing has a simple goal. Her challenge is to marry the unmarriable, and she does this by unorthodox means because orthodox ones would not serve. The process allows full scope for her abilities, but the goal is not empowering in itself. There is some suggestion that the mode of witty courtship will be prolonged into marriage itself. Hellena never makes Angellica's mistake of feeling safe and giving way to the spontaneous expression of love and desire which make the rake feel trapped and alienated. When Willmore names himself 'Robert the Constant', she responds that she is 'Hellena the Inconstant'. Yet Willmore makes two references to the troubles of married couples (V.i.450–1, 544–5). And there is no escaping the fact that Hellena has achieved her desire by exchanging the convent for a husband who will spend her inheritance. She has excelled at the 'game' but the game is over. Her autonomy can exist only in the liminal space of carnival.

If the fate of a lady of quality is inevitably confining, what of the prostitute? The first discussion between the men in the play in I.ii begins with the question of the merits of whores versus virtuous mistresses. Later in the same scene masquerading women who might or might not be prostitutes pass across the stage and stimulate both desire and discussion. Sometimes whores and 'women of quality' seem interchangeable to the men, especially Willmore; at other times the distinction is all-important. II.ii begins with discussion among the men of the courtesan Angellica Bianca who is advertising herself for sale by displaying her portrait. Angellica is resented, by Belvile in moral terms for setting herself up like a lady of quality (67–71), and by Willmore for charging too much. As usual with Willmore there is ambivalence between libertine ideas (sex should be freely given) and more mercenary motives: he cannot afford her. We can see this confusion in his first reaction to the portrait:

How wondrous fair she is – a Thousand Crowns a Month – by Heaven as many Kingdoms were too little, a plague of this Poverty – of which I ne're complain, but when it hinders my approach to Beauty: which Virtue alone ne're cou'd purchase. *Turns from the Picture* (II.i.98–101)

This scene in which Angellica gazes upon men who gaze in turn upon her picture focuses on the ambiguities of women's power. Who is in control of 'the gaze'? In one sense Angellica is a commodified object for male consumption; in another sense she is in control of the whole process, marketing herself and thus taking charge.

However, Angellica's power is illusory because it leaves no room for her own desire. Once she falls for Willmore she surrenders herself and loses everything. It would be easy to see Angellica as punished for pride and money-mindedness. She speaks of her vanity in II.i, and admits in V.i that loving Willmore has wounded her pride. Her focus initially is entirely on acquisition. She boasts: 'nothing but Gold shall charm my heart' (129–

30). When she subsequently falls for Willmore, sleeps with him for free and ends up giving him money, we could see this as Behn's critique of mercenary motives, especially since the play offers some explicit comment. Moretta laments that this is the general condition of prostitutes: 'Trophies, which from believing Fops we win, / Are Spoils to those who couzen us agen' (II.ii.430). As if to underscore the point, Lucetta, also, has a lover, Phillipo, to whom gives the money robbed from Blunt. Moreover, Willmore explicitly criticizes the selling of sex in the seduction scene (II.ii).

However, Willmore's critique is tainted in two ways. First, it is disingenuous, a bold seduction technique to undermine Angellica's defences, when more conventional love-rhetoric would bore her. As she says, 'I thought I shou'd have seen you at my Feet' (282); so Willmore's tactic of substituting criticism for flattery titillates, tantalizes and has the merit of surprise. Many critics have taken the critique of mercenary motives in this scene seriously; but its witty nature is suggested by the fact that Willmore's rebukes to Angellica alternate with his bantering barter with Moretta on how much sex may be obtained for a 'pistol' (punning on small coin, phallus and soldier's weapon). Yet wit alone would not be so seductive without the undercurrent of personal bitterness to appeal to her emotions.

Second, Willmore's critique is tainted because his own motives are far from pure, as we see when he is spending Angellica's money after deserting her, and boasting of having 'all the honey of Matrimony, but none of the sting' (III.i.109). In a sense he has done that for which he criticized Angellica: sold himself for money. Angellica herself points out the hypocrisy of men in general in criticizing whores when they buy and sell women in marriage:

Pray tell me, Sir, are you not guilty of the same Mercenary Crime, When a Lady is propos'd to you for a Wife, you never ask, how fair – discreet – or virtuous she is; but what's her Fortune – which if but small, you cry – she will not do my busines – and basely leave her, thou she languish for you, say, is this not poor? (II.ii.357–61)

Willmore scorns this 'Barbarouse Custome' (362), yet he is thrilled when he knows that Hellena (whom he ends up marrying) is an heiress: 'Ha! My Gipsie worth Two Hundred Thousand Crowns! – oh how I long to be with her – pox, I knew she was of Quality' (IV.ii.271–2). Of course there is no punishing of mercenary motives in Willmore's case.[16]

Angellica's story, then, is not to be reduced to a fable of avarice punished. Indeed, her motivation is quite complex. A song she plays from her balcony in II.i. suggests that virgins welcome 'kind force' (172) in sexual relations. She seems to construct herself as an emotional virgin who wants to be ravished by Willmore:

> I never lov'd before, tho oft a Mistress.
> – Shall my first Vows be slighted? (II.ii.380)

> Thou hast a Pow'r too strong to be resisted. (422)

It is hard to find an appropriate rhetoric of sexual submission. Angellica employs the discourse of romantic love. 'The pay, I mean, is but thy Love for mine. / Can you give that?' (418). The audience knows that Willmore is swearing love falsely; but Angellica effectively becomes a romantic heroine. Anita Pacheco gives an excellent explanation of her motivation:

> Behn depicts Angellica Bianca as a woman torn between immense pride and an equally formidable psychic burden of disempowerment – an inner division that dissociates her sexuality from her sense of self-worth. Romance offers her a dream of psychic wholeness in which desire and pride are harmonized, in which erotic surrender to male power signals not self-subversion but the ultimate confirmation of her own power and value. When Willmore's immediate betrayal explodes the dream of self-unity, Angellica's fragile constructed identity collapses with it, leaving behind a sense of utter worthlessness.[17]

For Pacheco, Willmore's treatment of Angellica is quasi-rape. Once Angellica has given herself she cannot re-assume self-control:

> But I have given him my Eternal rest,
> My whole repose, my future joys, my Heart!
> My Virgin heart, *Moretta*; Oh 'tis gone! (IV.ii 232)

It seems that what Behn is concerned with in Angellica's story is not moralistic treatment of selling sex, but exploring and exposing the double standard which allows Willmore to get away with behaviour that Angellica cannot get away with. Men and women alike are desiring subjects, but a woman who gives way to her desire is damned.

It may seem odd that Behn gives her prostitute a name meaning 'white angel'. This alerts us to the deconstruction of the virgin/whore binary which many critics have noticed in Behn's work. Far from being a vicious figure whose downfall satisfies, the tormented Angellica becomes a poignant figure. Indeed some critics have seen her as a tragic one. Jane Spencer notes, 'In the treatment of Angellica, both Killigrew and Behn were anti-

cipating the concerns of female-centred pathetic tragedy' (103). Whilst I
discuss below reasons for not considering Angellica tragic, there is certainly
some evidence to support Spencer's assertion. After Willmore's betrayal
Angellica's bitter blank verse speeches and soliloquies stand out amidst
the bawdy prose of others:

> He's gone, and in this Ague of my Soul
> The Shivering fit returns; ...
> In vain I have Consulted all my Charms,
> In vain this Beauty priz'd, in vain believ'd,
> My Eyes cou'd kindle any lasting fires;
> I had forgot my Name, my Infamie,
> And the reproach that Honour lays on those
> That dare pretend a sober passion here.
> Nice reputation, tho' it leave behind
> More Vertues than inhabit where that dwells;
> Yet that once gone, those Vertues shine no more.
> – Then since I am not fit to be belov'd,
> I am resolv'd to think on a revenge
> On him that sooth'd me thus to my undoing. (IV.ii.473)

Angellica thinks Willmore has deserted her because of her tainted past.
Yet Behn presents her as a woman wronged and not (or not primarily) as a
prostitute socially excluded. The passage from Pacheco's article quoted
above continues: 'Male dominance and female submission do indeed
define the world for Angellica Bianca as she confronts the truth that the
loss of her virginity outside wedlock is the essential and inescapable
meaning of her life' (341). However, it is not her condition as a prostitute
that alienates Willmore, nor is Behn so bound by conventional morality.
In the sequel, *The Second Part of the Rover*, Hellena has died and
Willmore is again torn between a prostitute and a lady of quality. This time
he chooses the prostitute, La Nuche. In *The Revenge* the prostitute Corina
is included in the play's closure-by-multiple-marriage. What alienates
Willmore in Angellica is her emotional constancy, her neediness and pleas
for commitment: 'pox o' this whining' (IV.ii.251). As an emotional virgin
she does not know how to play the game. In the world of wit she commits
the great solecism of being boring. When she becomes angry and tries to
kill Willmore, he is attracted again: 'By Heaven thou'rt brave, and I admire
thee strangely' (V.i.279). Angellica and Willmore are at cross-purposes, she
thinking he despises her lack of virtue, he bored and impatient at the very
mention of such a topic (IV.ii.239–78). Part of Angellica's tragedy is that

she has an outsider's rosy-tinted view of the cavalier world and takes it too seriously. This means that, first, she believes the romantic formulae which trip so easily from Willmore's tongue in the seduction scene; then, she believes without evidence that she is excluded by conventional moral parameters (V.i.270–8); and finally she attempts a heroic revenge in a comic context.

Since this revenge takes the form of threatening Willmore with a pistol, it could be seen as a woman seizing phallic power and initiative. Jacqueline Pearson likens Angellica at this moment to warrior viragos such as the amazon Cleomena in Behn's *The Young King*, and argues: 'Male sexuality in Behn is often an instrument of power, and she allows women to compete for this by allowing them to share the phallic power of swords, daggers and pistols' (158). Frances Kavenik, on the other hand, sees Angellica as still bound by convention, even here: 'When she assumes the ultimate male role and threatens him with a pistol, she also ironically speaks in the accents of a romantic hero(ine)' (186). Peggy Thompson sees Angellica's gesture as futile because she is easily disarmed: 'With a simple pull of the trigger, then, Angellica could symbolically explode male power as it has been inscribed in romantic comedy. But Behn is simply not ready to condemn her Tory cavalier' (80). There is no doubt that the audience feels sympathy for Angellica, and she is right when she tells Willmore, '[thou] dost wanton with my pain' (V.i.209). Yet there is also an uneasy laughter at Angellica as she melts at Willmore's words, and a rather disturbing (to the female reader at least) admiration for Willmore as he counters her threats with coolness and wit:

Angellica. And I have vow'd thy death, by all that's Sacred.
Willmore. Why then there's an end of a proper handsome Fellow,
      That might a liv'd to have done good service yet;
      – That's all I can say to't. (V.i.217–20)

Thompson refers to what she calls 'the conventional, sexist conclusion of *The Rover*' (80), from which Angellica is excluded. Many critics have noticed that Angellica's exclusion casts a shadow over the comic resolutions and conventional nuptials at the end. Two qualifications must be made, however. First, Angellica effectively concedes Willmore's argument that before his arrival her pride was excessive (V.i.255–67). Perhaps she will ultimately be the better for the lesson, and more capable of a fulfilling, reciprocal relationship. Second, it is Antonio who disarms Angellica, not Willmore, and he does it in a spirit of love for her and service. Nobody seems to have noticed that there is a strong hint that Antonio's love will offer Angellica balm for her emotional wounds. Thus, while Angellica verges on being a 'pathetic' figure, she is not ultimately a tragic one.

Much critical attention has focused on the episode in II.i. in which Willmore steals one of Angellica's portraits.[18] It is worth noting that he does this in response to a fight between wealthy Spaniards over who will be Angellica's new 'protector'.[19] His motive is a mixture of desire, envy and anger at his own poverty. His seduction of Angellica contains the same mixture of lust and revenge. The reason the sign-stealing seems significant is Behn's reference to it in a postscript to the play. Responding to accusations of plagiarism of Killigrew, she comments: 'I, vainly proud of my Judgment, hang out the Sign of *Angellica*, (the only stolen Object) to give Notice where a great part of the Wit dwelt' (p. 521). Whilst somewhat disingenuous about her indebtedness to *Thomaso*, Behn is right to claim that her play is wittier, and literary history has endorsed her belief in her work. These lines have led some critics to posit an identification between Behn and Angellica. Catherine Gallagher, in an influential and much reprinted article, argues: 'Aphra Behn embraced the title of whore ... By literalizing and embracing the playwright-prostitute metaphor, therefore, Aphra Behn was distinguished from other authors, but only as their proto-typical representative'.[20] Janet Todd gives the title *The Sign of Angellica* to her study of 'Women, Writing, and Fiction 1660–1800':

Despite Angellica's social and moral failure within the play, Aphra Behn, the first woman writer in England known to have earned a reasonable living through creative writing, associated herself with her prostitute, whose initials she shared. Accused of pilfering from men's works, she insisted in a postscript that she had hung out 'the sign of Angellica (the only stolen object) to give notice where a great part of the wit dwelt'. Clearly she was aware of the artifice of Angellica, for the plot punishes it; the identification of the two women indicates that Behn's professional literary concern is with the portrait, with the social construction of woman, the woman in business, in activity, in story, and in history, the female persona not the unknowable person. (p. 1)

It is a testimony to the force of these arguments that they have received widespread critique and modification.[21] Once again, it is necessary to remember the whole spectrum and interrelation of characters: just as no one character is to be valued in isolation, so also Behn as author is not to be identified exclusively with the commodified and traduced Angellica, but also partakes of Hellena's wit, Florinda's virtue and aristocratic values,

and even Lucetta's duplicity. Moreover, her multiple identification need
not be limited to women. Deborah Payne has argued that in her later plays
Behn adopts the persona of a male playwright.[22] Why may we not posit an
identification between Behn and her hero?[23] Certainly we are sometimes
discomfited by finding ourselves laughing with Willmore at female character's discomfiture. Behn resembled her hero in her poverty and social
precariousness, her travels, her royalism.[24] She is also herself a 'rover' in a
more literary sense: no one character has a transcendent subject position
or psychological supremacy; and it is difficult to identify Behn's own
character in her work. Of course it is methodologically dubious even to
attempt this, but critics are repeatedly tempted by the desire to recover the
female author, partly because of her elusiveness. Subtle critiques can sometimes replicate this error in more complex ways, while criticizing cruder
versions of it in others.

There are times when it seems problematic even to consider that
Behn writes from a female perspective. The best examples of this in *The
Rover* are the scenes of attempted rape. In the first of these scenes (III.v)
the drunken Willmore finds Florinda '*in an undress*' in the garden at night,
waiting for Belvile. He conducts his attempt on her virtue as a mock-
courtship, deploying various outrageous libertine arguments before
resorting to force. For example, when Florinda calls him a 'Filthy Beast'
(139) he says that they ought to lie together like animals in a state of nature
because 'there will be no sin in't' (141). There is also the familiar libertine
claim that her eyes 'gave the first blow' (150). Florinda is saved only by a
fortuitous interruption. Anita Pacheco, in one of the best articles on Behn's
drama in recent years, has argued that Behn exposes the play-world's
rape-culture.[25] However, this perspective depends on the spectator's
assumed abhorrence. Unfortunately, there is no escaping the fact that this
scene is comic,[26] and that, while some of the comedy is at Willmore's
expense,[27] there is also laughter at the floundering Florinda. While a reader
might remain impervious to this, it would be hard for a spectator in the
theatre (even a female one) to resist at least a temporary comic collusion
with male values. Moreover, III.v follows the scene of Blunt's humiliation,
so the audience is already in the mood to laugh at a victim's distress. If we
laugh at Blunt's discomfiture, why not at Florinda's?

In fact there is a close connection between the humiliation of the two
characters. Blunt is stripped, robbed and thrown into the sewer, and
immediately afterwards Willmore attempts to strip and rape Florinda.
Blunt's attempted rape of Florinda, which turns into a would-be gang

rape, is in response to his own humiliation and his desire to be revenged on women:

> Cruel, yes, I will kiss and beat thee all over; kiss, and see thee all over; thou shalt lye with me too, not that I care for the injoyment, but to let thee see I have tain deliberated Malice to thee, and will be reveng'd on one Whore for the sins of another; I will smile and deceive thee, flatter thee, and beat thee, kiss and swear, and lye to thee, imbrace thee and rob thee, as she did me, fawn on thee, and strip thee stark naked, then hang thee out at my window by the heels, with a Paper of scurvy Verses fasten'd to thy breast, in praise of damnable women – Come, come along. (IV.v.611-19)

This is presented as comic as well as nasty. By now the habit of laughing at Blunt is well established among the characters and the audience. However, it is questionable whether we also laugh at Florinda, who has after all broken her own rules as a 'lady of quality' by being out alone at night. It is a moot point whether we are expected only to feel pity and fear for her, or whether we might also be tempted to laugh at her naive expectation of chivalry. She certainly meets with none: Frederick mocks both her and Blunt and is ready to join in the rape until Florinda names Belvile, though it is fear of social consequences not of offending his friend which gives him pause: 'I begin to suspect something; and 'twould anger us vilely to be trust up for a rape upon a Maid of quality, when we only believe we ruffle a Harlot' (IV.v.682-4). Florinda is not entirely the passive victim here: her assertion of her 'quality' has worked, temporarily at least. The ring she gives Frederick reveals her identity to Belvile, but he cannot act without revealing her identity and shaming her. He is forced to watch as the men compare sword-lengths to see who will enjoy her first. The winner of this phallic byplay is Pedro the Spaniard, Florinda's own brother.[28] A grotesque parody of chivalry ensues as Pedro asserts that they are 'proper Gentlemen' (111) and they resolve to allow her to choose who will rape her first. She is saved by her quick-witted cousin Valeria, as Belvile stands bemused.

The gang-rape scene is darker than III.i. because more men are implicated, including those closest to the heroine, and the danger is more prolonged. Even Belvile seems tainted. In III.vi. he seemed outraged at the very idea of attempted rape of Florinda, and not just because the intended victim was his mistress: 'if it had not been Florinda, must you be a Beast? – a Brute? a Senseless Swine' (III.vi.198-9). However, in the gang-rape scene he shows no outrage or even opposition, and is feeble as a protector. Much of the comedy is at the expense of the men, and all of them are implicated. It therefore seems true to an extent that Behn reveals and questions the 'rape culture'. Against this, there are two factors. First, the female point of view is not made prominent. Florinda voices her distress, but as soon as she is safe easily forgives everyone concerned. No moral is drawn, and the implication seems to be that, if the woman concerned had not been Florinda, the gang rape could have gone ahead. Second, there is little doubt that Behn, disturbingly, implicates us in men's values by making us laugh at attempted rape. Skilful directing would be needed to make an audience ashamed of their laughter and force them to question their collusion in oppressive values.[29]

Men's sexuality in the play is presented as dangerous, desirable and ridiculous at the same time. Willmore is both predator and victim, damaging women but also tyrannized over by his own sex-addiction. I noted above that I.ii sees a group of disguised women who might be whores pass across the stage. They are swiftly followed by men 'drest all over with Horns of several sorts', suggesting both phallic potency and cuckoldry. Belvile sees that 'Tis a Satyre against the whole Sex' (I.ii.101–2). Male friendship displays a similar duality, being both elevated and ridiculous. As in *The Country Wife*, homosocial connections appear primary but are deeply problematic. There is no essential difference between the English and Spanish gentlemen: Belvile and Antonio respect one another's 'quality' and are chivalrous in enmity (IV.i). Behn always resists xenophobia, which she associates with Whigs. The English country fool Blunt is more of an object of ridicule than any Spaniard. Yet within the peer groups of the privileged, male friendship appears to be prized but often flawed. When there is unity it is often in nastiness, 'to ruffle a harlot' or mock at Blunt's distress.

Men's friendships often conceal covert mockery, deception and mutual disservice. Perhaps this is because true friendship cannot co-exist with an oppressive attitude to women, even though men think it can. Pedro and Antonio fight over Angellica, whom both seek to possess; but also over Florinda, possessed by Pedro as a brother but slighted by Antonio as a suitor. Willmore is not really sorry for sexually assaulting Belvile's beloved and, which Belvile seems to mind just as much, impeding Belvile's access to her by his intrusion. In IV.ii Willmore's clumsiness again betrays Belvile, revealing his identity to Pedro just when a successful disguise had almost brought about the lovers' union. It is he who suggests comparing swords in V.i., putting Florinda at risk and again causing Belviel to abuse him as an 'intollerable Sott' (V.i.101). Belvile is not uniformly high-minded: he encourages Pedro to join the mockery of

Belvile's own country man, Blunt, and leads the taunting in V.i. As I have already noted, he is passive in the face of Florinda's danger and distress in the same scene. Of course much of the bungling and byplay is for comic purposes; but the comedy is often at the men's expense.

Some critics have found the genre of this play difficult to determine, and many have argued that the comic ending is overshadowed by darker notes, especially for women: the recent scenes of attempted rape, Angellica's 'tragic' fate, uncertainty about Hellena's future.[30] In fact, as we have seen, Angellica has gone off with Antonio, and all the characters are comic targets. Whilst it is true that Behn offers a novel focus on women's perspective, she has little sympathy for victims of either gender. It is not only the women who must compromise: Willmore is forced with a nice irony into the marriage he fears and despises, precisely because of his overmastering desire to possess Hellena which he cannot fulfil any other way. What is as astonishing about Behn as any of her innovations is the sheer robustness of her comedy.

Behn is often singled out by critics because of her gender, but she was very much a writer of her own times, who had her finger on the cultural 'pulse'. She was the first to respond to the burgeoning political crisis of 1678/79, which led to a sharp break in the generic evolution of comedy. Sex comedy went quite suddenly into eclipse, following the astonishing failure of a series of sex comedies by major writers in the spring of 1678.[31] Then, as political crisis gripped the nation, there was a virtual cessation of comedies: only one in the 1678/79 season. That one, *The Feign'd Curtizans* (1679), was by Aphra Behn, and was a sign of what was to come: a revival of the satire of upstarts and puritans typical of 1660s comedy, coupled with a celebration of upper-class good taste across national boundaries. Behn's play associates Whiggish anti-popery and patriotism with puritan sexual hypocrisy, folly, pretension, philistinism and low-class money-grubbing.[32] This sets the tone for a new wave of political comedies which employ methods and modes reminiscent of 1660s comedy to attack the Whigs. Meanwhile, the crisis saw the emergence of tragedy, and it is to this form that we must now turn.

Notes

1 See Spencer, '*The Rover* and the Eighteenth Century'.

2 Potter, 'Transforming a Super-rake'; Munns, 'Barton and Behn's *The Rover*'; Copeland, 'Re-producing *The Rover*' and 'Reviving Aphra Behn'; and Goodman, 'Reviewing the Idea of the Canon'.

3 See DeRitter, 'The Gypsy, *The Rover*, and the Wanderer: Aphra Behn's Revision of Thomas Killigrew'; and *Works*, ed. Todd, vol. 5, introduction (446–50) and notes (556–70). All quotations are from this edition.

4 Critics debate how far the play's atmosphere is 'carnivalesque' in the Bakhtinian sense and how far the liberating potential of carnival is counteracted by its unleashing of male power, or recuperated by the re-assertion of social authority: see Hughes, *English Drama*, 208–12; Carlson, 'Cannibalizing and Carnivalizing'; Linda R. Payne, 'The Carnivalesque Regeneration of Corrupt Economies in *The Rover*'; Wiseman, *Aphra Behn*, 49–58; Boebel, 'In the Carnival World of Adam's Garden: Roving and Rape in Behn's *Rover*'. Since Italian carnival preceded Lent, John Franceschina in 'Shadow and Substance in Aphra Behn's *The Rover*' associates the carnival setting with political support for the royalism and Catholicism. On carnival in Restoration and eighteenth-century texts in general see Terry Castle, *Masquerade and Civilization: The Carnivalesque in Eighteenth-century English Culture and Fiction*, Stanford, Stanford University Press, 1986.

5 For a somewhat naive view of Behn as feminist see Langdell, 'Aphra Behn and Sexual Politics'. For a more qualified and subtly argued case for Behn as proto-feminist or quasi-feminist in important respects see Gill, *Interpreting Ladies*, 138, Munns, '"I by a Double Right Thy Bounties Claim"', and Pearson, *Prostituted Muse*, 153–68. For critiques of feminist interpretations see Mendelson, *The Mental World of Stuart Women*, chapter 3; Deborah C. Payne, '"And poets shall by patron-princes live": Aphra Behn and Patronage'; and Kavenik, 'Aphra Behn: The Playwright as "Breeches Part"'. For the strongest case against seeing Behn as feminist see Rogers, *Feminism in Eighteenth-century England*, 98–9, 115. Views depend partly on the critic's understanding of 'feminism', which may be seen in terms of female agency and/or subjectivity ('how far are women empowered in the plays?'), or on exposing women's oppression though representation of their disempowerment ('how critical is Behn's representation?').

6 Russell in the introduction to her edition likens Hellena and Florinda to Rosalind and Celia in *As You Like It*.

7 The name in *Thomaso* belongs to an old, decayed whore.

8 Todd in the notes to her edition (p. 558) comments that he is now in Spain, showing the cavaliers' 'easy changing of sides'. The point is good, though she is thinking of *Thomaso*: Behn's play is set in Naples.

9 See Goreau, *Reconstructing Aphra*, 213, 226; and Franceschina, 'Shadow and Substance in Aphra Behn's *The Rover*', 30. The likeness to James is made more explicit in the dedication to the sequel, *The Second Part of the Rover* (1681).

10 Critics who see the play as (with varying degrees of qualification) a celebration of the libertine masculinity which Willmore typifies include Duffy, *Passionate Shepherdess*, 145–8; Rogers, *Feminism in Eighteenth-century England*, 58; Cotton, 'Aphra Behn and the Pattern Hero', 215–18; Brown, *English Dramatic Form*, 60–1; and Markley, '"Be impudent, be saucy, forward, bold, touzing, and leud": The Politics of Masculine Sexuality and Feminine Desire in Behn's Tory Comedies', 121. For a darker view of Willmore and libertinism in the play see DeRitter, 'The Gypsy, *The Rover*, and the Wanderer', 85–91; Hobby, *Virtue of*

Necessity, 122–7; Pearson, *Prostituted Muse*, 153; Chernaik, *Sexual Freedom in Restoration Literature*, 206–8; Pacheco, 'Rape and the Female Subject in Aphra Behn's *The Rover*', 341; Kaufman, 'The Perils of Florinda'. Thompson in 'Closure and Subversion in Behn's Comedies' sees Willmore as ambivalently depicted but ultimately salvaged as a (problematic) hero.

11   For the politics of *The Rover* see Franceschina, 'Shadow and Substance', who finds personations of political figures in the play. For the politics of Behn's drama see Markley, 'Be impudent'; Owen, '"Suspect my loyalty when I lose my virtue": Sexual Politics and Party in Aphra Behn's Plays of the Exclusion Crisis'; Feldwick, 'Wits, Whigs, and Women: Domestic Politics as Anti-Whig Rhetoric in Aphra Behn's Town Comedies'; and Zook, 'Contextualizing Aphra Behn: Plays, Politics, and Party'.

12   See my '"Suspect my loyalty when I lose my virtue": Sexual Politics and Party in Aphra Behn's Plays of the Exclusion Crisis' for a discussion of the play (38) and the question of authorship of this play, published anonymously (45).

13   For Hellena's self-advertisement, paralleling that of the prostitute Angellica, see Copeland, '"Once a whore and ever?": Whore and Virgin in *The Rover* and its Antecedents'.

14   Examples of those who see Hellena as (within limits) a positive alternative include Link in the introduction to his edition, DeRitter, 'The Gypsy, *The Rover*, and the Wanderer'; Bobker, 'Behn: *Auth*-Whore or W*riter*?'; Nash, '"The sight on't would beget a warm desire": Visual Pleasure in Aphra Behn's *The Rover*'. The strongest argument for her being entirely recuperated into the patriarchal economy she rebels against is made by Diamond, '*Gestus* and Signature'.

15   Many critics assume Hellena is empowered in male dress, but Hutner in 'Revisioning the Female Body' points out that Hellena is abused and mocked by Willmore, who easily penetrates her male disguise. For a broader discussion of relevant issues see Lesley Ferris (ed.), *Controversies on Cross-dressing*, London, Routledge, 1993.

16   Possibly this is because, like the obnoxious but successful fortune-hunters Bassanio and Lorenzo in Shakespeare's *The Merchant of Venice*, he is a spendthrift. At the opening of the sequel, *The Second Part of the Rover* (1681), he has spent all the deceased Hellena's fortune. In Behn and Shakespeare there seems to be some equating of financial irresponsibility with generosity of spirit.

17   'Rape and the Female Subject in Aphra Behn's *The Rover*', 340.

18   See especially Diamond, '*Gestus* and Signature in Aphra Behn's *The Rover*'.

19   He does not do it in the interests of public morality, as Boebel bizarrely claims, misreading II.i.202–4.

20   'Who was that masked woman? The prostitute and the Playwright in the Plays of Aphra Behn', 71, 73.

21   Hutner, 'Revisioning the Female Body: Aphra Behn's *The Rover, Parts I and II*', 103; Hughes, *English Drama*, 209 (implicitly); Bobker, 'Behn: *Auth*-Whore or W*riter*? Authorship and Identity in *The Rover*', 33 and *passim*; D. Payne (see next note).

22 'And poets shall by patron-princes live', 117.

23 Gardiner in her seminal essay 'Aphra Behn: Sexuality and Self-Respect' argues: 'This cavalier pose helps her define an autonomous position for herself as a bright, sexually-active woman. There are few societies in which such a person could function freely. Behn invents one in her drama, where she can imagine herself as the dashing Rover of her most famous play' (69).

24 For Behn's life see the biographies listed in the bibliography, especially Duffy, *The Passionate Shepherdess*; Goreau, *Reconstructing Aphra*; Mendelson, *The Mental World of Stuart Women*; Todd, *Secret Life*; Jones, *New Light on the Background and Early Life of Aphra Behn*; and Caywood, 'Deconstructing Aphras'.

25 'Rape and the Female Subject in Aphra Behn's *The Rover*'; see also Stewart, 'Rape, Patriarchy, and the Libertine Ethos: The Function of Sexual Violence in Aphra Behn's "The Golden Age" and *The Rover, Part I*'; Boebel, 'In the Carnival World of Adam's Garden: Roving and Rape in Behn's *Rover*'; Marsden, 'Rape, Voyeurism and the Restoration Stage'; Kaufman, 'The Perils of Florinda'.

26 We may compare comic attempted rape scenes in films such as Costner's *Robin Hood: Prince of Thieves*.

27 John Franceschina has argued that after this scene Willmore changes from a Hobbesean rake to a 'fop'. The actor who played the part, William Smith, was also famous for Sir Fopling Flutter in Etherege's *The Man of Mode*. See 'Shadow and Substance in Aphra Behn's *The Rover*', 35.

28 Boebel observes: 'Behn opens her play with one kind of brotherly "kindness" and threatens to end it with another – incestuous rape – thus exposing both as different aspects of the same arbitrary patriarchal domination' (67).

29 Carlson's review of JoAnne Akalaitis's 1994 production (based on John Barton's 1986 Royal Shakespeare Company adaptation) says the audience (as well as the male characters) were implicated in the near gang-rape and not absolved from blame: 'Cannibalizing and Carnivalizing: Reviving Aphra Behn's *The Rover*'.

30 Hume, *Development of English Drama*, says that the play has elements of the intrigue play and comedy of manners, but is not wholly satisfactory as either: 305, 336. See also Gill, 137–57, Franceschina, 32–3, and Linda Payne, 40–1 and *passim*.

31 See Hume, '"The Change in Comedy": Cynical Versus Exemplary Comedy on the London Stage, 1678–83'.

32 See my *Restoration Theatre and* Crisis, 3, 63–5, 153–4, 172, 192.

4

Tragedy I:
Nathaniel Lee's *Lucius Junius Brutus*

There are several possible explanations for the shift from heroic drama to tragedy in the 1670s. The first is that Dryden, who had pioneered the heroic form, grew tired of it. As I noted in Chapter 1, Dryden collaborated in 1674 in an attack on Settle's heroic extravaganza *The Empress of Morocco*. Settle's play is written in imitation of Dryden's; and, in attacking Settle, Dryden may have felt that he was attacking his own youthful excesses.[1] By the end of 1675 Dryden was re-evaluating his approach. Possibly he was influenced by the attacks on his heroic plays, discussed in Chapter 1. In the prologue to *Aureng-Zebe*, produced at this time, Dryden praises Shakespeare, and says he is 'weary of his long-lov'd Mistris, Rhyme'. The play, though still in rhyme and in the heroic mould, has a softer, more domestic atmosphere emanating from women characters, Indamora and Melesinda, who have a prominent role. The hero is more virtuous and more reflective than Almanzor. His relationships with his father and with the woman he loves are more subtle and more tormented. The attitude to bloodshed is more restrained and ambivalent. After this, Dryden abandoned rhyming heroic tragi-comedy for blank verse tragedy in *All For Love; or, The World Well Lost* (1677), an adaptation of Shakespeare's *Antony and Cleopatra*.

Although Dryden popularized the turn from heroic drama to tragedy, Henry Neville Payne was the pioneer. His *The Fatal Jealousie* (1672) draws on Shakespeare's *Othello* and other Elizabethan and Jacobean tragic models, and he was the first to turn to blank verse tragedy in *The Siege of Constantinople* (1674). Other dramatists experimented with what might be called a transitional form of heroic horror plays, still within the heroic mould but preoccupied with villainy and tryanny: examples are Settle's

Love and Revenge (1674), Otway's *Alcibiades* (1675), Behn's *Abdelazer* (1676) and Lee's *Gloriana* (1676). However, Otway's *Don Carlos* (1676) has a similar domestic atmosphere to Dryden's *Aureng-Zebe*. Lee moved away from rhyme slightly before Dryden in *The Rival Queens; or, The Death of Alexander the Great* (1677); whilst Otway followed their example in his *The History and Fall of Caius Marius* (1679), a romanized adaptation of Shakespeare's *Romeo and Juliet. The Rival Queens* and *Caius Marius* are clearly tragedies, characterized by a darkness of tone absent in heroic drama, and by a sense of moral difficulty reminiscent of Jacobean tragedy. For example, Alexander in Lee's *The Rival Queens*, torn by love for two women, is an ambiguous figure, somewhere in between victim and tyrant, tragic lover and libertine. The world of the play is a dark and morally complex one in which the innocent are destroyed and Alexander's killer is both a villain and a victim of tyranny, who survives his deed.[2] However, Restoration tragedy differs from Elizabethan and Jacobean tragedy, and follows on from the heroic extravaganzas and semi-operas which preceded it, in making much greater use of elaborate stage effects, song and spectacle.[3]

The turn towards tragedy was not just a shift in theatrical fashion. It also had a political impetus. Payne's *The Siege of Constantinople* (1674) sets the tone for later tragedies in its peculiar combination of royalism with scepticism and pessimism. The wicked, plotting Chancellor, modelled on opposition noblemen such as Shaftesbury, is a model for subsequent villains of Tory tragedy; but Payne's play also evinces what was to become typical unease about the problems caused by unruly royal desire and caprice. The tension between the ruler's desires and political necessity is also central in Otway's last rhyming heroic drama, *Titus and Berenice* (1676), in Sir Charles Sedley's *Antony and Cleopatra* (1677) and in Dryden's *All For Love* in the same year, as well as being a subordinate theme in Lee's *The Rival Queens*. The theme was topical because enormous political anxiety was generated by Charles II's perceived enslavement to his unpopular French mistresses at a time when there was widespread concern about the growing power of France, and widespread suspicion about Charles's relationship with the French king, Louis XIV.

This theme of the ruler's irresponsible love may serve as an example of the way in which political meanings are contested in Restoration tragedy. Different tragedies offer differing perspectives on the problem. *Titus and Berenice* is a dark play set in a world of impossible choices. The pressure to renounce his foreign mistress corrupts Titus and turns him into a tyrant: a clear warning to the Charles II's political opponents that they might push him too far. Sedley's treatment of the issue is politically oppositional and prefigures Whig tragedy. His Antony is a critical portrait of Charles II, blind to the way in which his foreign mistress manipulates him, and inappropriately merciful and severe at the wrong times. The battle of Actium is a critical depiction of Charles's unpopular Third Dutch War. As in later Whig drama, the Roman Republic is viewed with nostalgia, while the common people are treated kindly, and Antony is glad to be set right by them. Poet Laureate Dryden's *All For Love*, as might be expected, treats the ruler's unruly passion for an unpopular foreigner more sympathetically. The proto-Whiggish values of Roman civic virtue and respect for law are treated correspondingly more negatively. Antony's wife Octavia is an unattractive character, demanding her rights to Antony according to the law while using his daughters to manipulate him. Dryden's play may well have been a response to Sedley's.[4] The difference between his play and Sedley's is nowhere more apparant than in the treatment of Cleopatra, whom Sedley portrays as a passionate seducer and Dryden as a virtuous and suffering heroine. It also seems pointed that Dryden makes his lovers sympathetic, concluding his play with the rousing encomium, 'No lovers lived so great or died so well'.

The tragedies contain good parts for women, perhaps better than the heroic plays. For example, the tone of Sedley's and Dryden's plays on the Cleopatra story is set by the actresses playing the parts: in Sedley's play Mary Lee, who had played villains in Pordage's *Herod and Mariamne*, Otway's *Alcibiades*, Behn's *Abdelazer* and Settle's *Pastor Fido*, and a passionate mistress in Etherege's *The Man of Mode*; in Dryden's play Elizabeth Boutell, who typically played young innocent girls. Conversely, Antony's Roman wife Octavia was played by Mary Betterton, wife of the famous Thomas Betterton who played Antony, and famous for a range of female parts, mainly virtuous; whilst in Dryden's play Octavia was played by Katherine Corey, who often played shrewish and unpleasant characters. Elizabeth Howe has suggested that tragedy developed precisely in order to offer actresses a scope which the heroic play did not afford them.[5] Certainly it is true that Restoration tragedy, sometimes labelled 'pathetic' or 'affective' tragedy, does stress the feminine and the sentimental. By the end of the seventeenth century a highly popular genre of 'she-tragedy' had developed, focusing on the pure and suffering woman. The term was coined by Nicholas Rowe, and is appropriate for plays such as his *The Fair Penitent* (1703). Early eighteenth-century she-tragedy equates suffering femininity with virtue.[6] We should be wary, however, of reading back this perspective into Restoration tragedy. There were a couple of Restoration precursors of she-tragedy, such as Otway's *The Orphan* (1680), a play which really gained popularity only later in the heyday of she-tragedy; and John Banks's *Vertue Betray'd; or, Anna Bullen* (1682), a play on a political theme (the execution of Anne Boleyn) which is nevertheless almost solely concerned with the suffering of its virtuous heroine. These plays are atypical, however. Women have a more central role in Restoration tragedy than in heroic drama, but their perspective is not a privileged one, and the meaning of their experience is sharply contested.

Howe's argument focuses particularly upon the extraordinary talents of Elizabeth Barry, who played the heroine in both of the plays which are the subject of this chapter and the next. Lee's *Lucius Junius Brutus* and Otway's *Venice Preserv'd* are supreme examples of Restoration tragedy. In both the trigger for the action is a rape or near-rape. Both also focus on the contested meaning of women's experience. The plays are quite similar in setting: both set in republics, both in an atmosphere of political contention, both focusing on the difficulties of rulers and subjects and on the tension between different kinds of love, loyalty and honour. In both fatherhood is a central concern, a theme which, as we shall see, has strong political overtones. However, the perspective taken by the two playwrights is quite different. In my *Restoration Theatre and Crisis* I have labelled *Lucius Junius Brutus* a Whig play and *Venice Preserv'd* a Tory play. It must be emphasized, however, that the labels 'Whig' and 'Tory' are provisional at this time when political polarization was something new and difficult; and that such terms should be used cautiously in relation to the drama. Moreover, the politics of *Lucius Junius Brutus* in particular are contested by critics. We shall need to look closely at the plays to see the differences in political perspective. I have decided to follow a somewhat different procedure in this chapter from that in previous chapters. Although I shall follow my usual practice of offering a reading of the play in its critical and historical context, I also want to argue strongly against what I see as misrepresentation of the play. Since I am a published participant in the debate about *Lucius Junius Brutus*, it seems more honest to defend my critical position than to affect an agnosticism which I do not genuinely feel. In previously published work I have gone to some lengths to identify and analyse the existence of oppositional or Whiggish drama, so I want to challenge criticism which denies its existence.[7] In particular, I want to contest the views of Victoria Hayne, who argues that *Lucius Junius Brutus* is anti-Whig, an extraordinary view which can be sustained only by quoting very selectively from the play. As far as I know, nobody has yet challenged her views, which appeared in an article in the prestigious journal *ELH* in 1996.

Lucius Junius Brutus was banned by the Lord Chamberlain after a few days' performance, owing to complaints from members of the audience about 'Scandalous Expressions & Reflections upon ye Government'.[8] This gives us our first clue that the play was seen as Whiggish by Lee's contemporaries.[9] There was a very good reason why Lee might have wished to offer a Whiggish play in the autumn of 1680: the Exclusion Parliament was sitting and there would have been large numbers of Whig MPs in the theatre audience.[10] Whig support was widespread at this time, and powerful figures such as the Earl of Sunderland, the French ambassador and even the King's mistress, the Duchess of Posrtsmouth, thought they might win. Lee needed a success after the banning of his anti-Catholic *The Massacre of Paris* and it would have seemed logical to write a play in keeping with the mood of the times.[11]

The play tells the story of the expulsion of the Tarquin monarchy and the founding of the Roman republic. In order to secure the new state, Brutus sacrifices his sons, condemning them to death for treasonably plotting to restore the monarchy. This heroic self-sacrifice is viewed with unqualified approval by Livy, one of Lee's chief sources. Machiavelli also commented favourably on Brutus's action in his *Discourses*, seeing it as necessary (from a pragmatic point of view) in suppressing 'tyranny' and establishing a new 'democratic regime'.[12] Hayne counterposes Livy's view of Brutus as 'principled' and Machiavelli's view of him as 'opportunistic', but Machiavellian 'virtu' is by no means simply the opposite of 'virtue'. Lee also expresses admiration for Brutus in his dedication:

I must acknowledge, however I have behaved myself in the drawing, nothing ever presented itself to my fancy with that solid pleasure as Brutus did in sacrificing his sons. Before I read Machivel's notes upon the place, I concluded it the greatest action that was ever seen throughout all ages on the greatest occasion. For my own endeavour, I thought I never painted any man so to the life before.

Hayne assumes a negative significance in Lee's mention in his dedication of Machiavelli's admiration for Brutus; but it is important to remember that Machiavelli was more positively regarded in the Restoration than in the Renaissance. Also, Machiavelli's comments appear in his *Discourses*, a text which had found some reception and was not simply caricatured and condemned like *The Prince*.[13] Hayne claims that the passage cited above is 'obscure and tonally puzzling'. Yet 'However I have behaved myself in drawing' is a standard humility topos, as is confirmed by the modest pose of the preceding and ensuing sections of the Dedication. It does not mean that Lee has drawn Brutus in negative outlines. Lee's intention to make Brutus 'great' is clear, even if we take 'greatest action' in a morally neutral sense, meaning to be wondered at, or having heroic grandeur, rather than moral sanction. Lee goes on to quote a passage from Virgil's *Aeneid* which concludes, '*Infelix utcunque ferent ea facta Minores!*' (Unhappy man, however posterity extols that deed!) This seems to confirm Brutus's personal misfortune and the positive judgement of posterity, aspects which Hayne would ignore and deny respectively.

The story of Brutus was well known as a tale of republican heroism, and was used by opposition pamphleteers and poets, as I have detailed in my article '"Partial Tyrants" and "Freeborn People" in *Lucius Junius Brutus*'. This, again, suggests that there is an oppositional potential in the play. Since every story which could be supposed to offer a lesson from history was contested in the seventeenth century, royalists inevitably tried to rework the tale for their own ends, but it was singularly difficult in this instance. When Sir Robert Filmer in 'Observations Upon Aristotle's Politics' wished to reinterpret the story for royalism, he knew he was arguing against the commonly accepted interpretation. To bolster his ingenious and controversial argument for the greatness of Roman kingly government and the tyranny of that of the consuls, Filmer has to play down Brutus's character and role. Hayne respectfully cites Filmer's account of partriarchal power within the Roman republic without noticing that Filmer, in trying to expose a contradiction, contradicts himself. He is so keen to glorify patriarchalism, praising the father's power in order to glorify the king's, that he is led into approval of Roman fathers who sacrifice their sons, and by implication of Brutus.[14] Most notable of all, however, is the fact that Filmer is forced to vilify the Lucrece whose rape by Tarquin's son was the catalyst for the expulsion of the Tarquins:

The fact of young Tarquin cannot be excused, yet without a wrong to the reputation of so chaste a lady as Lucrece is reputed to be, it may be said she had a greater desire to be thought chaste than to be chaste. She might have died untouched and unspotted in her body if she had not been afraid to be slandered for inchastity. Both Dionysius Halicarnasseus and Livy, who both are her friends, so tell the tale of her as if she had chosen rather to be a whore than to be thought a whore. To say truth, we find no other cause of the expulsion of Tarquin than the wantonness and licentiousness of the people of Rome. (259)

Filmer's argument is that Lucrece should have kept quiet. She made herself a whore in publicizing her wrongs. It is the greatest flaw in Hayne's argument that she effectively colludes in this denial of the raped woman's experience.

Lee's treatment of Lucrece is very different from Filmer's. Lucrece is on stage alive for only a short time, but she is an important figure in unfolding great events, and plays a key role in the play. The part was played by the imposing Mary Betterton, whose husband Thomas played Brutus. Lucrece's rape by Sextus, son of Tarquin, is portrayed as violation of her body and mind, and also of her hospitality, as Sextus was her guest. Lucrece controls the response to her experience in a series of effective and powerful speeches. Through superb rhetoric she builds up suspense and horror, telling her husband and father not to touch her; then describes the rape in some detail and the threats and force Sextus used. Finally, after a moment of faintness, she reaches her climax, 'Revenge the honor of the ravished Lucrece' (I.409). She then stabs herself, to 'set free / My soul, my life and honor all together' (417). The word 'revenge' recurs ten times in her dying speeches, the last line she speaks being a typical example of Lee's repetitive style at moments of intensity: 'Revenge me; O revenge, revenge, revenge' (418). Yet the word 'honor' is equally important. Lucrece is the embodiment of Roman virtue. Her suicide is an act to restore her honour which Sextus has violated, and to set an example to posterity. Her husband Collatinus can only weep. It is left to Brutus to organize the revenge which Lucrece wants, by instigating a ritual in which everyone swears to avenge her after kissing the dagger with which she has stabbed herself. Brutus gives Lucrece's suicide meaning as a sacrifice 'For chastity, for Rome, and violated honor' (426). He ensures that she will recieve what she desires, the positive judgement of posterity:

> O Lucrece! O!
> When to the clouds thy pile of fame is raised
> While Rome is free thy memory shall be praised. (455)

The raped woman in the seventeenth century – and in ancient Rome – was a dishonoured figure, not an innocent victim; but Brutus triumphantly continues the transformation which Lucrece herself began from shame to glory. Brutus and Lucrece are 'Romans' with all the connotations which

Roman virtue had in the seventeenth century, including honour, dignity, courage, self-sacrifice and public spirit. The words 'Rome' and 'Roman' recur repeatedly in Brutus's speeches.

Behind Filmer's argument that Lucrece should have kept quiet lies the royalist idea of quietism, which I discussed in Chapter 1: people should leave politics and public affairs to the king. Brutus frequently uses the term 'the world' (e.g. II.380) to mean the public sphere, the demands of society upon the individual. For royalists interference in the affairs of kings was presumptuous; for Brutus, as for the Whigs, it is every responsible citizen's duty, even if personal sacrifice is involved. The rape of Lucrece can find a political meaning in Brutus's world which it cannot have for royalists. For Lee's Brutus, as for Lucrece herself (but not for Filmer), the rape of Lucrece is a 'public wound' (II.149). Belvidera, the rape victim in Otway's *Venice Preserv'd*, envies Lucrece:

> O thou Roman Lucrece!
> Thou couldst find friends to vindicate thy wrong;
> I never had but one and he's proved false;
> He that should guard my virtue has betrayed it. (III.ii.8)

Belividera wants her near-rape to have an equal political significance to the rape of Lucrece. In *Venice Preserv'd*, as we shall see, it is rebels who are rapists. In *Lucius Junius Brutus* rape is associated with royalism, suggesting very different politics.[15] In fact Lee emphasizes that royalism equals rape. Lucrece's body is on stage in Act II as a very tangible reminder both of her own suffering and of the Tarquins' lust and tyranny. Despite her preference for stage spectacle over language, Hayne misses the effect of the violated woman's body on the audience. In case we should forget, it is repeatedly emphasized that royalists are rapists: the rape of citizens' wives by princes and courtiers has been common (II.51–60). Rome is a 'city filled with rapes, adulteries' (II.219). Demented royalist plotter Tiberius looks forward to raping the daughters of commonwealthsmen (IV.67).

The Roman virtue of Lucrece is contrasted with the sensuality of the young lovers, Titus, son of Brutus, and Teraminta, illegitimate daughter of Tarquin. Some critics have found the comparison to the lovers' detriment. The play's editor, John Loftis, for example, finds himself 'intermittently repelled by the luxuriance of [Titus's] passionate language' and sees the exchanges between the lovers as characterized by 'occasional mawkish passages' and emotional excess' (xxii–xxiii). Victoria Hayne goes to the opposite extreme and calls Titus and Teraminta 'passionately

principled lovers' (344). This says more about the difference in perspective between critics of different generations than it does about Lee's
play. The lovers are certainly pititable. Lee sets up a tension between love
and duty, as Brutus demands that Titus give up Teraminta for the sake of
Rome. The play works because we can sympathize *both* with Titus's love
for Teraminta *and* with his impulse of duty and respect towards Brutus
and the Roman republic.

It is very important to be aware, as Hayne is not, that Titus is torn
between love and duty, and that he is heroic when resolved to die for
Rome. Hayne's view of the play as organized around a tension between
persecuting father and oppressed lovers is wrong. Titus himself is divided
between loyalty to Brutus and love for Teraminta. This is a division
between two sides of his personality or two different codes of behaviour:
on the one hand, sentiment, as when the marriage of the lovers is 'Blessed
with a flood that streamed from both our eyes, / And sealed with sighs, and
smiles, and deathless kisses' (II.413); on the other hand, 'rigorous Roman
resolution' (II.377). Titus is very far from regarding his father simply as an
oppressor. In psychological terms he needs Brutus to be strong. For
example, he is glad when Brutus casts off his madness, even though Brutus
condemns his love:

> O, let me fall low as the earth permits me,
> And thank the gods for this most happy change,
> That you are now, although to my confusion,
> That awful, godlike, and commanding Brutus. (I.242)

In political terms he approves of his father's aims and shares his goals:

> The body of the world is out of frame,
> The vast distorted limbs are on the rack
> And all the cable sinews stretched to bursting,
> The blood ferments, and the majestic spirit,
> Like Hercules in the envenomed shirt,
> Lies in a fever on the horrid pile. (II.436)

This is a particularly interesting image because it reverses one in Crowne's
Tory drama *The Ambitious Statesman*. In that play the ambitious Constable
literally racks his virtuous, loyal son on stage. Here Brutus undoes the
damage to the 'world' by the torturing Tarquins, and heals the times.

Brutus helps Titus move from changeability to fixity of purpose. In
Act II the sight of Teraminta is enough to undermine Titus's resolve to put
Rome first: 'I did forswear myself / In swearing that, and will forswear

again' (II.416). Later, Titus is noble and firm and Brutus himself becomes divided: this time it is he who needs Titus to be strong and Titus who is glad to oblige.

Our attitude to the play's politics really depends on our view of Brutus and of his actions. Critics' views range from positive to entirely negative. For John Loftis there is a 'sustained grandeur of the tragic hero, Brutus, in whom a sense of duty enforces a suppression of private emotion'. The dramatization of Brutus's Roman restraint also has a positive effect on the verse, curtailing the worst excesses of Lee's typical repetitious and overblown rant, and confering on the climactic scenes a 'quiet dignity' (xxi). For Hayne, at the other extreme, the play is deliberately designed to undermine Brutus's oratory and criticize the Whigs by association. Everyone must form their own judgement, but it seems to me that Hayne's entirely negative view can be ruled out. The full title of the play is *Lucius Junius Brutus, Father of His Country*. Lee sets up an immediate identification with his central character by calling himself the father of his play in his Epistle Dedicatory of the published text to the Earl of Dorset: 'I was troubled for my dumb play, like a father for his dead child' (p. 5). When Lee says, in the passage quoted above, that he has painted Brutus more to the life than any of his previous protagonists, he may mean that he has given him more human and sympathetic qualities than, for example, his Nero in *The Tragedy of Nero* (1674), who embodies tyrannical excess; or that these human qualities are more successfully combined with the dignity of the republican hero than are the personal and political dimensions of that fractured character Alexander in *The Rival Queens*.

In the opening scene Brutus, like Hamlet, has adopted an 'antic disposition'. Betterton, who played Brutus, was also famous for his Hamlet. This initial resemblence enhances Brutus's stature. Brutus acts the part of a madman to protect himself from Tarquin who has killed his brother and father and confiscated their property. In his mad guise he is a privileged 'Fool', a truth-teller who utters jibes about royal adultery and priestly sexual hypocrisy, and about the Court. Yet this position is a painful one, as Lee establishes in a long soliloquy which establishes both Brutus's suffering and his Roman virtue:

> O Brutus! Brutus!
> When will the tedious gods permit thy soul
> To walk abroad in her own majesty,
> And throw this visor of thy madness from thee?

> O, but what infinite spirit, propped by fate,
> For empire's weight to turn on, could endure
> As thou hast done the labors of an age,
> All follies, scoffs, reproaches, pities, scorns,
> Indignities almost to blows sustained,
> For twenty pressing years, and by a Roman?
> To act deformity in thousand shapes,
> To please the greater monster of the two,
> That cries, 'Bring forth the beast, and let him tumble.'
> With all variety of aping madness,
> To bray, and bear more than the ass's burden;
> Sometimes to hoot and scream, like midnight owls,
> Then screw my limbs like a distorted satyr,
> The world's grimace, th'eternal laughingstock
> Of town and court, the block and jest of Rome.
> Yet all the while not to my dearest friend,
> To my own children, nor my bosom wife,
> Disclose the weighty secret of my soul.
> O Rome, o mother, be thou th'impartial judge
> If this be virtue, which yet wants a name,
> Which never any age could parallel,
> And worthy of the foremost of thy sons. (I.108–33)

The isolation of not even feeling safe enough to tell the truth his wife and children is the particular marker of Brutus's extreme suffering and superhuman fortitude, the sign that, as Edgar puts it in Shakespeare's *King Lear*, 'The oldest hath borne most'. There is also a particular indignity about the humiliation of animal postures being imposed on someone with a marked sense of what it means to be a Roman, and a man rather than a beast. Hayne, professing to consider the dramatic sequence, claims that the first scene establishes sympathy for the lovers before Brutus's exchange with Titus. Unfortunately she misrepresents the sequence by missing out the soliloquy which establishes sympathy for Brutus, also prior to this exchange. Moreover the sufferings of self-dramatizing, sensual youth are privileged in her analysis at the expense of tension and contradiction, while those of long-enduring middle age are denied. Furthermore, she is blind to the notion of Roman virtue, so important in the play and entirely familiar to Lee's contemporaries.

Brutus has not begun to shed his antic pose in public when he meets his son Titus and reacts to Titus's relationship with Teraminta, the illegitmate daughter of Tarquin:

> Who would be there at such polluted rites
> But goats, baboons, some chatt'ring old silenus
> Or satyrs grinning at your slimy joys. (I.212)

Brutus is still in his mad role here. The excessive, animalistic language is similar to that with which he earlier taunted the priests and courtiers in the guise of lunacy. Only gradually during the ensuing exchange does he become his true 'Roman' self, a change for which Titus gives thanks at line 242. Brutus's objection to Titus's relationship is political, but the way he expresses it at this early stage reflects a mood of personal bitterness. His resentment is comprehensible: he has suffered twenty years of isolation even from his family, while Titus has plunged without pause for thought into a relationship with the daughter of Tarquin, author of Brutus's own prolonged sufferings. The animal imagery he uses reflects his earlier disgust at his own animal posturings, his prostitution of reason in a loathsome but necessary pretence of imbecility. Hayne's view is that 'The play's dramatic sequence, which encourages the audience to enjoy and sympathize with Titus's lyrical evocation of marital sexuality before presenting Brutus's objections, suggests the audience is intended to choose bliss over slime' (344). This is wrong because the sequence is misrepresented, as discussed above; but also questionable for another reason.

What seems to Hayne to be a 'lyrical evocation of marital sexuality' by Titus, could be read as appetitive and even rather predatory. Titus is not at his most heroic when in the throes of his love. Titus responds to Teraminta's request for reassurance with a greedy emphasis on his own sexual pleasure. The play opens with her anxiety and insecurity and his response which is to insist on the pleasures of their forthcoming wedding-night:

> Cold as thou art, I'll warm thee into blushes. (I.38)
> This night, this night shall tell thee how I love thee. (I.64)

In Act II when he sees her again after promising Brutus to give her up, he falls upon her hungrily, as if he would devour her: 'thou mass of hoarded sweets' (II.423). When he pines for her in III.iii he is missing 'The softest bosom sweet, and not enjoyed' (7). When he sees her again later in the same scene he utters what must surely be one of the worst lines in sentimental drama: 'Leap to my heart and ride upon the pants' (61); and he urges 'Come to thy husband's bed' (65). At the end of Act III he falls upon her as if he would crush her almost to death:

Come to my breasts, thou tempest-beaten flower,
Brimful of rain and stick upon my heart.
O short-liv'd rose! yet some hours will I wear thee.
Yes, by the gods, I'll smell thee till I languish,
Rifle thy sweets, and run thee o'er and o'er,
Fall like the night upon thy folding beauties,
And clasp thee dead. Then, like the morning sun,
With a new heat kiss thee to life again,
And make the pleasure equal to the pain. (III.iii.171)

He has just saved her life at the cost of his own honour; yet she is a 'short-liv'd rose'; and his references to pain and death seem to go beyond the seventeenth-century association of death and orgasm to a perverse (though psychologically comprehensible) wish both to enjoy and to annihilate her.[16] When Teraminta is wounded at the end, Titus's reaction is characteristic: 'The very top of beauty ... Defiled and mangled thus' (V.i.54). Titus's attitude to Teraminta seems consistently inadequate. He is inclined inappropriately to objectify her, and he is unable to satisfy or protect her. He covers over this deficiency with tears and sighs, and exaggerated protestations of sentimentalized devotion. There is a sense that he is not at his best in the relationship, but, on the contrary, weak, and volatile; 'effeminate' in Restoration terms, co-dependent and over-emotional in modern ones.

Titus's weakness around Teraminta is in no sense an indictment of her. She is more heroic than him at times, for example when she pleads for his life in eloquent speeches and with all the 'saint-like virtue of a Roman wife' (IV.366). This phrase of the onlooker Valerius associates Teraminta at this moment with Lucrece. Lee's play is moving, and a tragedy, precisely because Teraminta is so sympathetic. Ultimately, Teraminta (unlike Lucrece) cannot have what she wants because it is counterposed to the interests of Rome. Faced with a choice between Teraminta and the royalists or his father and the good of Rome, Titus at first chooses wrongly. On his wedding night he suffers revulsion of mind and body, and is impotent because 'The horror of my treason shocked my joys' (IV.169). The word 'horror' is not lightly used here: as we shall see, it is repeatedly used in this scene to express the outrage of onlookers – and the audience – at royalist atrocities. The word 'treason' also recurs, as Titus proclaims his new resolve that 'Treason and tyranny shall not prevail' (IV.158). In Act IV the royalist counter-revolution leads to wholesale massacre in Rome. Unlike modern critics, Titus recognizes that he cannot put one individual's

good before that of the Roman people. The self-sacrificing heroism of this
is increased by Teraminta's beauty and virtue; but this does not mean that
Titus should abandon his duty for her sake: he has tried that and it has
failed. Even if civic duty is a less familiar concept today, we can relate to
the predicament: what possible future could there be in a relationship
entered into in defiance of 'the gods, / Glory, blood, nature, ties of reverence,
/ The dues of birth, respect of parents, all' (III.iii.138)?

However, Titus's progression from emotionalism to a fixed republican resolve can be quite hard for scholars today to grasp. This is partly
because we have lost a sense of Roman virtue, and perhaps also a sense of
any heroic or even viable political action or political alternatives. We may
also have problems with Brutus's masculinism.[17] In Act I he calls Titus
'degenerate boy' and wants to 'shake this soft, effeminate, lazy soul / Forth
from thy bosom' (I.227). Later he praises Titus's 'manly plainness' (II.282),
meaning honesty and straightforwardness. The early Titus takes a different
view:

> Give me a little time to rouse my spirits,
> To muster all the tyrant-man about me,
> All that is fierce, austere, and greatly cruel
> To Titus and his Teraminta's ruin. (II.362)

Titus the tearful lover is 'effeminate' both in the sense of being like a
woman and in the Restoration sense of being excessively susceptible to
woman's influence. At the end of Act II when Teraminta is taken away
from him, Titus describes himself as a woman, a 'soft mother' who cannot
believe her baby is dead and 'shrieks to see 'em wrap it in the shroud'
(II.520, 525). The later Titus, as we shall see, is very different, proud of
bearing his punishment without tears, and heroic in death.

Titus's sensitivity works not to undermine the idea of manliness but
to show its human cost, and make it the more heroic. It is important to
recognize that manliness was not a negative value for Lee's contemporaries. I discuss Dryden's masculinism in Chapters 1 and 6, and it is worth
quoting again here the passage from his preface to *Troilus and Cressida*:
'Friendship [i.e. between men] is both a virtue, and a Passion essentially;
love is a passion only in its nature, and is not a virtue but by Accident;
good nature makes Friendship; but effeminacy Love.'[18] As we shall see in
Chapter 6, Dryden's Hector and Andromache are scathing about Paris's
'effeminacy'. Their masculinism is echoed by Lee's Brutus, and their story
directly alluded to at the moment at which he sacrifices his sons:

Had Hector and the Greeks and Trojans met
Upon the truce and mingled with each other,
Brought to the banquet of those demigods
The fatal head of that illustrious whore,
Troy might have stood till now. (V.ii.13)

Masculinism is not a negative characteristic, though it does have its price.
For Brutus manliness is allied to the stringent heroism which can subordinate personal desire to public duty, to the very important idea of Roman
virtue: shortly after his reference to 'manly plainness' in Act II, Brutus
instructs Titus to stop crying and 'stand up now a Roman' (II.307). Later,
when Brutus learns of his sons' part in the royalist plot, he himself sheds
'unmanly tears'(IV.287). It is Titus who becomes the manly one. Manliness
for Brutus means dignity, the oppposite of animalism. At his low point
Brutus describes himself as 'unmaned' because he is reduced to bellowing
like a beast (IV.556–8). In Act V Brutus is resolved, but must submit to the
test of women's tears which he has to resist. This is presented as an ordeal
for him and a test of his courage. It is up to each reader or member of the
audience to decide what they feel about the positive value accorded to
manliness in the play; but, in deciding, it is important to take into account
the predatoriness of 'sentimental man' (the early Titus), otherwise we end
up with a skewed perspective which vilifies Brutus and whitewashes
Titus, instead of understanding the dramatic tension between them.

There are two kinds of women in the play: women who have Roman
virtue, and women who cry. Lucrece has Roman virtue, like Portia in
Shakespeare's *Julius Caesar*, or, in more extreme form, Volumnia in his
Coriolanus. Brutus's wife Sempronia falls into the weepy category. She
brings on an army of weeping women to undermine Brutus's resolve at the
end. But Teraminta does not fall simply into the weeping category. She is
also capable of moments of 'virtue', for example in her response to Titus
telling her that Brutus has demanded that he should renounce her:

I am your wife, and one that seeks your honor.
By heaven, I would have sworn you thus myself.
What, on the shock of empire, on the turn
Of state, and universal change of things,
To lie at home and languish for a woman!
No, Titus, he that makes himself thus vile,
Let him not dare pretend to aught that's princely,
But be, as all the warlike world shall judge him,
The droll of th'people and the scorn of kings. (II.495)

Here Teraminta is more 'manly' than Titus, just as Titus in his turn later sustains Brutus's manhood when it falters. So not only is Titus divided between love and honour, but Teraminta herself at times espouses the cause of Roman virtue over that of love, a clear sign that the 'manly' Roman way cannot be simply dismissed as inimical to love and therefore despicable.

Lucius Junius Brutus offers the contrast between two rival versions of sexual politics, one Whiggish and one Tory. The Whig perpective which is Brutus's, which prevails, and which the play seems to endorse, combines masculinism with respect for the liberties of the virtuous woman, in this case Lucrece. We find this perspective in other Whig plays such as Shadwell's *The Lancashire Witches* and *The Woman-Captain*.[19] The royalist sensibility, drawn from cavalier drama, the Court culture of Charles I and Henrietta Maria and French romance, endorses passion and sentiment, and celebrates the type of hero (like the early Titus) who, as Dryden says of his Antony in *All For Love*, 'Weeps much; fights little; but is wond'rous kind'.[20] In this royalist culture women are favoured more as lovers but less as citizens and political subjects.

To say that the play seems to endorse a Whiggish perspective does not mean that Lee is partisan in a facile way, or that he is unaware of complexities or of the human cost of political virtue. On the contrary, he exploits difficult situations to poignant effect. What is essential is to recognize that Brutus is acting from a position of principle and at some personal cost; otherwise nothing in the play makes sense. Brutus sacrifices his dignity in his guise of madness, as well as intimate contact with others. In the end, of course, he sacrifices his sons. Another of the sacrifices he has to make is to deny his feminine side, to stifle his tears. Hayne's portrayal of Brutus as a mere opportunist is an astonishing exercise in political crudity and literary imperviousness. It would be possible to argue that Brutus is opportunistic at certain moments, for example when he vows to exploit the rape of Lucrece:

> ... For now's the time
> To shake the building of the tyrant down.
> ... So from the blackness of young Tarquin's crime
> And furnace of his lust, the virtuous soul
> Of Junius Brutus catches bright occasion.
> I see the pillars of the kingdom totter. (I.266)

Yet it is equally possible to read in the lines a combination of real disgust, heroic purpose and outrage sharpened by Brutus's own sufferings under

Tarquin. The echoes of Milton's 'Samson Agonistes' lend weight to the idea that Brutus is to be seen as a hero, destroying 'Philistines' through noble self-sacrifice. I have already made the point that Brutus carries out Lucrece's own wishes. It is necessary also to appreciate that the cause of liberty and the Roman republic can be seen as a 'bright occasion'.

For Brutus this is a particular moment in history 'when honor, / When Rome, the world, and the gods come to claim us' (II.380). All these things are equally important: honour, concern for one's country, public spirit and religion. These are alien values to critics today, and perhaps were so at the Restoration court; but they were values dear to the heart of the political majority in Lee's England. Brutus respresents people's genuine concerns, the kinds of concerns which had resulted in the overwhemlimng victory of the Whigs in elections to successive Parliaments during the Exclusion Crisis. Brutus could be talking about Charles II's subjects as much as Tarquin's when he says:

> You that were once a free-born people, famed
> In his forefathers' days for wars abroad,
> The conquerors of the world. (II.192)

Andrew Marvell in his *An Account of the Growth of Popery and Arbitrary Government* (1677) expresses at great length Parliament's concerns about Charles's supine, francophile foreign policy.[21] Many in Lee's audience, not least the MPs, would have shared these concerns. Thomas Jordan had reflected the popular mood in his Lord Mayor's Show, performed just over a month before *Lucius Juinus Brutus*. Jordan introduces the figure of Sir John Hawkwood, 'an ancient English Hero' who tells the spectators what they want to hear:

> I flourish'd in those daies *Edward* the Third
> Did conquer *France*, with his Victorious Sword.
> He purchas'd Fame, Wealth, Honour in that Nation,
> But all the purcahse now, is a new *Fashion*.
> What your Fore-fathers gain'd by Blood and Sweat
> Is now exchang'd for a *French* Flagellet.[22]

The word 'forefathers', echoed in Brutus's speech, invites the audience to become personally involved, identifying with the speaker's concern about the country's decline. Tories retaliated to such concerns by sneering at excessive patriotism, and by stressing upper-class bonds over national ones. Strong patriotism is a positive value in Whig drama, and a negative value in Tory drama.[23]

Lee also reflects the current mood of extreme concern about religion. The Exclusion Crisis was precipitated by genuine fears that the English Protestantism and the liberties it guaranteed were under threat.[24] The founding of the republic in Lee's play is an act of religious piety. Brutus is frequently described as god-like, and as having godlike virtue (e.g. II.237, 245; IV.8; V.ii.68), not only by admiring Romans but also by his son Titus (e.g. II.488; IV.365, 503). The quasi-Catholic priests, in contrast, are the plays' villains. In league with the royalists, they lie, cheat, torture and murder, then deny that the gods are angry or even interested:

> Fumes, fumes; the phantoms of an ill digestion.
> The gods are as good quiet gods as may be,
> They're fast asleep and mean not to disturb us. (IV.163)

Titus in this scene is sure the gods play an active role in human affairs (IV.132, 144), and he is echoed by Valerius (184) and Brutus (246).

Concern about the law was also widespread. Brutus is strongly commited to the law, and wants to establish:

> Laws, rules, and bounds, prescribed for raging kings,
> Like banks and bulwarks for the mother seas,
> Though 'tis impossible they should prevent
> A thousand daily wracks and nightly ruins,
> Yet help to break those rolling inundations
> Which else would overflow and drown the world. (III.ii.11)

Brutus's execution of his sons at the end is a legal action, not to be confused with royalist arbitrary violence. Though both sides in the Exclusion Crisis claimed that the law was on their side, a focus upon law and liberty as transcendent values was Whiggish, both in politics and in drama.[25] Law, patriotism and piety were the Whigs' strong cards in 1680, and Brutus holds all three.

So much for Brutus's ends. What about his means? Hayne makes much of the fact that Brutus uses crowd politics in Act I, and that the mob under Vinditius's leadership are shown executing summary justice on the courtier Fabritius in Act II. We could scarcely expect Lee to depict the common people heroically. There is no play produced in the theatres in the Exclusion Crisis in which the common people are depicted positively; though artisans are depicted as (comic) popular heroes in *The Coronation of Queen Elizabeth*, a three-act entertainment performed at the London fairs in August 1680; and they are positively represented in Thomas Jordan's Lord Mayor's Shows, as one might expect since they were financing and performing the spectacle.[26] In the theatres commoners are typically represented in Exclusion Crisis drama as an unruly mob. It is striking, then, that Lee's artisans are not fickle, and do not yearn for change and destruction for their own sake. This distinguishes them from the mobs in Tory plays who change their allegiance with every new speech, and want simply to cause trouble and unrest.[27] There are notable differences between the crowd scenes in this play and those in other plays. The people's leader Vinditius, played by the great comic actor Nokes, is an amusing figure who is, as David Vieth remarks, 'surprisingly positive'.[28] Vinditius is less evil than rabble-rousers such as Creon in Dryden's and Lee's *Oedipus* or Cade in Crowne's *The Misery of Civil-War*, plays performed in the previous season to *Lucius Junius Brutus*. Vinditius is somewhere in between such villainous types and a comic, meddling and ambitious busybody like Valeria in Tate's *The Ingratitude of a Common-wealth*. At times Vinditius rises to the status of wise 'Fool': the action bears out the truth of his comments on the priests' hypocrisy in III.i and on their violence and treachery in Act IV.

The victim of mob violence is Fabritius, the ridiculous 'crack-fart of the court' (II.69). Fabritius taunts Brutus in Act I and arrogantly despises the people in Act II. Brutus addresses the people in the tones of Shakespeare's Mark Antony: 'Patricians, people, friends, and Romans all' (II.139). Fabritius abuses them in terms which resemble less Brutus in *Julius Caesar* than Bottom in *A Midsummer Night's Dream*:

> How long at length, thou many-headed monster,
> You bulls and bears, you roaring beasts and bandogs,
> Porters and cobblers, tinkers, tailors, all
> You rascally sons of whores in a civil government,
> How long, I say, dare you abuse our patience? (II.61)

The comedy is at Fabritius's expense, and at the expense of the Court of which he is a part. The laughter is increased because Fabritius, for all his pretensions, is from common origins himself, elevated for his role as Court pimp.

Lee's crowd are not a fickle mob who change with every wind. They are unmoved by Fabritius, but swayed by Brutus because he has right on his side. Hayne misses the point of the contrast between Brutus's successful oratory and the failed rhetoric of other characters, seeing this as undermining the basis of all language. Language is a site of contestation in *Lucius Junius Brutus*, but this does not mean there is no meaning. On the contrary, there is an intersection between language and history. Brutus's language makes more sense than other people's because it is appropriate to the historical moment. This is why he is able to oppose fixity of purpose to Titus's initial emotionalism and changeability. It is not that he represents transcendant values, but that his language and vision embody the future. Hayne disallows all Brutus's inspiring speeches by the simple expedient of declaring all language 'vile' (taking her cue, and indeed her title, from the sex-obsessed Titus of Act I, as he anticipates the primacy of sense over talk on his wedding night). However, the point about Brutus's sacrifice of his sons is precisely that it shows his rhetoric is *not* empty; he is prepared to put his actions where his mouth is. Fabritius's alliterative and bombastic royalist rant is empty of signification. Brutus's language embodies a new political reality. It is true that Vinditius plays a comic, slightly debunking role in relation to Brutus's oratory. Fabritius plays a similar role in relation to the royalist speech of Tiberius in Act II, discussed below. Brutus's tolerance of Vinditius is proof of his verbal repudiation of pride and ambition, discussed below. He is as happy to let his words stand the test of vulgar associations as he is to submit to the challenge of history. Moreover, Brutus's rhetoric transcends ridicule effortlessly with speeches which must stir a chord in anyone not utterly impervious to (or incapable of imaginatively entering into) democratic or libertarian hopes. Of course there are moments when Brutus's own language fails, moments of his greatest distress; but, far from proving language vile, these moments are proof of Brutus's humanity, and Titus's 'bright occasions', or chances to prove himself.

Hayne fails to make sense of the contrast between Brutus's success with language and others' failed oratory, seeing this merely as evidence of his oppressiveness and their victim status. Behind Hayne's analysis also seems to lurk an affection for victims: Teraminta in victim rather than heroic mode, Titus in victim mode (his republican moods being entirely ignored), the loathsome Fabritius. Brutus is effective and successful and therefore oppressive and nasty by definition. Without explicit reference to Foucault, there is a sense of his influence in this preference for the marginal, and discounting of real, effective opposition. However, Brutus is the man of the moment, the agent of destiny and the gods, the voice of the future. It is not necessarily a moral question (although of course a strong moral argument against the Tarquins and in favour of Brutus's better government can be made). The point is that the moment has come when, because of propitious circimstance, or a 'ripeness' within the old order, courageous individual action can make a difference. It is a historical crux; or what chaos theorists call a bifurcation point.[29]

Hayne makes much of the fact that Brutus uses prodigy-mongering, for example when he claims to see in the skies a monstrous dragon with flaming eyes (I.321). This is quite a successful way to get the people's attention. At other times Brutus uses more elevated political rhetoric, as I noted above. The scene in Act I has comic overtones as the plebians bully ones of their number who cannot see the dragon into saying he can see it. More to the point, however, Vinditius's interpretation of Brutus's flaming-eyed dragon as representing the tyrannical Tarquins is instantly confirmed by the entry of Lucrece, who describes her rapist's 'red and sparkling eyes' (I.367). Far from being a complete chimera, the dragon is a symbol of the very real violence of 'lustful, bloody Sextus' (I.359). Although he 'works the crowd', Brutus is far from being an exploiter of the people. Indeed, he has a positive attitude to the people, within limits. Collatinus's sneers, 'Brutus does indulge the people' (III.ii.26), but he fails to smear his opponent with the charge of rabble-rousing, for Brutus immediately replies:

> Consul, in what is right I will indulge 'em.
> And much I think 'tis better so to do,
> Than see 'em run in tumults through the streets,
> Forming cabals and plotting against the senate,
> Shutting their shops and flying from the town,
> As if the gods had sent the plague among 'em.
> I know too well you and your royal tribe
> Scorn the good people, scorn the late election …
> Yet wise men know 'tis very rarely seen
> That a free people should desire the hurt
> of common liberty. (III.ii.27)

The reference to the 'late election' is strikingly topical, and must surely have raised a cheer from the MPs in the audience, who had been angered by the King's delay in calling Parliament after repeated Whig electoral victories. In Tory drama populism and rabble-rousing are used again and again to demonize Whig leaders. Brutus's defence of the 'good people' is strikingly different.

The crucial point about Brutus is that, unlike demagogues in other plays, he is not motivated by personal ambition, but on the contrary is willing to make personal sacrifices for the people's good. Villainous ambition was a charge Tories repeatedly tried to level against the Whigs.[30]

But Brutus scorns self-aggrandizement and has no thought of personal reward. He scorns 'ceremonious honors' (II.239). Thanking him on behalf of the senate, Valerius says:

> Next we, as friend, with equal arms embrace thee,
> That Brutus may remember, though his virtue
> Soar to the gods, he is a Roman still. (II.244)

Brutus's reply is significant:

> And when I am not so, or once in thought
> Conspire the bondage of my countrymen,
> Strike me, you gods; tear me, O Romans, piecemeal,
> And let your Brutus be more loathed than Tarquin. (247)

This distinguishes Brutus absolutely from ambitious, quasi-Whiggish rebels and plotters in Tory plays, such as Creon in *Oedpius*, the Constable in Crowne's *The Ambitious Statesman*, Marius Senior and Metellus in Otway's *Caius Marius* and the various rebels in Whitaker's *The Conspiracy*. Brutus wants to create a society 'Where rancour and ambition are extinguished' (III.ii.62). As we shall see, in this play destructive ambition is a royalist quality.

Brutus is also moderate in his behaviour, in contrast to royalist violence and excess. In III.i we see Collatinus, Lucrece's widower and Brutus's fellow-consul, breaking faith with his dead wife and conspiring with the royalists to restore the Tarquins. In the next scene we find Brutus merely replacing Collatinus as consul. This judicious action is vindicated when we see that the new consul Valerius is virtuous and ultimately heroic. Moreover, Brutus even compensates Collatinus for loss of office: 'The city renders thee what is thy own / With vast increase' (III.ii.76). Collatinus gets off lightly, and Brutus's just – indeed merciful – proceeding is in keeping with his commitment to the law.

In contrast to Brutus's modesty and moderation, the royalists are proud and ambitious. In III.i we see the royalist plotters work upon Collatinus's personal ambition to get him to join them. We hear of Tarquin's 'fathomless ambition / And ocean luxury' (III.ii.17). In general, the royalists are characterized by violence and excess. Even Tarquin's daughter Teraminta judges that 'Tarquin, although my father, is a tyrant, / A bloody black usurper' (III.iii.111); though like Dryden's Benzayda she dutifully begs Titus to spare her cruel father's life. Tarquin's queen threatens to kill Teraminta if Titus does not join the royalist conspiracy. However, Teraminta urges Titus to be true to his ' honour' (III.iii.136) and stay true to Brutus's cause. Though Titus capitulates to save her, he knows he is plunging into dishonour (131, 138, 170). There is never any suggestion that the royal cause has the slightest legitimacy.

Events bear out Brutus's view that the royalists violate sacred institutions:

> Invading fundamental right and justice,
> Breaking the ancient customs, statutes, laws,
> With positive power and arbitrary lust. (II.179)

This is not just abstract rhetoric but a reference to Tarquin's grounding his personal rule upon 'the horrid slaughter / Of all the princes of the Roman senate' (177). However, Lee does not rely upon descriptions of past atrocities, but twice uses horrific spectacle to arouse anti-royalist feeling. The first spectacle we have already considered: the suicide of the raped Lucrece and the ritual of swearing revenge for her wrongs. The second is the horrific sacrifice of two 'commonwealth's men' in Act IV. The victim's only crime is saying "'twas possible / That kings themselves might err and were but men, / The people were not beasts for sacrifice' (IV.30). Terms such as 'commonwealth's men' and 'royalists' (IV.53) have a topical resonance, recalling the English Civil War and Exclusion Crisis. Here the royalists and their priest accomplices are unambiguously villains, dementedly plotting the rape and massacre which will accompany the restoration of Tarquin. Tiberius in particular gleefully anticipates the forthcoming slaughter in Rome, cheerfully acquiescing in the planned murder of his own father (IV.59), despite a promise to Titus at the end of Act II that this was not intended. Tiberius is prone to false promises, just as his priestly companions are to false oaths.

Lee also plays on the audience's religious feelings, as Tiberius looks forward to burning down Rome's temples (16). The priests' treachery and hypocrisy exploit anti-Catholic feeling. They are linked to the devil as they 'Swear by the gods celestial and infernal' (IV.93), and engage in 'so damned a conjuration ... devilish sacrifices, / A sacrament of blood' (230, 232). The association between popery and diabolism was common in Whig propaganda.[31] There is a particular attempt to arouse the horror of the watching MPs, as the sacrificial victims 'begin to roar', and the gloating Tiberius wishes:

> O that the hearts of all the traitor senate,
> And heads of the foul hydra multitude,
> Were frying with their fat upon this pile. (IV.98)

This is a reminder that the royalists are murderers of 'parliamentarians'. Tiberius is almost a pantomime villain here, ranting vengeance on his shocked and titillated audience. Then: *'The scene draws, showing the sacrifice: one burning and another crucified; the* Priests *coming forward with goblets in their hands, filled with human blood'*. Then, as if the twin horrors of burning and crucifixion were not enough, the priests chant while the royalists proceed to drink the blood and swear loyalty to Tarquin. These actions are not chosen at random: burning (of heretics and of cities) was the chief atrocity cited in anti-Catholic propaganda; crucifixion of course recalls the death of Christ; and drinking human blood suggests diabolism as well as the Catholic mass. Lee offers an exemplary anti-royalist and anti-Catholic spectacle resembling the anti-Catholic spectacle in other plays such as Settle's *The Female Prelate*, a Whiggish play about Catholic destruction of a nobleman's liberty, property, family and ultimately life. In Settle's Act III the persecuted hero, Saxony, is taken into a chamber where the scene opening 'discovers variety of Hereticks in several Tortures' (p. 40); in Act IV the imprisoned heretics set the prison on fire and the ghost of the old Duke of Saxony, murdered by Pope Joan in her youth, writes 'MURDER' on the wall in 'bloudy fire' (IV.iii, p. 50); and in Act V 'The Scene opens, and discovers a Stake and Faggots, with Priests with Lighted Torches to kindle the Fire, and the Rabble hurrying Saxony to the Fire' (V.ii, p. 70).

The spectacle in Lee's Act IV reverses the meaning of spectacle in royalist plays such as William Whitakers *The Conspiracy*, in which royalists are ritually murdered while gloating rebels watch:

Scene drawn, discovers a Room hung all with black; the Old Queen, Lentesia, Bectas, Kara, and Kulcaiha seated, while several of the Royal Party are plac'd in Order, with Coffins before them, on which stand a dim Tapier, and Mutes standing ready as to strangle them; then Enter eight or ten Blackmoors, drest like Fiends, and dance an Antic; having done, they go out, and after fearful groans and horrid shriekings; some of them return with burnt Wine, which they fill, out in Sculls to the King's Friends, who as fast as they drink, dy: at which the Queen and all the rest seem pleas'd. (V, p. 51)

In the same way Nahum Tate piles up atrocities to increase pity and strengthen his message against rebellion at the end of *The Ingratitude of a Common-wealth*, his adaptation of Shakespeare's *Coriolanus*: the villain Nigridius gloats that he has killed Menenius and tortured Coriolanus's little son and thrown the mangled body into Volumnia's arms, thus driving her demented. Coriolanus does not die until he has been subjected to

Volumnia's ravings and the boy's pathetic dying speech, in addition to the wounding and threatened rape of his wife.

Lee also reverses the political meaning of dead babies, an emotive image in propaganda in all ages. In a Tory play such as John Crowne's *The Misery of Civil-War* the image of babies impaled on soldiers' pikes is used to arouse horror at rebellion. Here it arouses horror against the royalists, as Titus describes.

> Nothing but images of horror round me,
> Rome all in blood, the ravished vestals raving,
> The sacred fire put out; robbed mothers' shrieks
> Deaf'ning the gods with clamors for their babes
> That sprawled aloft upon the soldiers' spears. (IV.175)

The word 'horror' is repeated by Valerius (183) and reiterated by Titus (202). Titus's rejection of the royalists is fourfold: disgust at 'Horrors and midnight murders' (131); emotional resistance as 'My heart rebelled / Against itself'; rational revulsion, as 'My reason and my faculties were wracked' (138); and religious insight: 'The gods, the gods awake you to repentance / As they have me' (132). The royalists, in contrast, are monstrous, heartless, irrational and irreligious. Their demented blood-letting contrasts sharply with the Brutus's lawfulness and commitment to 'universal peace' (III.ii.63). The 'trial' of Fabritius by Brutus's supporters in Act II (not witnessed or condoned by Brutus himself, it must be noted) showed that the republicans are not perfect either, but it pales into insignificance beside royalist crimes. It is significant that, whilst the royalists planned the wholesale slaughter of the senate and consuls, the senate and consuls 'will see strict justice done upon the traitors' (IV.215).

Mystifyingly, Hayne discusses these spectacles, but 'writes out' their effect in arousing antipathy against the royalists, and even twists the royalist atrocities into an indictment of Brutus. Her argument is that the cumulative violence taints Brutus's sacrifice of his sons at the end. In fact the royalist atrocities allow both a context for and a contrast with Brutus's actions. Spectacle, says Hayne, undercuts political rhetoric. True; but the spectacle of royalist atrocities undercuts *their* rhetoric, and reinforces the anti-tyrannical speeches of Brutus which might otherwise seem rather abstract.[32]

Brutus speaks of the 'vanity and ambition' of his royalist son, Tiberius, and condemns his companions, 'the young hot blood of Rome, / ... Such headlong youth as, spurning laws and manners, / Shared in the

late debaucheries of Sextus, / and therefore wish the tyrant here again'
(III.i.107, 110). Then in Act IV we see Tiberius and his companions not
only shedding but drinking the hot blood of their victims, and Tiberius
revelling in fantasies of rape and slaughter, and dreaming of drinking the
blood 'Of Rome's best life, drawn from her grizzled fathers!' He continues,
'That were a draught indeed to quench ambition' (IV.117–18), echoing and
vindicating his father's earlier criticisms. Thus the events of Act IV bear
out Brutus's words. Hayne's account of Brutus's language undermined by
what we witness on stage is the opposite of the truth: the action of Act IV
and Tiberius's own words show the literal truth of Brutus's words. In
contrast to Brutus's inspiring rhetoric, most of Tiberius's speeches are
aggressive and appetitive, revelling in bloodlust.

The only exception is a speech at the beginning of Act II:

> Remember this in short. A king is one
> To whom you may complain when you are wronged;
> The throne lies open in your way for justice.
> You may be angry, and may be forgiven.
> There's room for favor, and for benefit,
> Where friends and enemies may come together,
> Have present hearing, present composition,
> Without recourse to the litigious laws,
> Laws that are cruel, deaf, inexorable,
> That cast the vile and noble all together,
> Where, if you should exceed the bounds of order,
> There is no pardon. O, 'tis dangerous
> To have all actions judged by rigorous law.
> What, to depend on innocence alone,
> Among so many accidents and errors
> That wait on human life? (II.9)

This is the only good royalist speech in the play, and might well have been
a sop to royalists in the audience. What are we to make of it? It seems quite
persuasive at first. However, we have just witnessed the suicide of Lucrece,
raped by her royal guest and relative. We are already aware that there is a
disparity between theory and practice, that the justice and mercy of the
throne is a rhetorical construct. We are shortly to see the low-born
Fabritius admit that he obtained a knighthood for acting as pimp to royalty
(II.113–15), which will cast an ironic light on the fact that 'There's room for
favour, and for benefit'. The elevation of the unworthy and slighting of
those with long and loyal service was a constant complaint from 1660

onwards, whether in the laments of royalists who felt that their loyalty during the interregnum deserved greater reward or in the attacks on the King's mistresses.

An ironic light is cast In III.ii on the claim to offer 'present hearing, present composition', rather than lengthy legal delays. The priests come to the senate and demand the restitution of Tarquin's property, swearing profusely and falsely that Tarquin intends no further harm. Brutus's reply is reasonable and judicious: 'The things you ask being very controversial / Require some time' (114). The priest sneers that under consular government:

> A very trifle cannot be resolved;
> A trick, a start, a shadow of a business
> That would receive dispatch in half a minute
> Were the authority but rightly placed
> In Rome's most lawful king. (III.ii.142)

Of course the restitution of Tarquin's property is not a trivial question. The fact that the priest is flagrantly lying is soon revealed in his reference to 'the royal plot' (149), and his bad faith and specious argument taint the point made by Tiberius.

Moreover Tiberius's attack on the law would not necessarily have been well received. His objection to the fact that laws 'cast the vile and noble all together' may be taken to imply that nobles should be above the law, an attitude which the Restoration audience, and the MPs in particular, would have found problematic to say the least.[33] Tiberius's desire for favored treatment may be a sign of the arrogance and aristocratic 'scorn' which Brutus rebukes in Collatinus (III.ii.34). If Tiberius's speech is indeed intended to carry conviction, one might expect Brutus's expulsion of Tarquin to be presented as problematic in itself. However, it occurs almost as a natural process. In contrast, as I noted above, the attempted counter-revolution is presented as 'the royal plot', with all the negative connotations which the word 'plot' had in 1680.[34]

Brutus tries to achieve dignity and to adhere to his resolution and his duty despite personal appetite and inclination. The royalists have the nature and behaviour of animals in the seventeenth-century conception. Tiberius seems like a cross between Shakespeare's Lady Macbeth and Edmund in *King Lear* as he casts off natural ties:

> I here put off all nature ...
> All blood, all reverence, fondness be forgot.

> Like a grown savage on the common wild
> That runs at all and cares not who begot him,
> I'll meet my lion sire and roar defience,
> As if he ne'er had nursed me in his den. (III.i.166, 169)

This animalism is in direct contrast to the reason and virtue of Brutus and the filial piety of Titus. Sempronia can't have her way at the end because she pleads for Tiberius too.

Brutus's behaviour at the moment when his sons' involvement in the conspiracy against him is revealed is exemplary in its piety and humility. First, he is 'at a loss for thought, and must acknowledge / The councils of the gods are fathomless' (IV.274). Then, he wonders at

> Fate, or the will of heav'n, call't what you please,
> That mars the best designs that prudence lays,
> That brings events about perhaps to mock
> At human reach and sport with expectation. (IV.281)

He sheds uncharacteristic tears, 'To see his blood, his children his own bowels, / Conspire the death of him that gave them being' (IV.288). He goes through the same stages of spiritual doubt, philosophical paralysis and reaffirmation as Shakespeare's Hamlet, only more quickly, and ends like Hamlet believing in a divinity that shapes our ends:

> Yet after all I justify the gods,
> And will conclude there's reason supernatural
> That guides us through the world with vast discretion,
> Although we have not souls to comprehend it. (IV.293)

There are echoes here also of Milton's aim to justify the ways of God to man. Both his human distress and the metaphysical scope of his thought distinguish Brutus entirely from the royalists, who are creatures of pure appetite.

Brutus pardons his sons as a father, but condemns them as a consul. His understanding of the gods' will is that his personal feelings must be sacrificed:

> Since then, for man's instruction, and the glory
> Of the immortal gods, it is decreed
> There must be patterns drawn of fiercest virtue,
> Brutus submits to the eternal doom. (IV.299)

Teraminta then pleads for Titus's life. Her courage and dignity at this point surpass Titus, who grovels on the ground in 'streaming tears', kissing his father's feet and howling for mercy (IV.399–42). Teraminta is not critical of Brutus; on the contrary, her argument is that Titus resembles him, bearing 'The portraiture of all your manly virtues' (332). She also tells Brutus of Titus's repentance and attempts to stop the conspiracy. Far from being impervious or obdurate, Brutus listens courteously and is moved, promising to spare Titus. He is thus the very reverse of a tyrant.

Moreover, it is vital to our understanding of the play that it is Titus who demands to die for Rome. Brutus has now forgiven him fully, and Titus is 'in the calm of nature', the 'tempest' of emotion 'quite overblown' (456–7). It is his turn to be the strong one. He plays the active role, and Brutus is passive, gentle, seemingly exhausted. Titus is goaded by 'All those reproaches which the eyes and fingers / And tongues of Rome will daily cast upon me' (IV.462). He is tormented by 'the stings of my own conscience' (466), and concerned for 'my blotted honor' (469). Titus's changeability is a thing of the past. He has 'a mind resolved' (472). The values he will die for are the gods' will, filial piety, justice and the liberty of Rome:

> Yes, sir; I call the powers of heav'n to witness,
> Titus dares die if so you have decreed;
> Nay, he shall die with joy to honor Brutus,
> To make your justice famous through the world
> And fix the liberty of Rome forever. (IV.478)

When Brutus hesitates, Titus insists: 'The gods will have it so' (505). Finally, Brutus agrees:

> It seems as if the gods had preordained it
> To fix the reeling spirits of the people
> And settle the loose liberty of Rome. (512)

Yet the decision is too much for his composure. He is 'unmanned', in tears, and prostrate on the ground, finally reduced again to animal status as he bellows like a beast in his grief and despair, (536–7, 549, 556–8). It is Titus who raises him up, Titus who seizes the moment, takes charge of their fate and decrees their joint statement to posterity. Brutus ends the Act dumb: 'But, O, my tears run o'er, / Groans choke my words, and I can speak no more' (IV.5 84). Hayne leaves out all mention of either the pathos or the role-reversal in this scene.

At the end Titus submits to whipping without 'one groan' or 'woman's tear' (V.i.46), for, 'I have borne it well, and like a Roman' (48). But Brutus has forgotten to protect Teraminta. Her entry, wounded and furious, is for Titus 'this last wound, this stab to all my courage' (73). Teraminta is now reduced to a pitiable and childlike state and wishes:

> To murmur, sob, and lean my aching head
> Upon thy breast, thus like a cradle babe
> To suck thy wounds and bubble out my soul. (V.i.85)

Brutus's failure to protect Teraminta is a serious error and it sets up a dramatic tension and conflict.[35] However, it is immediately followed by the excessive and venomous rantings of the subhuman Tiberius, who is impervious to his own guilt, and whose accusations of Brutus are clearly false: 'Thou more tyrannical than any Tarquin' (V.i.116). A more balanced view is offered by Valerius, who agrees to give Titus a Roman death at his sword's point, to spare him the indignity of the executioner's axe, but will not try to save him from death:

> For when I weigh with my more serious thought
> Thy father's conduct in this dreadful justice,
> I find it is impossible to save thee. (V.i.166)

Tiberius is incapable of this 'more serious thought'; and impervious to the 'never fading glory' which inspires both Valerius (V.i.174) and Titus (181). Tiberius can think only of himself, whereas Titus and Brutus are alike in thinking first and foremost of the good of Rome and the future. They represent a higher and more heroic order of humanity.

In V.i we have seen the human cost of Roman justice (in Teraminta) and the necessity for it (in Tiberius); as well as the inspiring dignity and courage that commitment to justice and the Roman code of honour can bring (in Titus and Valerius). Now Brutus enters and prays to Jupiter and the gods to 'Guard and defend the liberty of Rome' (V.ii.5). He also explains his purpose:

> Jove having from eternity set down
> Rome to be head of all the under world,
> Raised with this thought, and big with prophecy
> Of what vast good may grow by such examples,
> Brutus stands forth to do a dreadful justice. (V.ii.18)

In other words, he is inspired by God, his country and its future empire, the needs of the historical moment, the judgement of posterity and good principles even at personal cost: just as the Whigs claimed to be, when they continued to urge the safeguarding of the Protestant succession at the risk of their personal property, livelihoods and even their lives.[36] Brutus will heal the times by setting an act of self-sacrifice against the rampant appetite and ambition of Tarquin and his followers. We hear how his own personal example of Roman virtue will help create a brighter future, and inspire Rome and the world:

> Thus shall we stop the mouth of loud sedition,
> Thus show the difference betwixt the sway
> Of partial tyrants and of a freeborn people,
> Where no man shall offend because he's great,
> Where none need doubt his wife's or daughter's honor,
> Where all enjoy their own without suspicion,
> Where there's no innovation of religion,
> No change of laws, nor breach of privilege,
> No desperate factions gaping for rebellion,
> No hopes of pardon for assassinates,
> No rash advancements of the base or stranger,
> For luxury, for wit, or glorious vice;
> But on the contrary a balanced trade,
> Patriots encouraged, manufactures cherished,
> Vagabonds, walkers, drones, and swarming braves,
> The froth of states, scummed from the commonwealth,
> Idleness banished, all excess repressed,
> And riots checked by sumptuary laws. (V.ii.42)

This contains some phrases which must indeed have seemed like 'Expressions & Reflections upon ye Government' as they rang out in the theatre, and bears a striking resemblance to Whig ideology. Brutus enumerates Whig concerns here: good firm government but without tyranny, and with a positive concern for morality, property, religion and law; an end to court corruption, favouritism, luxury and vice; and the promotion of trade and the conditions of peace and order under which trade can flourish. Pride in trade and manufacture was particularly evident among the Whigs and those who formed their base of support, and was celebrated annually, together with peaceful order, in Thomas Jordan's Lord Mayor's shows.[37] The Whig leader Shaftesbury believed in an enlightened capitalism and was keenly committed to colonialism.[38] 'All the senate' (V.ii.68), like the House of Commons in 1680, are supportive of these ideals.

The senators who formerly pleaded with Brutus to spare his sons now understand his actions and call him excellent and godlike. Their expressions of gratitude to Brutus are still ringing in our ears when Sempronia

enters. She brings with her the female relatives of all the royalist plotters,
and urges them to assault Brutus with their tears:

> ... haste, haste, and run about him,
> Groan, sob, howl out the terrors of your souls,
> Nay, fly upon him like robbed savages,
> And tear him for your young. (V.ii.79)

This is oddly similar to Tiberius's 'Like a grown savage on the common
wild' speech in III.i. Tiberius and Sempronia recognize nothing outside
their own will. Sempronia pleads for both her sons and for all the
conspirators. Unlike Teraminta, she has no sense of the cause at stake or of
Titus's moral superiority. There is no question of Brutus giving in to
Sempronia, though her pleading is a trial for his fortitude. Sempronia
reminds us of the manipulative Octavia in Dryden's *All For Love*, as she
brings in her young son Junius to try to manipulate his father with a
mawkish speech. Crucially, moreover, Titus most emphatically does not
want what the women want for him: life at any price, at the expense of
honour. As Titus receiveds his death-wound, the women 'shriek' and
'swoon', but Titus praises Valerius for stabbing him 'bravely' and 'nobly'
(V.ii.146–7).

Teraminta dies cursing Brutus; but she has lost her vision, both
literally and metaphorically:

> The heav'n is all benighted, not one star
> To light us through the dark and pathless maze.
> I have lost thy spirit; O. I grope about
> But cannot find thee. Now I sink in shadows. (V.ii.161)

The dying Titus has a very different perspective. Unlike other tragic
heroes such as Oedipus in the play of that name, or Castalio in Otway's
The Orphan, he does not die cursing the gods, or even in a state of reproach.
On the contrary, he feels he has died for a reason, as he tells Brutus: 'I hope
the glorious liberty of Rome, / Thus watered by the blood of both your
sons, / Will get imperial growth and flourish long' (V.ii.168). In
psychological terms, he dies at one with his father and in a state of psychic
unity with himself:

> What happiness has life to equal this?
> By all the gods I would not live again;
> For what can Jove or all the gods give more,
> To fall thus crowned with virtue's fullest charms,
> And die thus blessed in such a father's arms? (V.ii.182)

Valerius tries to sentimentalize the situation, describing Brutus as a 'noble vessel ... floating in this world of ruin' (V.ii.188, 190). He is rebuked and contradicted. Instead, the play ends on a note of piety and moderation, as Brutus prays for peace, and asks Jove, once again, to 'Guard and defend the liberty of Rome' (V.ii.210). The effect is the same as at the end of Shakespeare's *Richard III*, where it is made clear that we have seen not mindless violence, but a move 'To reap the harvest of perpetual peace / By this one bloody trial of sharp war' (V.ii.15). To deny the force of the play's climax in the name of the supremacy of young love is to impose on the play an ideology very different from that which the ending actually encourages us to admire.

I argued in Chapter 1 that heroic drama tends to contain or gloss over ideological contradictions, and in Chapter 2 that sex comedy tends to collapse into its contradictions. With an oppositional tragedy such as *Lucius Junius Brutus* the critic's task is to rescue the play from the morass of contradiction in which other critics have collapsed it and to clarify that the play's contradictions are resolved in the direction of the emergent ideology of Whiggism. This ideology may not be very congenial to modern taste, which tends to be anti-masculine (in the academy at least), and to privilege the youthful and the sensual; but it is one thing to find the play's ideology distasteful and another to 'write it out'.

Notes

1 This suggestion is made by Dryden's biographer James Winn in *John Dryden and His World*, 256.

2 For a fuller survey see Hughes, *English Drama* , chapters 3 and 7; and Cannan, 'New Directions in Serious Drama on the London Stage, 1675–1678'.

3 See Cannan, 230–1.

4 I refer to a politically 'pointed' reworking. Of course it was common for playwrights to be influenced by one another. For example Crowne's *The Destruction of Jerusalem* (two parts) (1677) reworks similar subject matter to Otway's *Titus and Berenice*; Banks's *The Rival Kings* (1677) and Pordage's *The Siege of Babylon* (1678) are clearly influenced by Lee's *The Rival Queens*. Dryden's method seems to go beyond this normal exploiting of material seen as good 'box office'.

5 *The First English Actresses*, chapter 5.

6 See Howe, 124, and Brown, *English Dramatic Form*, chapter 5.

7 For a full discussion of the differences between Whig and Tory drama see my *Restoration Theatre and Crisis*, chapters 4, 5, 6 and 8. For a full discussion of the politics of *Lucius Junius Brutus* see my '"Partial Tyrants" and "Freeborn

People" in *Lucius Junius Brutus*'. Broadly speaking the play is seen as Whiggish by (apart from myself) Frances Barbour, 'The Unconventional Heroic Plays of Nathaniel Lee'; Loftis, Introduction to *Lucius Junius Brutus*; Hume, 'The Satiric Design of Nathaniel Lee's *The Princess of Cleve*' and *The Development of English Drama*, 344; Brown, *English Dramatic Form*, 76–81; Staves, *Players' Scepters*, 79, 245; and Braverman, *Plots and Counterplots*, 161–7. Canfield in 'Royalism's Last Dramatic Stand' denies the existence of other Whig plays but acknowledges this one. However, in *Heroes and States*, 57–8, his reading is more qualified, stressing the patriarchal elements in the new commonwealth. The play is seen as politically ambiguous and negative about the commonwealth by Vieth, 'Psychological Myth as Tragedy'; Armistead, *Nathaniel Lee*; Hammond, 'The Greatest Action'; Parker, 'History as Nightmare'; and Brown, 'Nathaniel Lee's Political Drama'. Hayne in 'All Language then is Vile' argues that the play is anti-Whig.

8 London, Public Record Office, L.C. 5/144, p. 28 cited in Loftis's introduction to the play, xii.

9 Hayne implausibly suggests that the play was banned because of a scene in Act II in which Vinditius and the mob stage a summary trial of the courtier Fabritius. This, she argues, recalls the trial of the Earl of Stafford for Catholicism and hence reflects on the government. I discuss the scene (a standard mob scene, identical in kind to those in other plays, though perhaps more comic) below. The point to make here is that, if one short scene had offended, the censor would merely have insisted that that scene be cut out, just as earlier in 1681 several scenes were cut from Shadwell's *The Lancashire Witches* at the censor's order (and later printed in italics in the published version).

10 For a detailed account of the effect of the Exclusion Parliament on the audience and on the drama, see my *Restoration Theatre and Crisis*, chapter 3.

11 For the banning of *The Massacre*, probably written in 1679, see my *Restoration Theatre and Crisis*, 301–2. Lee had had difficulty also in obtaining a licence for his anti-Catholic *Caesar Borgia* (1679). That Lee wrote oppositional plays is thus clear; but that he also wrote to suit his times is suggested by his collaboration with Dryden in the strongly Tory *The Duke of Guise* in the Tory Reaction period (1682). In this play Lee allows material from his own *The Massacre* to be adapted with an opposite political slant. In *The Vindication* Dryden says Whigs accused him of corrupting Lee politically. From 1684 Lee was confined in the Bethlehem lunatic asylum. He was released after the revolution of 1688 and given a pension. *The Massacre of Paris* was performed in 1689 but Lee never wrote anything new and died in poverty and alcoholism in 1692.

12 Machiavelli, *Discourses*, I, 466.

13 For the argument that 'the formulations of Machiavellian and Harringtonian republicanism came to appear appropriate in the parliamentary monarchy of Restoration England' see Pocock, *The Machiavellian Moment*, 405, 378–422 and *passim*.

14 Filmer, *Patriarcha and Other Writings*, 260. It is not the case, as Hayne

suggests, that the Brutus story was used impartially by royalists and the opposition alike. She also argues, contradictorily, that Brutus's republicanism associates him with 'the most extreme opposition positions' (352). This argument also needs some modification: it is true that republicans were the extreme wing of the Whigs, but not that the history of the Roman republic was regarded as extremist in itself. Brutus himself is certainly no extremist, but, on the contrary, wants to create a society in which 'The people do agree and live secure, / The nobles and princes loved and reverenced' (III.ii.66).

15 See my '"He that should guard my virtue has betrayed it": the Dramatization of Rape in the Exclusion Crisis', and *Restoration Theatre and Crisis*, 175–6, 205, 226, 231–2, 254.

16 We may compare the language of Dryden's Aureng-Zebe to Indamora:

> Oh I could stifle you with eager haste!
> Devour your kisses with my hungry taste!
> Rush on you! Eat you! Wander o'er each part,
> Raving with pleasure, snatch you to my heart!
> Then hold you off and gaze! Then, with new rage
> Invade you, till my conscious limbs presage
> Torrents of joy which all their banks o'erflow! (*Aureng-Zebe*, IV.ii.146)

17 However, as recently as the mid-1950s Lee's editors could state that the play had 'greater nobility and greater virility than any other' of his plays: *Works*, II, 219.

18 *Works*, XIII, 247.

19 See my *Restoration Theatre and Crisis*, 90, 93, 166, 173, 193, 199.

20 *Works*, XIII, 20.

21 See my 'The Lost Rhetoric of Liberty: Marvell and Restoration Drama'.

22 *London's Glory*, p. 7. A flagellet or flageolet is a small wind instrument.

23 See my *Restoration Theatre and Crisis*, 122–4, 153–4.

24 See Downie, *To Settle the Succession of the State*, chapter 1.

25 See my *Restoration Theatre and Crisis*, 120–2, and other passages indexed under 'law'.

26 See my *Restoration Theatre and Crisis*, 149–51, and other sections indexed under 'common people'. For the Lord Mayor's Shows see chapter 9.

27 In the previous season see e.g. Dryden's and Lee's *Oedipus*, Crowne's *The Misery of Civil-War*, Otway's *The History and Fall of Caius Marius* and Behn's *The Young King*. Other examples include Tate's *Richard the Second*, around the same time as *Lucius Junius Brutus* or slightly later, and *The Ingratitude of a Common-wealth* (autumn to winter 1681).

28 'Psychological Myth as Tragedy', 59. Vieth follows Loftis who, in his introduction to the play, identifies Vinditius with Popish Plots informer Titus Oates (xvi). I find the alleged similarities ('ambition, 'supposed service' to the nation) unconvincing: these are typical characterisitics of mob-leaders and busybodies. I have argued against a too-ready resort to personal parallels in my

'Interpreting the Politics of Restoration Drama', and *Restoration Theatre and Crisis*, 27-8.

29 See my 'Chaos' article.

30 For a discussion of the treatment of ambition in Exclusion Crisis drama see my *Restoration Theatre and Crisis*, 134.

31 See my *Restoration Theatre and Crisis*, 94, 142-3, 148, 189-90, 270-1.

32 Hayne also says that anti-Catholicism is politically neutral, despite the fact that the play was performed at a time when the political nation was polarized around fear of 'popery' in high places and attempts to exclude the King's Catholic brother from the succession. For the politics of anti-Catholicism see my *Restoration Theatre and Crisis* and 'The Politics of John Dryden's *The Spanish Fryar*'.

33 See Nenner, *By Colour of Law*, 48, 198.

34 Accusations of plots and counterplots proliferated. Marvell's *An Account of the Growth of Popery and Arbitrary Government* (1677) claimed that influential courtiers had been plotting for years to introduce the twin evils of his title into England. Roger L'Estrange responded in *An Account of the Growth of Knavery* with accusations of an opposition plot to impugn the government and introduce rebellion on the model of 1641. Then from autumn 1678 onwards Whigs exploited the Popish Plot scare and Tories accused Whigs of a plot against the government. Many thought the Popish plot a sham, but there were also sham plots organized by royalists and Catholics, with the aim of incriminating the Whigs, such as the 'Meal Tub Plot' of 1679.

35 Though lesser in dramatic scope, we may compare the 'tone' of Shakespeare's Coriolanus's forgetting his benefactor's name in *Coriolanus*, I.x.78-90, and thus exposing him to slaughter. Brutus's forgetting, similarly, is the behaviour of a flawed hero (exhausted by care for his country) rather than that of a villain.

36 For Whig loyalty to king and cause at personal cost see my *Restoration Theatre and Crisis*, 112-3. For persecution of the Whigs see 41, 43-4.

37 See my *Restoration Theatre and Crisis*, 61, 119, 122-4, 276-9, 287, 291, 293, 299.

38 See Haley, *The First Earl of Shaftesbury*, 227, 262-4.

5

Tragedy II:
Thomas Otway's *Venice Preserv'd*

Whereas *Lucius Junius Brutus* showed a heroic aspect to republicanism, *Venice Preserv'd; or, A Plot Discovered* is a Tory play which criticizes republicanism in power through its depiction of the corrupt Venetian senate; and also attacks rebellion, in keeping with Tory advocacy of non-resistance, through its portrayal of the corrupt conspiracy against the senate, led by the Spanish ambassador. The play's Toryism is strongly avowed in the various prologues and epilogues, and the circumstances surrounding their composition and delivery. Whereas *Lucius Junius Brutus* was performed at the height of the Whig ascendancy, *Venice Preserv'd* probably had its première in February 1682. This was the Tory Reaction period, when a reconsolidation of Stuart ideology accompanied the King's use of French subsidies to rule without Parliament. Otway's prologue for the first performance follows the ideology of the Tory backlash in questioning the existence of the Popish Plot, out of which the Whigs had made so much political capital. The epilogue is strongly Tory and makes an explicit application of the play's conspiracy to Whig factionalism.

The play was specially performed before royalty in April, when James returned from exile to London, the Whigs' attempt to exclude him from the succession having failed. Another performance in May celebrated the return of James's wife Mary.[1] Dryden and Otway wrote special, loyal prologues and epilogues respectively for these occasions, which were published as broadsides. Otway went on to dedicate the published text of *Venice Preserv'd* to the King's mistress, Louise de Kéroualle, Duchess of Portsmouth. The Whigs had made political capital out of the unpopularity of Charles II's French, Catholic mistresses, and the Duchess of Portsmouth was probably the most unpopular of all, despite her attempt in 1680 to curry favour with the Whigs. Otway's dedication therefore seems a defiantly Tory gesture. In his dedication Otway refers to the illegitimate son the Duchess had borne Charles, and hopes that he will 'defend [Charles II's] right against the encroachments of republicans in his senates' (p. 4). This distinguishes the Duchess's son from another of Charles's bastards, the Duke of Monmouth, who had thrown in his lot with the Whigs, and hoped to displace James as heir to the throne. The wording also associates the corrupt senators of the Venetian republic in the play quite explicitly with the Whigs. Otway's Tory intentions, then, seem not to be in doubt.

Yet there are undercurrents of doubt beneath the play's apparent Toryism, and a complex 'sexual politics'. If we look again at the various prologues and epilogues we can discern a cynical tone which somewhat undercuts the fervent Toryism. The February prologue, for example, opens with the author's mockery of his own motives:

> In these distracted times, when each man dreads
> The bloody stratagems of busy heads;
> When we have feared three years we know not what ...
> What makes our poet meddle with a plot?
> Was't that he fancied, for the very sake
> And name of plot, his trifling play might take? (p. 5)

Otway mocks the political opportunism of dramatists here. He suggests that his intention in subtitling the play 'A Plot Discover'd' was to attract attention and to give rise to all sorts of interesting speculation in the light of the accusations and counter-accusations of plotting which had been flying between the Whigs and Tories for the previous few years. As a poverty-stricken playwright, Otway is ready to place his play at the disposal of the dominant political faction, but the mocking and jaundiced tone alerts us to the need to be wary of looking for fervent political commitment.

Lucius Junius Brutus is a play with a clear and fairly vigorous ideology which over-determines its contradictions. *Venice Preserv'd* is an ideologically complex play, more discussed by critics than other Restoration tragedies, perhaps for that very reason. Critics' views have ranged from seeing the play as unambiguously Tory[2] to seeing it as per-meated by a sense of darkness, uncertainty and pessimism.[3] Some have seen the play's politics as incidental, a background for the play of emotion.[4] Others have tried, with varying success, to spot topical allusions and parallels.[5] Some confusion has been engendered, also, by attempts to resolve the play's plot into a straightforward political allegory or parallel.[6] Laura Brown and Susan Staves take account both of politics and of darkness and difficulty, without reducing political reference to topical allusions or allegory. They do this by locating the play within the framework of their broader arguments according to which our sympathy for those who suffer and rebel in a corrupt society points to the need for the new political order which was to come after 1688.[7] Recently Derek Hughes, who did much to reorient scholars' approach to the play in 1971, has returned to it in an anlysis which, though not primarily focused upon politics, takes account of the play's contradictions;[8] whilst the complexity of the plays' politics and sexual politics have been discussed by myself, by J. Douglas Canfield and by Jessica Munns.[9]

The play opens with a row between the hero Jaffeir and his father-in-law, the senator Priuli. Priuli is a 'cruel father' (I.10), and his bad fatherhood reflects adversely upon the senate of which he is a member. He is guilty of 'proud oppression' (I.6), casting his daughter and son-in-law out to starve because they have married without his consent, with a stream of 'unnatural' curses:

> A sterile fortune, and a barren bed,
> Attend you both; continual discord make
> Your days and nights bitter and grevious; still
> May the hard hand of a vexatious need
> Oppress and grind you; till at last you find
> The curse of disobedience all your portion. (I.53)

This echoes Metellus, a cruel father in Otway's *The History and Fall of Caius Marius* (1679), set in the Roman republic. In both plays bad fatherhood is used to demonize the republican condition.

We might also detect some personal bitterness. Bad or indifferent fathers are a recurring theme for Otway. There is an undertone of resentment beneath the avowed loyalism of the dedication, as he tells the Duchess of Portsmouth: 'a steady faith, and loyalty to my prince, was all the inheritance my father left me, and however hardly my ill-fortune deal with me, 'tis what I prize so well that I ne'er pawned it yet, and hope I ne'er shall part with it' (3-4). Loyalty to the King was *all* Otway's father left him.[10] Nor was Otway much more successful with the father/king, Charles II. He refers in the dedication to powerful enemies at court 'that with malicious power kept back and shaded me from those royal beams, whose warmth is all I have, or hope to live by' (3). In fact Otway lived and died in poverty, and persistently complained of lack of reward as a son, lover, author, soldier and loyal subject.[11] Personal bitterness permeates his plays, creating an atmosphere of pessimism rather than fervent Toryism.

As well as being cruel, Priuli is guilty of ingratitude, a charge frequently levelled at Whigs by Tories.[12] Jaffeir has saved the life of Priuli's daughter Belvidera, which Priuli himself endangered by his selfishness and cowardice:

> Your unskilful pilot
> Dashed us upon a rock; when to your boat
> You made for safety, entered first yourself;
> The affrighted Belvidera following next,
> As she stood trembling on the vessel side,
> Was by a wave washed off into the deep –
> When instantly I plunged into the sea,
> And buffeting the billows to her rescue,
> Redeemed her life with half the loss of mine. (I.33–4)

There seems to be an allusion here to political misleadership. We may compare the political use of similar imagery in Dryden's political poem *Absalom and Achitophel*, where Whig leader Shaftesbury is described as:

> A daring Pilot in extremity;
> Pleas'd with the Danger, when the Waves went high
> He sought the Storms; but for a Calm unfit,
> Would Steer too nigh the Sands, to boast his Wit.[13]

The republican Senator Priuli is an unfit father, and also unfit to steer the ship of state.

As a father Priuli is a negative version of Lee's Brutus. Brutus must overcome his agony and stifle his tenderness, ultimately finding peace and republican resolve. Priuli is simply cruel and thoughtless, until the very end when both his daughter and his son-in-law are dead, and he feels a futile regret:

> Sparing no tears when you this tale relate,
> But bid all cruel fathers dread my fate. (V.iv.36)

Also like Brutus, Priuli has republican manliness, but here it is unambiguously negative: 'she [Belvidera] is gone, and if I am a man / I will forget her' (I.71).

Otway thus manages to taint republicans with excessive manliness; and simultaneously with effeminacy, as another senator Antonio cringes before his mistress. Meanwhile the rebels also use manly rhetoric in a negative context, as when Bedamore tells two other conspirators to behave like men with a glorious purpose rather than like quarrelling boys (II.iii.32), or praises a 'show of manly virtue' (II.iii.121). The hero Jaffeir, conversely, is a more positive version of the early Titus in Lee's play. He is much prone to sentimentality, and is ruled by his emotions: 'My heart that awes me is too much my master' (I.85). This would seem to suggest that Otway reverses Lee's gender values, disparaging Whiggish 'manliness' and placing a positive connotation upon the emotionalism and 'effeminacy' which Lee treats negatively.

However, nothing in Otway's play is straightforward. Jaffeir's emotionalism is far from being an unmixed blessing. He experiences extreme conflict about his manhood, and is torn apart by the clash between loyalty to his wife and to his male friend. Excluded by temperament from the political world of men, Jaffeir lacks agency and becomes a pawn for others:

> How cursed is my condition, tossed and jostled
> From every corner; fortune's common fool,
> The jest of rogues, an instrumental ass
> For villains to lay loads of shame upon,
> And drive about just for their ease and scorn. (III.ii.213)

Here Jaffeir resembles Belvidera and women in general. There are also echoes of the figure of fun, masochistic Senator Antonio, driven about the room by his scornful mistress.

If 'effeminacy' is not all good, 'manliness' is far from being entirely bad. There is a positive (or partly positive) example of vigorous manhood in Jaffeir's anti-republican soldier friend Pierre, who can 'own myself a man' (I.153). Pierre is Whiggish in being a rebel, though his political cause is the opposite of that of Lee's Brutus: Pierre conspires against the republic. However, like Brutus, Pierre thinks the cause makes him a man in the sense of not suffering like a beast:

> Rats die in holes and corners, dogs run mad;
> Man knows a braver remedy for sorrow:
> Revenge! (I.285)

This is a man in the sense that Hamlet praises in Fortinbras:

> What is a man,
> If his chief good and market of his time
> Be but to sleep and feed? A beast, no more. (IV.iv.33)

Fortinbras is leading his army into battle for a small cause, but, in the 'manly' code, this is 'greatly to find quarrel in a straw / When honour's at the stake' (IV.iv.55). Fortinbras seems heroic (to Hamlet at least), and so does Pierre to Jaffeir, at least some of the time. It is by no means clear that there is any privileged perspective in the clash between the male and female perspectives in *Venice Preserv'd*. Rather, there is an unresolved contradiction between them.

Jaffeir's bitterness at Priuli's neglect, Belvidera's resulting poverty, and his own social exclusion make him open to Pierre's rebellious rhetoric:

> ... our Senators
> Cheat the deluded people with a show
> Of liberty, which yet they ne'er must taste of.
> They say, by them our hands are free from fetters,
> Yet whom they please they lay in basest bonds;
> Bring whom they please to infamy and sorrow;
> Drive us like wracks down the rough tide of power,
> Whilst no hold's left to save us from destruction. (I.153)

This is powerful anti-republican rhetoric. The references to the senate recall the Whig-dominated Parliament; there may also be a reference to Whig control of the City of London when Pierre says the Venetian rulers 'make us slaves and tell us 'tis our charter' (I.164). Charles II's manœuvres against the City culminated in the Tory Reaction period in the removal of its charter, and similar attacks were made on the charters of other cities and boroughs. However, there is no one specific topical allusion in Pierre's speeches. That would be to limit Otway's political force and effect. In showing the Venetian senate as tyrannical, Otway follows his source, Saint-Réal's *A Conspiracy of the Spaniards Against the State of Venice*, in invoking what David Wootton has called the anti-myth of Venice, a model widely accepted in the late seventeenth century as a negative example of republicanism.[14]

Brutus's emphasis on the common good, and on trade and prosperity, is reversed in Pierres's attack on oligarchy:

> Curse on the common good that's so protected,
> Where every slave that heaps up wealth enough
> To do much wrong, becomes a lord of right! (I.181)

There is also a jibe here at the rich merchants who supported the Whigs, a satiric target in Otway's *The Souldier's Fortune* (1680). We can discern a personal element too: Pierre's mistress Aquilina has been stolen by a

'wealthy fool' (I.187), the senator Antonio. The lines are also coloured by
Otway's own bitterness about poverty, and by the general resentment of
royalists whose loyal service had been overlooked while former parliamentarians prospered.

One by one the high goals of Lee's Brutus are shown as corrupted: not
only trade and the common good, but the social order, public safety,
national unity and law:

> In such a wretched state as this of Venice,
> When all agree to spoil the public good,
> And villains fatten with the brave man's labors.
> We have neither safety, unity, nor peace,
> For the foundation's lost of common good,
> Justice is lame as well as blind amongst us;
> The laws (corrupted to their ends that make 'em)
> Serve but for instruments of some new tyranny
> That every day starts up to enslave us deeper. (I.207)

Pierre's skill lies in linking the political to the personal. Earlier references
to Priuli's oppression of Jaffeir and Belvidera are echoed when he describes
Venice suffering 'under vile oppression' (I.255). Later Jaffeir will describe
the goal of the conspiracy as 'To restore justice and dethrone oppression'
(II.iii.126).

However, Jaffeir has to be urged towards political action. He is even
more prone to sentimentality than Titus in the early scenes of *Luicus
Junius Brutus*. In him the seventeenth-century and modern uses of the
word 'effeminate' meet: he is easily swayed by a woman (Belvidera), and
also 'womanly' in his emotionalism. Unlike Titus, he remains very change-
able, not only easily moved by women, but also highly sensitive to the
claims of male friendship. Thus he says to Pierre:

> But when I think what Belvidera feels,
> The bitterness her tender spirit tastes of,
> I own myself a coward. Bear my weakness,
> If throwing thus my arms about thy neck,
> I play the boy, and blubber in thy bosom. (I.272)

The infantilism and the tears remind us of Teraminta as well as Titus.

Pierre wants revenge and speaks of his 'cause' (I.289), but Jaffeir's
instincts are those of the self-stifling, quietist heroes of royalist drama: 'No,
there's a secret pride in bravely dying' (I.284).[15] Whereas Lee's Brutus
condemned the 'ocean luxury' of Tarquin's court in a play performed

before an audience of MPs, Otway's Jaffeir, in a play patronised by the
royal family and their entourage, is openly luxurious. He tells Priuli:

> I have treated Belvidera like your daughter,
> The daughter of a Senator of Venice.
> Distinction, place, attendance, and observance,
> Due to her birth, she always has commanded.
> Out of my little fortune I have done this,
> Because (though hopeless e'er to win your nature)
> The world might see I loved her for herself,
> Not as the heiress of the great Priuli. (I.88)

This passage has caused some confusion, as it appears Jaffeir is contra-
dicting himself: he has treated Belvidera 'like your daughter' to show he
'loved her for herself, / Not as the heiress of the great Priuli'. However,
Jaffeir simply means that he has supported her in the style to which a
senator's daughter is accustomed in order to show he did not want her for
her money and status. To him, loving Belvidera for herself means spending money on her. In Renaissance drama 'luxury' is negatively presented,
but there is no irony or criticism in Otway's presentation of Jaffeir's desire
for wealth. Indeed violation of Jaffeir's rich possessions is a source of
horror, as we see in the passage in which Pierre describes the eviction of
Belvidera:

> Here stood a ruffian with a horrid face
> Lording it o'er a pile of massy plate,
> Tumbled into a heap for public sale;
> There was another making villainous jests
> At thy undoing; he had ta'en possession
> Of all thy ancient most domestic ornaments,
> Rich hangings, intermixed and wrought with gold;
> The very bed, which on thy wedding night
> Received thee to the arms of Belvidera,
> The scene of all thy joys, was violated
> By the coarse hands of filthy dungeon villains,
> And thrown among the common lumber. (I.238)

Critics commonly stress the sexual humiliation entailed in the violation of
the marriage bed here, and of course this is a big factor in Jaffeir's grief.
However, when Jaffeir gives ironic thanks to have heard 'the worst that can
befall me' (I.269), he is thinking, first and foremost, 'I am not worth a
ducat' (I.251). It is common in tragedy for the protagonist to ask God (or
the gods) why he has been created to aspire, only to be humiliated. Jaffeir

is the first example, to my knowledge, of a hero whose disappointment includes the unabashed desire for a refined lifestyle:

> Tell me why, good Heav'n,
> Thou mad'st me what I am, with all the spirit,
> Aspiring thoughts *and elegant desires*
> That fill the happiest man? (I.307, my emphasis)

Eighteenth-century actor David Garrick knew what he was doing when he broke with tradition and portrayed Jaffeir not as scruffy but as splendidly dressed (intro., xix).[16]

When Jaffeir joins the conspiracy at Pierre's urging, he goes against his nature, for he is not naturally a man of action. His natural inclinations are masochistic. He is religious in a morbid way: when he meets Pierre in II. ii, he is on his way to pray, and is convinced he is going to Hell. Pierre's gift of money only confirms this suspicion: 'What must this buy, rebellion, murder, treason? / Tell me which way I must be damned for this' (II.ii.37). Jaffeir is obsessed with the idea of his own death: 'A thousand daggers, all in honest hands; / And have not I a friend will stick one here?' (II.ii.63). His newfound adherence to the 'cause' seems histrionic rather than based upon conviction.

What are we to make of Jaffeir's joining the conspiracy? This is a complex question. Not only is Jaffeir's commitment suspect but it is also not clear exactly what we are to make of the plot itself. The conspiracy contains men with good and bad motives, ranging from Pierre's political idealism to the selfish ambition of Bedamore and Renault. Pierre sounds like Lee's Brutus at his most heroic: 'I have told thee that which only gods / And men like gods are privy to' (II.ii.73). However, when this is echoed by the repulsive Renault, it sounds simply blasphemous: '[We are] men separated by the choice of providence / From the gross heap of mankind' (II.iii.28–9). Pierre in II.iii likens himself to Brutus, murderer of Julius Caesar; but Renault prefers the analogy of Catiline, an archetype of ambition and bloodlust. The cause itself has some heroic aspects. Its goal of cleansing the corruption of the republic is presented positively: we witness the loathsomeness of Senator Priuli before we hear Pierre's arguments against the senate. The plotters' grievances reflect Otway's own. For example, Venice suffers from 'A tattered fleet, a murmuring unpaid army / … This wretched state has starved them in its service' (II.iii.72, 87). Otway had been one of the soldiers who suffered the vagiaries of Stuart foreign policy and were disbanded, in many cases without seeing action, and without being paid.[17]

However, the conspiracy also has the negative qualities of rebellion, familiar from many Tory tragedies.[18] II. iii opens with Renault soliloquizing about the apsiring heights and shaky foundations of his overweening personal ambition, a quality regarded as typical of rebels. This would immediately have alerted a contemporary audience to the fact that this conspirator is a villain. Like the royal plot in *Lucius Junius Brutus*, the conspiracy is bloodthirsty. Renault conjures up 'a spectacle of horror' (382) and urges:

> Shed blood enough, spare neither sex nor age,
> Name nor condition; if there live a Senator
> After tomorrow, though the dullest rougue
> That e'er said nothing, we have lost our ends.
> If possible, let's kill the very name
> Of Senator, and bury it in blood. (III.ii.333)

Even Pierre revels in the prospect of the wholesale slaughter of senators in II.ii. Above all, like the royalists in Lee's play, the conspiracy is tainted by rape. In a typically histrionic and rash gesture, Jaffeir leaves Belvidera with the conspirators as a pledge of his own commitment, prioritising the homosocial bond with his male collaborators over loyalty to his wife. Renault attempts to rape her. After this secret sexual attack he hypocritically claims to be a champion of the cause of moral purity:

> Let's consider
> That we destroy oppression, avarice,
> A people nursed up equally with vices
> And loathsone lusts, which Nature most abhors,
> And such as without shame she cannot suffer. (III.ii.366)

Hypocrisy was a quality Tories associated with Whig and puritan 'rebels'.

It seems clear, however, that the conspiracy represents rebellion in general terms rather than any specific historical plot. All attempts at a topical parallel have something against them. Thus, the fact that the plot's leader is the ambassador of Catholic Spain might suggest an analogy with Popish Plot; but against this is the fact that, as Pierre says:

> For it is founded on the noblest basis,
> Our liberties, our natural inheritance.
> There's no religion, no hypocrisy in't. (II.ii.89)

The reference to liberties here, like much of Pierre's rhetoric, sounds Whiggish. Yet there are also similarities with royalism. When Pierre tells Jaffeir: 'Thou shall be freed from base Priuli's tyranny, / And thy sequestered fortunes healed again' (II.ii.97), he sounds exactly like royalists plotting against Cromwell in the interregnum and scheming to recover their sequestered estates.[19] It was possible for the conspiracy to be portrayed as Jacobite in revivals of the play after the rebellion of 1715.[20] The conspiracy does not represent any one particular grouping, but offers fleeting resemblances which the audience can apply themselves. Above all, it provides the spur for Belvidera's arguments against rebellion. Her sufferings at the hands of the conspirators make her Tory arguments for non-resistance all the more compelling.

Belvidera was played by Elizabeth Barry, who had also played Teraminta. Like Teraminta, Belvidera is ultimately marginalized by masculine values, but she is a powerful presence in the play and a tragic hero in her own right.[21] Her stature is undisputed: there is no Lucrece figure to steal her thunder, only the courtesan and dominatrix Aquilina. Like Teraminta, Belvidera is emotional. Almost her first words tell of her 'heavy heart' (I.318), and references to her heart are frequent thereafter. She is also openly passionate, telling Jaffeir, 'I swell, and sigh, and labor with my longing' (I.346), and giving herself 'loose to love with kisses, kindling joy' (I.353). This sensuality has aroused hostility in male critics, beginning with Lord Byron, who called her: 'that maudlin bitch of chaste lewness and blubbering curiosity ... whom I utterly despise, abhor, and detest'.[22] This tells us more about Byron than Belvidera. Poor Belvidera also has to contend with male misunderstanding in the play. Whereas Titus turned Teraminta into an object of sexual passion, Jaffeir fails to respond adequately to Belvidera's passion, and instead objectifies her as 'his choicest treasure' (I.390). Again, we see his obsession with worldly riches. Whereas Titus hugs Belvidera to him in a frenzy of desire, Jaffeir, continuing the wealth metaphor, will 'Thus hug my little, but my precious store' (393).

The gesture of hugging (and the avoidance of hugging) focuses a nexus of gender issues in the play. Renault, seeing two men embrace, mutters 'I never loved these huggers' (II.iii.146). This shows a negative masculinism, as well as a lack of finer feelings or sensitivity. However, Jaffeir also experiences conflict about hugging. He finds it easier to embrace his friend with passion than his wife, yet has to do it as if his friend *is* his wife. Jaffeir ends Act II in an orgasmic frenzy of gender confusion: he hugs Pierre, ostensibly in place of Belvidera, but actually seeming to find it easier to show passion to him than to her; and paradoxically swearing love to him in a way which shows doubts about loyalty to him and his cause are already creeping in:

> Oh Pierre, wert thou but she,
> How I could pull thee down into my heart,
> Gaze on thee till my eye-strings cracked with love,
> Till all my sinews with its fire extended,
> Fixed me upon the rack of ardent longing;
> Then swelling, sighing, raging to be blest,
> Come like a panting turtle to thy breast,
> On thy soft bosom, hovering, bill and play,
> Confess the cause why last I fled away;
> Own 'twas a fault, but swear to give it o'er,
> And never follow false ambition more. (II.iii.228)

The framing discourse of heterosexuality here cannot contain the unsettling of sex and gender categories which results both from the language and from the spectacle of male–male passion on stage.

Jaffeir has an ambivalent relationship to the masculine world, whereas Pierre has a stable one. When Pierre says, 'A soldier's mistress, Jaffeir, 's his religion' (I.199) he does not mean he worships women, but that he will fight to the death to avenge the insult of Antonio's 'theft' of his mistress Aquilina. The woman herself is only good for one thing, as far as Pierre is concerned. When she shows interest in politics, he snubs her: 'How! a woman ask questions out of bed?' (II.54). Pierre taunts Jaffeir for spending time with his wife: 'What feminine tale hast thou been listening to, / Of unaired shirts, catarrhs and toothache got / By thin-soled shoes?' (III.ii.223). His rage leads him to personify Venice as a whore whom 'real men' will punish: 'How lovely the Adriatic whore, / Dressed in her flames, will shine!' (II.iii.97). Pierre's real love is for his friend Jaffeir, as is clear when he defends him against the conspirators at the risk of his own life in III.ii. Jaffeir's attitude to women prefigures the idealization of the eighteenth century: 'Oh Woman! lovely Woman! Nature made thee / To temper Man: we had been brutes without you' (I.336). However, such idealization has no grounding in reality and can easily flip over into betrayal. Jaffeir leaves Belvidera with the conspirators, exposing her to risk, because he suddenly decides to idealize male friendship instead: 'I have henceforth hopes to call ye friends' (II.iii.153). Belvidera tries to claim him: 'My dear! my life! my love!', but he responds, 'Oh friends! … Take her from my heart' (II.iii.191). These are men he has just met, political associates rather than friends in the sense that Pierre is a friend. Yet at this moment their claims are paramount. What is at stake is Jaffeir's relationship to the male world, the world of social connection and status that he is desperate to rejoin one way or another. Jaffeir's 'manly' conduct in leaving Belvidera in II.iii earns reward from his male friend, as Pierre calls him 'my honor's brother' (II.iii.224). Jaffeir is acting emotionally rather than politically. In III.ii he impulsively returns for Belvidera, unable to keep away despite his promise to the plotters and telling her: 'the heart within my bosom / Moans like a tender infant in its cradle / Whose nurse had left it' (III.ii.18). These lines are very revealing. They show Jaffeir has lurched from seeing Belvidera as a pawn in his relations with other men to seeing her as a controlling parent/ nanny figure for whom he has a childish need. At no point does he have a clear perspective either of her as a person or of his obligations as her husband.

In these circumstances it is hardly surprising that Belvidera does not have as much success as Lee's Lucrece in asserting the importance or the political significance of her near-rape. In III.ii she echoes Lucrece as she tells of her experience, and contrasts their situations:

> No sooner was I to my bed repaired,
> To weigh, and (weeping) ponder my condition,
> But the old hoary wretch, to whose false care
> My peace and honor was entrusted, came
> (Like Tarquin) ghastly with infernal lust.
> Oh thou Roman Lucrece!
> Thou couldst find friends to vindicate thy wrong;
> I never had but one, and he's proved false;
> He that should guard my virtue has betrayed it. (III.ii.8–11)

Whereas Lucrece had witnesses who responded with appropriate horror, Belvidera is soliloquizing, giving her account only to the audience. In the ensuing scene with Jaffeir she delays revealing her experience during an extraordinary debate about sexual politics. Jaffeir's response to her distress (before he knows its cause) is to wish that she would be a 'pitying angel' (III.ii.49) to him in his unhappiness. The child in him takes no responsibility for having abandoned her, but simply says he feels bad and demands comfort. Then he adds insult to injury by contrasting her unfavourably with the stoic Portia, an example of Roman virtue. Belvidera struggles to assert that she is worthy to be trusted as Brutus trusted Portia, and to contest the exclusion of women from political knowledge. She also asserts that it is wrong for Jaffeir to have treated her simply as a token of exchange with the male conspirators:

> Must I
> Be made the hostage of a hellish trust?
> For such I know I am, that's all my value. (III.ii.106)

She seems very articulate, unusually aware of the impossible position of women, idealized and despised at the same time. With grotesque naïvety, Jaffeir then gloats that he has sworn to kill her father and revels in the plan for slaughter he and his friends have hatched:

> ... how rich and beauteous will the face
> Of ruin look when these wide streets run with blood;
> I and the glorious partners of my fortune
> Shouting and striding o'er the prostrate dead,
> Still new to waste; whilst thou far off in safety
> Smiling, shalt see the wonders of our daring,
> And when night comes, with praise and love receive me. (III.ii.143)

He is living in a fantasy world. Although women are excluded from politics, Belvidera shows more political realism as well as more moral responsibility than Jaffeir does:

> Murder my father! Though his cruel nature
> Has persecuted me to my undoing,
> Driven me to basest wants, can I behold him
> With smiles of vengeance, butchered in his age?
> The sacred fountain of my life destroyed?
> And canst thou shed the blood that gave me being?
> Nay, be a traitor too, and sell thy country;
> Can thy great heart descend so vilely low,
> Mix with hired slaves, bravoes, and common stabbers,
> Nose-slitters, alley-lurking villains! join
> With such a crew, and take a ruffian's wages,
> To cut the throats of wretches as they sleep? (III.ii.154)

Here Belvidera is as moving and as powerful as Lee's Lucrece; as virtuously loyal to a cruel father as Dryden's Benzayda; as patriotic to the republic and as nobly contemptuous of base behaviour and bloodlust as Lee's Brutus.

When he finally learns of Renault's sexual attack on Belvidera, Jaffeir's response is an impotent horror, the reverse of the active determination with which Brutus avenges Lucrece. Jaffeir is angry, but the cause appears to be his own 'dishonor' (III.ii.262) as a husband whose rights have been infringed. He is unable to act even upon this motivation, incapable either of denouncing Renault or of conciliating him, and commenting sarcastically aside on his cruelty throughout the remainder of III.ii. Pierre's reaction is legalistic: 'He used no violence?' (247). In moral terms we can say this response is uncomprehending of women's humiliation. It is a reaction shared by some of the play's male critics.[23] What the critics also miss is the political importance of the fact that the rape is not completed: by making Renault impotent and cowardly as well as a would-be rapist, frightened off by his victim's screams even though he holds a dagger, Otway doubly damns him in terms of the Restoration construction of manhood. In political terms, Belvidera's revelation makes Jaffeir regret his involvement in the conspiracy: 'our cause / Is in a damned condition: for I'll tell thee, / That canker-worm called lechery has touched it, / 'Tis tainted vilely' (III.ii.231).

Belvidera demands that Jaffeir denounce the men who have abused her, but he is torn apart by competing loyalties. This is not just because he is uncertain about betraying his friends for moral reasons, but also because he is reluctant to exchange the social connection he has achieved with other men for the 'soft authority' of Belvidera (III.ii.26). Belvidera's revelation has given her, temporarily at least, the mastery over Jaffeir. In II. iii she asked him, 'Alas, where am I? Whither is't you lead me?' (177). Now, he asks her:

> Where dost thou lead me? Every step I move,
> Methinks I tread upon some mangled limb
> Of a racked friend. Oh my dear charming ruin!
> Where are we wandering? (IV.i.1)

Jaffeir has attempted to use Belvidera to cement his connection to other men. Now she has revealed the reality and the rivalry beneath idealized male friendship: men will screw other men's wives if they can.

Already we can see that for both Jaffeir and Belvidera the near-rape has become transformed from an experience of personal suffering into a political signifier. Just as the conspirators work up their courage by imagining the praise of posterity, so Belvidera appeals to Jaffeir:

> Thy renown
> Shall be the future song of all the virgins,
> Who by their piety have been preserved
> From horrid violation. (IV.i.7)

The idea of being remembered by women means nothing to Jaffeir:

> Rather, remember him, who after all
> The sacred bonds of oaths and holier friendship,
> In fond compassion to a woman's tears
> Forgot his manhood, virtue, truth and honor. (IV.i.14)

There is a struggle going on here over social and emotional priorities. To Jaffeir's question, 'Must I betray my friends?' (IV.i.76), Belvidera responds, 'Hast thou a friend more dear than Belvidera?' (79).

Belvidera is more than a victim, however. She has her own political agenda. In Act IV she seems as much of an idelogue as Pierre in Act I. She advocates denouncing the conspiracy to the senate as a course of action which will bring 'eternal honor' (IV.i.4), and, like Pierre, manipulates Jaffeir politically by reference to the personal and the painful, working on his morbid imagination and 'pressing his buttons'. She paints a vivid picture of the results of the conspiracy: babies impaled on swords and mothers dripping blood and breast-milk (IV.i.49). However, this is less effective in overcoming Jaffeir's doubts than a reminder of her near-rape: 'Last night, my love!' (32), and her account of her own likely rape if the conspiracy succeeds:

> Think what then may prove
> My lot! The ravisher may then come safe,
> And midst the terror of the public ruin
> Do a damned deed. (IV.i.63)

Her rape touches his honour as well as his very real love for her. Jaffeir lets himself be persuaded by her to denounce the conspiracy, though he is still obssessing about 'the man I love' (IV.i.99), and his acquiescence is masochistic. He likens himself to a lamb, being led to sacrifice by an 'enticing flattering priestess' (IV.i.90), imagines being tied up on the altar, and 'hardly bleats, such pleasure's in the pain' (IV.i.94).

Both Jaffeir's self-positioning as an animal here, and the eroticized conjunction of pain and pleasure, recall the sadomasochism of the so-called 'Nicky-Nacky scenes' in which Senator Antonio is sexually dominated by Aquilina. Aquilina calls Antonio 'that old hideous animal' (III.i.10) and he is like an animal as he bellows like a bull, and sits under the table barking like a dog. He begs her: 'Spit in my face', 'use me like a dog', and 'kick on ... kick again – kick harder' (III.i.84, 91, 102); and provokes her until she whips him. Antonio is an extreme version of a stock figure of fun: the impotent, elderly lecher. Aquilina calls him 'old, silly, impertinent, impotent' (III.i.31). His over-use of silly endearments such as 'Nicky-Nacky' is typical of impotent old lechers in the drama, such as Mr. Limberham in Dryden's *The Kind Keeper*, or Sir Davy Dunce in Otway's own *The Souldier's Fortune*. Antonio's sado-masochism is in one sense merely an extreme form of the cringing before the mistress which is typical of these characters. However, there is clearly also an element of political satire. The February prologue hints at a double portrait of the Whig leader Shaftesbury in Renault and Antonio.[24] Whilst Renault does not have much in common with Shaftesbury, Antonio has the same name, is the same age (sixty-one) and has the same facility at speech-making. The topic of his speech in V.ii recalls Shaftesbury's insistence on the reality of the Popish Plot, and is presented ridiculously: 'That there is a plot, surely by this time no man that hath eyes or understanding in his head will presume to doubt, 'tis as plain as the light in the cucumber' (10). Moreover, Antonio is sexually corrupt and, though Shaftesbury was not in fact particularly lewd, he had a reputation for lechery. A tap in his side for medical reasons gave his enemies the opportunitiy to make jibes about venereal disease. The popularity of *Venice Preserv'd* as a Tory drama rested at least in part on a perceived caricature of Shaftesbury in the Nicky-Nacky scenes. Moreover, it is obvious that the corruption of Antonio reflects upon the republican senate of which he is a member, so that the Nicky-Nacky scenes contribute to Otway's Tory satire of republicanism.[25]

However, the situation is complicated by the fact that sadomasochism is not simply a marker of sexual perversion for Otway. Ideed, Otway seems to have an affinity for erotically charged masochism. Sir Jolly Jumble in *The Souldier's Fortune* is masochistic as well as voyeuristic. *The Orphan* has three masochistic characters, Monimia and two brothers, Castalio and Polydore, who desire her. All three are masochistic in their superhuman efforts to stifle their inclinations and conform to impossible ideals. All three almost revel in their ultimate pain, Polydore and Monimia almost gleefully devising tortures for one another. Jaffeir in *Venice Preserv'd* is intensely masochistic. To win Pierre's forgiveness he will 'Lie at thy feet and kiss 'em though they spurn me' (IV.ii.235). When Pierre is on the scaffold awaiting execution, Jaffeir asserts: 'stripes [from a whip] are fitter for me than embraces' (V.333–4). Jaffeir has a a masochistic psychology. He lacks a sense of his own and other people's boundaries. As we have seen, he opens himself to the claims of male acquaintances, barely known. He sees his friends' problems as his own, and his own as all-consuming. He fantasizes about being penetrated with a dagger (II.ii.63), and offers to stab himself with is sword if the conspirators find him lacking (II.iii.127). There are clear homoerotic overtones here, as well as a longing for pain.

Critics have frequently noted that Jaffeir's masochism resembles Antonio's, as if to suggest that Jaffeir is thereby tainted with Antonio's corruption. Kelsall, for example, says in his introduction to the play, 'are

not Antonio's sexual perversions, his subservience to Aquilina, his masochism, all too close to being a gross reflection of the latent tensions
between Jaffeir and Belvidera?' (xx). For Kelsall, subservience to a woman
is the crucial factor: Jaffeir 'has lost his virtue, his manliness' (xx).
However, there are two points to make. First, Jaffeir's masochism is in one
way quite distinct from Antonio's. Antonio engages in masochism as
sexual play in a context he thinks is safe. He has no desire whatsoever to be
annihilated. Then as now, sexual masochism in this sense is a 'safety valve',
and has no necessary connection to a morbidly masochistic psychology.
Second, in so far as a resemblance between Jaffeir and Antonio remains, it
works to Antonio's advantage as much as to Jaffeir's disadvantage; or,
more precisely, it works to confuse our boundaries of perception and
judgement. *Venice Preserv'd* is suffused with a diffuse eroticism, or in,
Freudian terms, a polymorphous perversity.

Eroticized masochism reaches its climax in Jaffeir's death, in which he
is joined not with Belvidera but with Pierre. In an ecstasy of masochism,
Jaffeir approaches his friend: 'Crawling on my knees, / And prostrate on
the earth' (V.iii.28). He praises Pierre's 'manly virtue' (32), and says that
he himself deserves to be whipped. He feels that Pierre is too kind to
forgive him and longs to be tortured. To see how this resonates for the
audience, we need to look at the build-up to it and the context. In the last
two acts, the focus has shifted from the horror of the conspiracy to the
treachery of the senate. Just as Jaffeir has broken his oath of loyalty to the
conspirators, the senators break their oath that Jaffeir's friends will be
immune from prosecution. All the conspirators, including Renault, choose
'honorable death (IV.ii.160, 162) over the shame of confession and
pardon. Later, we learn 'They've all died like men' (V.ii.53). This manliness now seems positive. Pierre in the final scenes takes on the heroic
aspect of the soldier character.[26] He is a military hero whose service the
Duke and senate have despised:

> Are these [chains] the trophies I've deserv'd for fighting
> Your battles with confederated powers,
> When winds and seas conspired to overthrow you.
> And brought the fleets of Spain to your own harbors?
> When you, great Duke, shrunk trembling in your palace,
> And saw your wife, 'th'Adriatic, ploughed
> Like a lewd whore by bolder prows than yours,[27]
> Stepped I not forth, and taught your loose Venetians
> The task of honor and the way to greatness. (IV.ii.125)

Here Pierre resembles another military hero despised by his country, James Stuart, and perhaps also that despised soldier Thomas Otway. Pierre's construction of the Duke and government as unmanly is born out by the cowardly and treacherous behaviour of the senators. Of course it also casts aspersions on Jaffeir; the Duke is unmanly because he lets his 'wife', the Adriatic sea, be 'ploughed' by invaders, just as Jaffeir has failed to defend his wife from the invasions of other men. Pierre calls Jaffeir a 'whining monk', a 'hypocrite', and 'a wretched, base, false, worthless coward' (IV.ii.180, 183, 192). Jaffeir responds not by defending his manhood but by 'effeminizing' himself with wishful thinking, tears and protestations of a devotion which seems both spiritual and passionate:

> I have not wronged thee, by these tears I have not.
> But still am honest, true, and hope too, valiant;
> My mind still full of thee; therefore still noble.
> Let not thy eyes then shun me, nor thy heart
> Detest me utterly. Oh look upon me,
> Look back and see my sad sincere submission!
> How my heart swells, as even 'twould burst my bosom;
> Fond of its jail, and laboring to be at thee! (IV.ii.197)

Act IV ends with Jaffeir shifting all the blame for his own betrayal of Pierre on to Belvidera, and trying to stab her, 'for dire revenge / Is up and raging for my friend' (IV.ii.383). He fails in his resolve, moved by her love and shamed by her willingness to die. Yet the Act ends with Jaffeir placing conditions upon reconciliation: 'Fly to thy cruel father; save my friend, / ... conquer him, as thou hast vanquished me' (IV.ii.423, 430). This shows a resentment of the women's power over men, and an ingenious attempt to channel this power into helping the male friend. The attempt is futile, as Pierre has already said he does not want to live and be dishonoured.

Belvidera prays a high price for trying to manipulate Jaffeir politically against his inclinations. Jaffeir rejects her with a deadly courtesy: 'Thy father's ill-timed mercy came too late. / I thank thee for thy labors though, and him too' (V.ii.104). She begs him to stab her, explicitly recalling their moments of mutual orgasm 'When joys have left me gasping in thy arms' (V.ii.123), and preferring the consummation of his death-giving thrust to continued separation. However, he will only leave her with a killing politeness, and she descends into madness. He has passed his agony to her. Earlier he cursed creation and urged the heavens to burn the world and everyone in it to a cinder (V.ii.93). Now, she curses, 'Blasted be every herb and fruit and tree,/Cursed be the rain that falls upon the earth,/And may

the general curse reach man and beast' (V.ii.225). This rage is assuaged in
her madness, when she talks of 'Murmuring streams, soft shades, and
springing flowers, / Lutes, laurels, seas of milk, and ships of amber' (V.ii.242).
Jessica Munns has pointed out that milk here is 'the female essence',[28] and
it is true that Belvidera has continued vainly to assert a woman's perspective, rather than trying to be accepted on men's terms like, for example,
Andromache in Dryden's *Troilus and Cressida*. However, what we
principally find in Belvidera's words of madness are images of luxury.
Luxury is not a trivial or frivolous issue in this play. The mainspring of the
tragedy is Priuli's failure to offer financial support to Jaffeir and Belvidera.
This is Belvidera's first thought when she sees her father in V.i:

> He's there, my father, my inhuman father,
> That, for three years, has left an only child
> Exposed to all the outrages of fate,
> And cruel ruin. (V.i.19)

It was material deprivation which rendered Jaffeir almost demented right
from the start, and made him open to Pierre's rebellious promptings.
Similarly, Otway in the epilogue to *The Souldier's Fortune* describes
himself as 'half grown mad', refers to 'starving Poets' and curses his fate. In
the last analysis it is poverty which is the death of Jaffeir and Belvidera, just
as it was to be the death of their author at the age of thirty-three.

It would be hard to argue, then, that the play privileges the assertion
of a feminine perspective. There is, however, some tempering of the play's
most manly figure. Pierre, facing death, appears, for the first time, tearful.
His tears are the more moving because, as Jaffeir says, 'I never saw thee
melted thus before' (V.iii.70). Pierre wrings Jaffeir's sensitive heart with
the words:

> Is't fit a soldier, who has lived with honor,
> Fought nations' quarrels, and been crowned with conquest,
> Be exposed a common carcass on a wheel? (V.iii.75)

There is little diminution in Pierre's essential toughness, however. What
he wants is, like Lee's Titus, to be killed by his friend and spared the
humiliation of a public execution. With typical extravagence and inap-
propriateness, Jaffeir, at first misunderstanding, replies, 'I have a wife and
she shall bleed, my child too / Yield up his little throat, and all t'appease
thee' (85). The tragedy all along has been that Jaffeir has assumed that
Pierre's urgings to manliness have to be taken literally, and that loyalty to
friends involves the actual sacrifice of his family: nobody asked him to

hand over Belvidera and a dagger to the conspirators. That was his own extravagant notion. Nobody wants him to kill Belvidera now, except, ironically, Belvidera herself, and that is only because she cannot have connection with him on any other terms.

In a gesture which is both heroic and futile at the same time, Jaffeir then stabs Pierre and himself. The priest says this double suicide is a 'Damnable deed' (V.iv.98), but he has already been marginalized in the scene. There was a strong feeling at the time against priests in general, and Catholic priests in particular, so we need not assume that his words offer a privileged perspective. The audience is equally if not more likely to give credence to Pierre, the patriotic soldier who has fought for his country, and who sounds like a Protestant Englishman as he asserts that he is true to his conscience, but rejects the priest as one who gets money by gulling 'silly souls' (V.iii.20). Pierre asserts, 'This was done nobly' (V.iv.99), and Jaffeir's responds, 'Bravely' (100). The Officer comments: 'Heav'n grant I die so well' (111). It is not that the suicide offers hope of any kind of transcendence. The 'heroic' alternative to masochism is simply a more defiant self-destruction. 'We have deceived the Senate', says Pierre (99), and he dies laughing. What the moment represents for Jaffeir is the consummation of his friendship with Pierre, a kind of mutual penetration, and, as he says, 'mingling' of their blood (102). He asks that the dagger be given to Belvidera, as 'A token that with my dying breath I blessed her' (107); but as usual there is a gap between his belief about his own intentions and the effect of his actions on others. He is actually sending her a token of her own exclusion. Jaffeir's is a tainted gesture: Belvidera can have the dagger she earlier begged for when there is no thrust behind it, when it has been used for the 'climax' between the men.

Throughout the play there has been an obsession with daggers. There are three references to daggers as better than curses in Act II. Jaffeir imagines a dagger in his own heart, almost with longing (II.ii.63), and offers to stab himself with his sword if the conspirators wish (II.iii.127). Pierre offers to cut his own tongue out with a dagger if Jaffeir prove false to the conspiracy in II.iii, wherupon we get the stage direction, '*Enter* Jaffeir *with a dagger*'. Jaffeir hands the conspirators his dagger together with Belvidera, so they may 'strike it to her heart' (II.iii.199) if he breaks faith. After she is sexually attacked, Belvidera begs Jaffeir to stab her with his dagger (III.ii.66), to 'strike thy sword into this bosom' (III.ii.152), before she reveals how Renault brandished Jaffeir's own dagger at the moment of his sexual assault. Later in the same scene Renault threatens to bury his dagger in Jaffeir's heart (III.ii.426). Again, the dagger reference is followed by references to – and byplay with – swords, as the conspirators exchange hard words about friendship and treachery. In IV.i when Jaffeir wavers on his way to denounces the conspiracy, Belvidera urges, 'let thy dagger do its bloody office. / Oh that kind dagger, Jaffeir, how 'twill look / Stuck through my heart, drenched in my blood to th' hilts!' (23). In IV.ii Pierre gives Jaffeir back his dagger as it has become a token of their violated friendship. Jaffeir then '*Holds the dagger up*' and soliloquizes about his pain at the loss of his friend and his memories – quickly suppressed – of Belvidera's experience, before fantasizing about plunging the dagger into his heart (IV.ii.269). Then Belvidera reveals that Pierre and the others are to die. As she leans on his breast, Jaffeir tries to stab her in revenge for his friend and in requital of his own violated honour, but fumbles and cannot bring himself to do it. Belvidera first begs for mercy, but then accepts death, kissing him and even longing for his thrust, so she can 'die in joys' (IV.ii.411). Here the dagger offers her the consummation she is not likely to find in sexual union. In Act V Belvidera persuades her father to secure the conspirators' pardon by recalling this moment:

> Oh my husband, my dear husband
> Carries a dagger in his once kind bosom
> To pierce the heart of your poor Belvidera.
> … think you saw his one hand
> Fixed on my throat, while the extended other
> Grasped a keen threat'ning dagger. (V.i.77, 88)

In an inversion of this, but for the same goal of saving Pierre, Aquilina threatens Antonio with a dagger in V.ii. He is titillated to ecstasy: 'Why what a bloody-minded, inveterate, termagant strumpet have I been plagued with! Ohhh, yet more! Nay then I die, I die – I am dead already. [*Stretched himself out*]' (V.ii.90). In V.ii Jaffeir draws his dagger and threatens to kill himself if Belvidera will not let go of him. As he leaves, she begs, 'Leave thy dagger with me. / Bequeath me something' (V.ii.206). As she descends into madness, she cries, 'Oh give me daggers, fire or water; / How I could bleed, how burn, how drown' (V.ii.228). As noted above, she is finally sent the dagger only after it has been used in the men's mutual suicide: a mockery of her hopes.

The circulation of this particular dagger reflects the circulation of power: it passes from Jaffeir to the conspirators as a token of exchange, sealing the bond between men; is used in the rape attempt as an emblem of phallic power; is restored to Jaffeir by Pierre as a sign of the failure and repudiation of friendship. Through the same dagger the marginalized Belvidera tries and fails to find inclusion and meaning in the male world, if only in death. Finally this dagger becomes a token of the consummated male friendship exchange, then is carried to the marginalized woman to bear witness to that fact.

It is not clear that Belvidera ever receives the dagger. The play ends with her pitiable and deluded ravings, as love, desire for Jaffeir to 'come to bed' (V.iv.2), loss, her father's tyranny and Renault's nastiness jostle one another in her thoughts. Then the bloody ghosts of Jaffeir and Pierre rise and drag her down into death. What are we to make of this melodramatic but also powerful moment? There are predatory and vengeful aspects to the ghosts' gesture; but, on the other hand, the woman and the male friends are at least united now, if only in the grave. They have made a defiant gesture against rulers and fathers, in a situation of extreme power-lessness. Priuli, the representative father and ruler, is powerless too, left to pity and self-reproach. The other powerful man, Antonio, has welcomed his own stabbing in an orgasmic ecstasy, epitomizing the self-destructive futility of this world. Everyone's attempts to exercise power through controlling others have been disastrous. No one has achieved agency, except in suicide. Political power is both all-pervasive and chimeric. Attempts at transformation have proved fantasy. Opponents, whether of the senate's power or of the power of the male bond, are marginalized and broken, but so are the wielders of power.[29]

It is ironic, then, that, in this world of brokenness and fragmentation, the dagger is the recurring sign. The dagger serves both as a marker of violence and death, and as substitute phallus and a symbol of desire. Indeed, it is through the dagger that Otway has associated all the principal driving forces in the play: sexual desire, male friendship, pain, betrayal, bad fatherhood, masculinity in crisis, femininity in eclipse, masochism, love and death. It seems apt that the only unity in this dark play is through the unifying image of the dagger, an instrument of death.

Notes

1 See Danchin, *Prologues and Epilogues of the Restoration*, IV, 413. Quotations from the later prologues and epilogues are from Danchin's text.

2 For example, Harry M. Solomon in 'The Rhetoric of Redressing Grievances: Court Propaganda as the Hermeneutical Key to *Venice Preserv'd*' interprets the play as clearly Tory and criticises those who have 'depoliticized' it (294).

3 For interpretations which privilege darkness of tone, ambiguity, psychological complexity or moral difficulty over political partisanship see e.g. Rothstein, *Restoration Tragedy*; Marshall, *Restoration Serious Drama*; Warner, *Thomas Otway*; Waith, *Ideas of Greatness: Heroic Drama in England*; Parker, 'The Image of Rebellion in Thomas Otway's *Venice Preserv'd* and Edward Young's *Busiris*'; Schille, 'Reappraising "Pathetic" Tragedies: *Venice Preserv'd* and *The Massacre of Paris*'.

4 Taylor, *Next to Shakespeare: Otway's* Venice Preserv'd *and* The Orphan *and Their History on the London Stage*, 55; Williams, 'The Sex-Death Motive in Otway's *Venice Preserv'd*', 63.

5 Montague Summers suggests that the Senate in the play represents the English Court: *Complete Works of Thomas Otway*, I, lxxxviii. John Moore suggests more plausibly that it stands for the Whig-dominated Parliament: 'Contemporary Satire in Otway's *Venice Preserv'd*'. Moore's view is endorsed by Ham: *Otway and Lee*. Zera S. Fink suggests more persuasively still that the Venetian Senate in the play is the Whig ideal discredited: *The Classical Republicans*, 124–48. Solomon in 'The Rhetoric of Redressing Grievances' agrees. Fink, Ham and Solomon suggest that the conspiracy against the Senate represents a Whiggish plot. David Bywaters counters with the suggestion that the conspiracy represents the Tory idea of the Popish Plot as hollow and silly, while the Senate represents the Whig leadership of the City of London: 'Venice, Its Senate, and Its Plot in Otway's *Venice Preserv'd*'. This is supported by Milhous and Hume in *Producible Interpretation*, 175–200. Jessica Munns accepts the identification of the Senate with the City Whigs, but insists that the conspiracy is real, dangerous and Whiggish: '"Plain as the light in the Cowcumber": A Note on the Conspiracy in Thomas Otway's *Venice Preserv'd*'.

6 For example Kelsall in his introduction says, 'Both the Senate and the conspirators are corrupt, and if either may stand for the Whigs, both can scarcely do so' (xiii). However, if we see the play as politically allusive, rather than allegorical, there is no problem with saying that Otway problematizes both corrupt republican authority and rebellion, and thus makes a twofold attack on the Whigs. In 'Political Interpretations of *Venice Preserv'd*', Philip Harth argues that the play offers a historical parallel rather than an allegory, but this still involves distortions in the interests of consistency: the parallel consists of the existence of a plot against the state. So, according to Harth, the government cannot be Whiggish, and the corruption which all critics agree permeates the Venetian government must be explained away.

7 Staves, *Players' Scepters*, 42, 79, 85–8, 192–3; Brown, *English Dramatic Form*, 89–95.

8 Hughes, 'A New Look at *Venice Preserv'd*'; *English Drama*, 300–6.

9 See my *Restoration Theatre and Crisis*, 175–6, 229–38; Canfield, *Word as Bond*, 300–10, and *Heroes and States*, 101–10; Munns, *Restoration Politics and Drama: The Plays of Thomas Otway*, chapter 5.

10 See Canfield's entry on Otway in *Restoration and Eighteenth-century Dramatists*, ed. Backscheider.

11 For Otway's complaints of lack of reward see prologue and epilogue to *The*

History and Fall of Caius Marius, and Dedication and epigraph to *The Orphan*, epistle and epilogue to *The Souldier's Fortune*. For (later) accounts of his suffering from unrequited love for Elizabeth Barry see *The Works of Thomas Otway*, ed. Ghosh, I, 13–14. For accounts of his poverty and his death, possibly from starvation, see *ibid.*, 28–37.

12 Whigs were supposedly ungrateful for the King's good government. They reversed the charge, speaking of royal or paternal ingratitude: see my *Restoration Theatre and Crisis*, 67, 119, 131–3, 163, 205, 226, 232, 261, 266.

13 See the text in Dryden, *Works*, II, lines 159–62.

14 See Wootton, 'Ulysses Bound? Venice and the Idea of Liberty from Howell to Hume'.

15 For example, Theocrin in Tate's *The Loyal General*: 'Fate wills, and 'tis expedient that I die!' (III, p. 25). For contradictions in the notion of quietists heroism see my *Restoration Theatre and Crisis*, 68–8, 200–1, 215–16.

16 Jaffeir's longing for wealth and social connection associates him also with his poverty-stricken author. There is a debate to be had about whether Otway's uncritical depiction of the desire for wealth and luxury is aristocratic and decadent or capitalistic and emergent, ideologically.

17 See my *Restoration Theatre and Crisis*, 218–19. Otway's grievances were the subject of his *The Soudier's Fortune* (1680).

18 See my *Restoration Theatre and Crisis*, 76, 129–30, 134–7, 170–1, 175, 205.

19 This had also been the theme of many 1660s comedies. A notable example is Sir Robert Howard's *The Committee*, the committee of the title being precisely the Committee of Sequestration which confiscated royalist lands and property.

20 See MacKenzie, 'A Note on Pierre's White Hat'.

21 For the tension between male and female values in the play see Rogers, 'Masculine and Feminine Values in Restoration Drama: the Distinctive Power of *Venice Preserv'd*'.

22 Letter to John Murray, 2 April 1817, cited in Taylor, *Next to Shakespeare*, 67. For negative views of Belvidera from a male viewpoint see Williams, 'The Sex-Death Motif', 66; Canfield, *Word as Bond*, 305; Hughes, 'A New Look at *Venice Preserv'd*', 448. For an illuminating discussion of Belvidera and critics' response to her see Munns, *Restoration Politics and Drama*, 186–94.

23 See my "He that should guard my virtue has betrayed it': the Dramatization of Rape in the Exclusion Crisis', 62.

24 Many critics have taken at face value this reference, which is clearly flippant and facetious. There is no resemblance between Renault and Shaftesbury, as Philp Harth has pointed out: 'Political Interpretations of *Venice Preserv'd*', 361. But see also Munns, *Restoration Politics and Drama*, 246, note 10.

25 Most Whigs were not, in fact, republicans, though there were exceptions such as Algernon Sidney. Tories tarred them with the brush of anti-monarchism, and compared them to the regicides of 1649.

26 See Teeter, *Political Themes in Restoration Tragedy*, 182ff.

27 The reference is to the ceremony at which the Duke or Doge cast a ring into the sea to symbolize the marriage of Venice to the Adriatic, also referred to at I.32.

28 *Restoration Politics and Drama*, 194.

29 Otway and Lee were also in a sense marginalized and perhaps also broken figures. Both lived and died in poverty, both were heavy drinkers. Lee went mad and was confined to Bedlam in 1684, being released after the revolution of 1688, only to sink into obscurity and die in the street in a drunken stupor in 1692. Otway died in 1685 at the early age of thirty-three, possibly of starvation. See introudctions to Lee's and Otway's *Works* and entries in *Restoration and Eighteenth-century Dramatists, A Dictionary of Literary Biography*, ed. Backscheider.

Shakespeare adapted:
John Dryden's *Troilus and Cressida*

In 1660 Shakespeare's reputation was not particularly high. There had been no performances of his work since the late 1630s and no collected edition of his plays had appeared since the Second Folio of 1632. Dryden and others set about constructing Shakespeare's reputation as a cultural icon.[1] There were several contenders for the role of 'national poet'. Fletcher was popular. Shadwell championed Jonson and modelled his own 'humours' comedies on Jonson's plays. Dryden's promotion of 'the Divine *Shakespeare*' was partly an aspect of his continuing literary battle with Shadwell.[2] Dryden's prologue to his and Davenant's adaptation of *The Tempest* in 1667 expresses his attitude:

> Shakespear, who (taught by none) did first impart
> To Fletcher wit, to labouring Jonson, Art.
> He Monarch-like gave those his subjects law
> And is the Nature which they paint and draw.
> Fletcher reached that which on his heights did grow
> Whilst Jonson crept and gather'd all below …
> But Shakespear's magick could not copied be,
> Within that circle none durst walk but he.

In Dryden's view 'Shakespear's power is sacred as a king's'. In the prologue to *Aureng-Zebe* Dryden says of himself that 'spite of all his pride, a secret shame / Invades his Breast at Shakespear's sacred name'.[3]

Despite this reverence for Shakespeare, almost all the Shakespeare plays performed during the Restoration period were altered or adapted. At first sight, this might seem to contradict the idea that Dryden and others held Shakespeare in high esteem. However, the Restoration playwrights altered Shakespeare not to devalue his achievement but to make him worthy of his exalted status; not to denigrate his plays but to elevate them (as they saw it) and also to popularize them.

Sometimes the chief motive was to increase entertainment-value. This was done by adding music and spectacle. The full resources of the new Dorset Garden theatre were used in the operatic version of *Macbeth* (1664) by Sir William Davenant. *The Tempest* was adapted by Davenant and Dryden in 1667, and was turned into an opera in 1674, with libretto by Shadwell and music by Matthew Locke. The 1667 version had already added various operatic elements, such as a song and masque dramatizing the crimes of Antonio and Alonzo, and Ferdinand and Ariel singing antiphonally in III.iv. The added spectacle includes a banquet brought in by 'eight fat spirits' in III.ii: a magical but also comic touch. The 1674 version turns the play into a full-scale opera with even more elaborate scenery and machinery for spirits to fly about, banquets to vanish and so on. Sometimes sensationalism is increased by adding sex and violence. A good example is Tate's adaptation of *Coriolanus* as *The Ingratitude of a Common-wealth* (1681), with all its added atrocities and horrific ending which I described in Chapter 5. Another example is Crowne's *The Misery of Civil-War*, an adaptation of Shakespeare's *2 Henry VI*, Acts IV and V, and *3 Henry V*. The play was produced at a time of political polarisation, when royalists accused the opposition of raising the spectre of the civil war of 1641, so to increase his royalist message Crowne adds in III.ii an exemplary spectacle of the horrors of civil war. Soldiers are shown robbing and tormenting peasants and raping their daughters. The peasants have only themselves to blame for they have railed seditiously in ale houses instead of living 'honestly and quietly'. The soldiers repeatedly sneer, 'How do you like Rebellion?' Then '*The Scene is drawn, and there appears Houses and Towns burning, Men and Women hang'd upon Trees, the Children on the tops of Pikes*' (III.iii, p. 36).[4]

In Shakespeare's *Titus Andronicus* Edward Ravenscroft found plenty of horrors already, but managed to add more and to make sensational use of racism. He does this by increasing the part and enhancing the villainy of the black man Aron (*sic*). For example in Act II, as in Shakespeare, Aron advises Tamora's sons to rape Lavinia, but he also encourages them to murder Bassianus. Ravenscroft concludes the scene with the villainous sons praising the black man in racial terms: 'Brave Moor!', 'Excellent Moor' (III.iii, p. 36). In Act III Ravenscroft adds bloodthirsty relish to Aron's speeches and stresses the premeditated nature of the villainy: 'This is the day of Doom for *Bassanius*, / His *Philomell* must lose her tongue to day' (p. 20). Ravenscroft also draws out Aron's and Tamora's lust. Partly, this is to satisfy audience taste for sexual titillation. Tate, for example, develops the triangular lust between Edmund, Goneril and Reagan in *Lear*. However, Ravenscroft also aims to get the maximum effect from the idea of the black man violating the white man's woman. Thus in Aron's soliloquy boasting of Tamora's love for him, Shakespeare's 'Away with slavish weeds and servile thoughts!' (II.i.18) becomes 'Hence abject thoughts that I am black and foul, / And all the Taunts of Whites that call me Fiend' (II, p. 15). Aron's defence of blackness in Act V is extended. There are racist insults in Shakespeare, but Ravenscroft adds more (e.g. V, pp. 52, 56). Ultimately Aron is racked on stage in the gruesome banquet scene to which even more horrors have been added. Titus shows Tamora *'the heads and hands of* Dem[etrius] *and* Chir[on] *hanging up against the wall. Their bodys in Chairs in bloody Linnen'* (V, p. 54). After telling her she has eaten the hearts and drunk the blood of her sons, Titus stabs her, but she hears Aron's confession and stabs her child by him before she dies, whereupon Aron says he will eat the child and is subsequently burnt alive on stage. Yet Ravenscroft also manages to gratify Restoration tastes for pity as well as horror, sensation and spectacle. He finds material ready to hand in Titus's grief in Act IV, his weeping in the dust for his sons, his agony over the violated Lavinia. He adds to the effect by including a pathetic exchange between Titus and the boy, Junius, who asks innocent questions about his father's and grandfather's fate. In case this does not provoke enough outrage at the plotters' actions, he adds the touching, 'Ah! but you shan't die yet Grandfather, / I Love you' (IV, p. 35).

Given this predilection for titillating horrors and emotional excess, it might seem strange that another impulse for adapting Shakespeare came from a desire for refinement and decorum. In the first place the dramatists wanted to purify Shakespeare's language, purging it of impurities. As Dryden put it, 'The English Language was then unpolished, and far from the perfection which it has since attained'.[5] Dryden's attitude to Shakespeare's language varied over time and depending on the context of his argument. In the postcript to *The Conquest of Granada*, as we saw in Chapter 1, the grammar and diction of Shakespeare and his contemporaries is criticized to exalt the heroic play. However, in *Heads of an Answer to Rymer's Remarks*, written but not published in winter 1677/8, Dryden praises Shakespeare's language for being natural and passionate. In the Preface to *All For Love* Dryden takes a respectful but somewhat superior attitude to Shakespeare's language:

I have not Copy'd my author servilely: Words and Phrases must of necessity receive a change in succeeding Ages: but 'tis almost a Miracle that much of his Language remains so pure; and that he who began Dramatique Poetry amongst us, untaught by any, and, as *Ben Johnson* tells us, without Learning, should by the force of his own Genius perform so much, that in a manner he has left no praise for any who come after him.[6]

In *The Grounds of Criticism in Tragedy*, the prefatory essay to *Troilus and Cressida*, Dryden takes a more critical attitude, accusing Shakespeare of overblown language and figurative excess:

Yet I cannot deny that he has his failings; but they are not so much in the passions as in his manner of expression: he often obscures his meaning by his words, and sometimes makes it unintelligible. I will not say of so great a poet, that he distinguish'd not the blown, puffy stile, from true sublimity; but I may venture to maintain that the fury of his fancy often transported him, beyond the bounds of Judgement, either in coyning of new words and phrases, or racking words which were in use, into the violence of a Catachresis: 'Tis not that I would explode the use of metaphors from passions, for *Longinus* thinks 'em necessary to raise it; but to use 'em at every word, to say nothing without a metaphor, a simile, an Image, or description, is, I doubt, to smell a little too strongly of the buskin.[7]

As we shall see, Dryden aims to prune and purge Shakespeare's language. However, we must be cautious about taking all the dramatists' assertions about their alterations of Shakespeare at face value. For example, linguistic refinement may not be as thorough as they claim. For instance, Crowne asserts in his prologue to *The Misery of Civil-War* that '*The Divine* Shakespear *did not lay one Stone*' of his '*poor Work*'. This is patently false. Indeed, it seems rather odd. The motive may be modesty, or alternatively self-aggrandizement, or perhaps it is to draw attention to Crowne's own politically motivated alterations. The fact remains that Crowne has taken much more from Shakespeare than he is prepared to admit. Moreover, sometimes, under the guise of linguistic 'refinement', the dramatists insert passages in the Restoration vernacular which are no more 'pure' than the Shakespearean original. We have to be aware that the picture is a little more complicated and contradictory than it at first appears.

The urge to refine Shakespeare also had a moral aspect. This affects the plots, which are often altered to introduce poetic justice: the bad must be punished and the good vindicated. This is a striking feature of Nahum Tate's *The History of King Lear* (1681), in which the ending is altered so that Lear is restored to the throne and abdicates in favour of the married couple, Edgar and Cordelia. The desire for moral refinement also affected the treatment of Shakespeare's heroines who suffer more (usually in love) and become sentimentalized, feminine, often victimized and more virtuous. Tate's Cordelia keeps silent in Act I not from militant honesty or dislike of flattery but from love of Edgar and fear of being forced into a distasteful marriage. In equally striking departure, Dryden turns Cleopatra in *All For Love* into a 'Mistress true'.[8] Even the iron matron Volumnia in *Coriolanus* is made to feel in Tate's *The Ingratitude* a 'Womans Tenderness ... / The Mothers Fondness, and her panting fears (III.ii, p. 36). The hero's wife Virgilia is similarly sentimentalized. Imogen in *Cymbeline* becomes, by a similar process, the feminine and sentimental Eugenia in D'Urfey's *The Injur'd Princess* (1682). The treatment of women in the adaptations is contradictory: on the one hand, Restoration playwrights substantially increase women's parts and add 'love interest' to Shakespeare's plays. In the Dryden–Davenant *Tempest* both Miranda and Caliban are given sisters. In *The Misery of Civil-War* Crowne creates the character of Lady Elianor Butler, a mistress for the future King Edward. On the other hand, making Shakespeare's heroines virtuous and sentimental, and privileging the feminine, may be considered to undermine the strength of Shakespeare's women and to disempower them. In stark contrast to Shakespeare's 'serpent of old Nile', Dryden's Cleopatra cries:

> Nature meant me
> A Wife, a silly harmless household Dove,
> Fond without art; and kind without deceit;
> But Fortune, that has made a Mistress of me,
> Has thrust me out to the wide World, unfurnish'd
> Of falsehood to be happy. (IV.i.91)

Yet this is not to say that the heroines of the adaptations are devoid of complexity or human interest, or that they are entirely lacking in spirit.[9] They have a different kind of heroism from Shakespeare's women, which is heroism none the less.[10] Tate's Cordelia seems more emotional and perhaps more victimized, but is also quite brave:

> Now comes my Trial, how am I distrest,
> That must with cold speech tempt the chol'rick King
> Rather to leave me Dowerless, than condemn me
> To loath'd Embraces! (I.i.92)

The addition of a love motive makes her in some ways a more appealing character than Shakespeare's. As we shall see, Dryden's Cressida also exemplifies these alterations and contradictions.

Sometimes the impetus for adaptation was a desire to enhance the political message, as in Crowne's *The Misery of Civil-War* and *Henry VI, the First Part* (1681); or Tate's *The History of King Richard the Second* (1680–81) and *The Ingratitude of a Common-wealth*. Political significance may be added, as for example when the rape of Lavinia in Ravenscroft's *Titus Andronicus* is presented as an 'Invasion on a Princes right' (II, p. 16) by plotters. Quite often the dramatists' alterations enhance a perceived royalist, patriarchal or authoritarian message. In his dedication to *The Ingratitude of a Common-wealth*, Tate says his adaptation of *Coriolanus* emphasizes the parallel between the Roman plebs and tribunes who reject Coriolanus and 'the busie [Whig] Faction of our own time ... those Troublers of the State that out of private Interest or Mallice, Seduce the Multitude to Ingratitude, against Persons that are not only plac't in Rightful Power above them; but also the Heroes and Defenders of their Country'. This clearly associates his hero Coriolanus with James Stuart, whose military heroism was much celebrated by royalists. Tate's aim is clear: 'The Moral therefore of these Scenes being to Recommend Submission and Adherence to Establisht Lawful Power, which in a word, is Loyalty'.[11] Tate makes alterations to Shakespeare to sharpen the political lessons. He strains every nerve to offer an exemplary spectacle of the dangers which can befall a nation which is ungrateful to its military heroes and natural leaders. Yet, as with linguistic and moral alterations, the process of politically motivated adaptation may produce a new set of contradictions. The glorifying of loyalty to flawed or corrupt royal or quasi-royal authority may creates a sense of bleakness and pessimism; or the depiction of royal faults may undermine the ideal of loyalty professed.[12] To take the example of Tate's Coriolanus: Tate mitigates the unfortunate contemporary resonance of a man betraying his country to a foreign enemy, since the Stuarts' fraternization with Catholic France had caused a political crisis. Tate improves his hero, playing down in his Coriolanus the uncompromising temperament for which James was famous, and omitting Menenius's disloyal criticism that things 'might have been much better, if / He could have temporized' in the exchange with the Tribunes (Shakespeare's IV.vi.16). Yet Tate's improvement of the James figure does not really work: nothing can assuage the uncomfortable resonance of a man in league with his country's enemies making a war on his own people, and there was enough apparent criticism of James in the play for it to be revived as an anti-Stuart one after the Jacobite rebellions of 1715 and 1745. The complexities of politically motivated alterations are exemplified in Dryden's *Troilus and Cressida*, and will be explored further below.

The subject of this chapter, Dryden's *Troilus and Cressida*, was important in the development of a theory of adaptation. The published text is prefaced by an essay, *The Grounds of Criticism in Tragedy*, which was an significant landmark in developing Shakespeare scholarship. Dryden in his dedication praises 'plainness and sincerity' in language, and 'moderation' rather than fulsomeness in style.[13] He urges his dedicatee, Robert Spencer, Second Earl of Sunderland, to lend his name to a project for purifying and stabilizing the English language on the model of French and Italian. In his preface Dryden laments the absence of 'a perfect Grammar' which would be the foundation of a stable language; but says that he has 'undertaken to correct' Shakespeare's play from the standpoint of an age in which there is greater linguistic refinement:

Yet it must be allow'd to the present Age, that the tongue in general is so much refin'd since *Shakespear's* time, that many of his words, and more of his Phrases, are scarce intelligible. And of those which we understand some are ungrammatical, others course [i.e. coarse]; and his whole stile is so pester'd with Figurative expressions, that it is as affected as it is obscure. (225)

Let us take the example of Hector's speech in the Trojan debate in Act II about whether to return Helen to the Greeks. In Shakespeare Hector takes nine lines to reach his conclusion:

> Though no man lesser fears the Greeks than I,
> As far as toucheth my particular, yet, dread Priam,
> There is no lady of more softer bowels,
> More spongy to suck in the sense of fear,
> More ready to cry out 'Who knows what follows?'
> Than Hector is. The wound of peace is surety.
> Surety secure; but modest doubt is called
> The beacon of the wise, the tent that searches
> To th'bottom of the worst. Let Helen go. (II.ii.8)

It is easy to see what Dryden's objections to this passage would be. The seductive sibilants have led Shakespeare into alliterative extravagance which distracts from the sense. There is indeed something coarse about 'spongy' and 'suck'. There is unnecessary repetition and possibly tautology in 'surety. / Surety secure.' Two different and conflicting metaphors are offered for 'modest doubt'. The speech displays interest in the sound of

words, and in metaphor, to the detriment of rhetorical force. Dryden
reduces the number of lines to five:

> Though no man less can fear the *Greeks* than I,
> Yet there's no Virgin of more tender heart
> More ready to cry out, *Who knows the consequence?*
> Then *Hector* is; for modest doubt is mix'd
> With manly courage best: let *Helen* go.

Dryden has omitted linguistic ornaments and extravagant flights of fancy.
He has brought out the central paradox of the speech more clearly. He has
made Hector assert his point and lead up to his conclusion more bluntly
and forcefully. In the process, Dryden displays Hector's true 'manliness' more
effectively, which accords with his notions of character, described below.

Yet it would be a mistake to see Dryden as simply refining Shakespeare: 'but I am willing to acknowledg, that as I have often drawn his
English nearer to our times so I have sometimes conform'd my own to his;
& consequently, the Language is not altogether so pure, as it is significant'
(226-7). Here we see Dryden under Shakespeare's spell. In his preface
Dryden has several criticisms of the language of the speech in *Richard II* in
which Shakespeare arouses pity for the humiliated Richard, but he cannot
help but praise also: 'the painting of it is so lively, and the words so
moving, that I have scarce read anything comparable to it, in any other
language' (246). In Hector's speech, quoted above, the first line and final
sentence are kept virtually the same as in Shakespeare: 'Though no man
less can fear the *Greeks* than I, … let *Helen* go.' Here the vigour of Shakespeare's language brings out the power of the central idea: the greatest
warrior-hero advocates the option of public safety, and true courage
means caring for the people's welfare. This is an instance of the 'significance' to which Dryden refers.

Moreover, Dryden does not always follow his own precepts about
figurative language, as we can see from the parting of Troilus and Cressida
at the end of IV.i:

Cressida: But as a careful traveller who fearing
      Assaults of Robbers, leaves his wealth behind,
      I trust my heart with thee; and to the *Greeks*
      Bear but an empty casket.
Troilus: Then, will I live; that I may keep that treasure:
      And arm'd with this assurance, let thee go
      Loose, yet secure as is the gentle Hawk

> When whistled off she mounts into the wind:
> Our love's like Mountains high above the clouds,
> Though winds and tempests beat their aged feet,
> Their peaceful heads nor storm nor thunder know,
> But scorn the threatning rack that roles below. (IV.i.107)

Here we have a heaping up of conflicting similes at a poignant moment. Yet in the preface Dryden was critical of a passage in his own *The Indian Emperour* in which Montezuma describes his danger in a somewhat far-fetched simile: 'he destroy'd the concernment which the Audience might otherwise have had for him; for they could not think his danger near, when he had the leisure to invent a Simile' (244). At the most poignant moment in his own play, Dryden has followed the Shakespearean practice which he condemns elsewhere.

With genre, as with language, Dryden is justified in his claims to have attempted refinement, but only up to a point. Shakespeare's play is usually defined by the non-definition 'problem play'. It is not called a tragedy but is listed in the Stationers' Register as a history and described on the title page of the 1609 quarto as *The Famous Historie of Troylus and Cresseid*. The epistle added to the quarto even suggests that the play is comic. Dryden measures the play against a definition of tragedy and finds it lacking: 'the latter part of the Tragedy is nothing but a confusion of Drums and Trumpets, Excursions and Alarms' (226). His essay, *The Grounds of Criticism in Tragedy*, which forms part of the preface says that tragedy needs unity of action and a proper beginning, middle and end. Shakespeare's history plays are measured and found wanting, 'rather Chronicles represented, than Tragedies' (230). Dryden simplifies the action, to remove the 'confusion of 'Drums and Trumpets, Excursions and Alarms':

I made with no small trouble, an Order and Connexion of all the Scenes; removing them from the places where they were inartificially set: and though it was impossible to keep 'em all unbroken, because the scene must be some-times in the City, and sometimes in the Camp, yet I have so order'd them that there is a coherence of 'em with one another, and a dependence on the main design: no leaping from *Troy* to the *Grecian* Tents, and thence back again in the same Act; but a due proportion of time allow'd for every motion. (226)

There is some truth in Dryden's perception that the action of Shakespeare's play is rambling, and he is right in some instances to say that his order makes more sense. For example, in Shakespeare's play Hector's challenge to the Greeks precedes the debate in Troy, appearing 'out of the blue' and to some extent pre-empting the Trojan debate; Hector's position in the debate is then anomalous when he advocates submission just after sending his challenge. In Dryden's version the challenge follows the debate, and is itself the subject of heated discussion, so that what is at stake in the single combat is more clearly brought out. The terms of the challenge, that Hector fights for a wife who is superior to any Greek woman, have more force because we have just encountered the noble Andromache and witnessed Hector in his domestic role, which we never do in Shakespeare; and also because Hector himself extols his lady's worth, rather than leaving it to Aeneas (II.i.180; compare I.iii.271 in Shakespeare). However, Dryden does not always follow his own intentions. For example, Pandarus suddenly appears in the Greek camp in IV.ii, with no account of how he got there, a solecism or failure of 'artifice' which Dryden would normally be quick to condemn.

Dryden also finds his Shakespearean original lacking in a proper ending: 'The chief persons, who give name to the Tragedy, are left alive: *Cressida* is false, and is not punish'd' (226). By increasing poetic justice and by killing off the mian characters, Dryden makes the play conform more strictly to classical notions of tragedy. For Dryden, good tragedy should have a 'Moral that directs the whole action of the Play to one center' (234). In his case, there are two possible morals, corresponding to the pity and fear which Dryden says (following Aristotle) that tragedy ought to arouse. The first, deriving from the pitiable story of the lovers, concerns the dangers of hasty judgement. The second, from the action set in the Greek camp, rests more upon fear, and is summed up in the play's final words: 'since from homebred Factions ruine springs, / Let Subjects learn obedience to their Kings' (V.ii.325).[14]

However, Dryden is not entirely in favour of classical rules, but, on the contrary, finds much to praise in the power of Shakespeare's writing. This is clear not only in the preface but also in the prologue, spoken by Thomas Betterton as the ghost of Shakespeare. Shakespeare is represented as rough, but also English, manly, bold and vigorous:

> And, if I drain'd no *Greek* or *Latin* store,
> 'Twas, that my own abundance gave me more.
> On foreign trade I needed not rely,
> Like fruitfull *Britain*, rich without supply.
> In this my rough-drawn Play, you shall behold
> Some Master-strokes, so manly and so bold,
> That he, who meant to alter, found 'em such,
> He shook; and thought it Sacrilege to touch. (249)

Dryden, then, has an ambivalent attitude to Shakespeare, both superior and awed at the same time. Moreover, even where he is in favour of classical rules, Dryden does not always follow his own recommendations. He says of the tragedian, 'If his business be to move terror and pity, and one of his Actions be Comical, the other Tragical, the former will divert the people, and utterly make void his greater purpose' (230). Yet Dryden adds comic bits to the tragic story of *Troilus and Cressida*, especially in his development of the comic potential of Thersites and Pandarus, and in his jibes at priests.[15]

Pandarus was played by renowned comedian Antony Leigh. His part is increased, as are both his lewdness and his voyeurism: 'when I had her in my arms, *Lord*, thought I, and by my troth I could not forbear sighing, *if Prince* Troilus *had her at this advantage, and I were holding of the door –* ' (I.ii.39). Thersites was played by the great specialist in low comedy, Cave Underhill. The development of this character by Dryden distracts from the focus upon 'great Persons' (231) which Dryden supposedly thinks proper to tragedy. His additions to Thersites's part tend to militate against dramatic 'propriety' and generic purity. For example, Dryden invents a meeting between Troilus and Diomedes in the Greek camp at the end of IV.ii, just after Troilus has witnessed what he thinks is Cressida's betrayal. Hot words are exchanged and Aeneas is only just able to persuade them to postpone fighting to the following day. Thersites concludes the scene with a speech less cynical and sardonic, more vengeful and more eager for mischief, than anything in Shakespeare:

Now the furies take *Aeneas*, for letting them sleep upon their quarrell: who knows but rest may cool their brains, and make 'em rise maukish to mischief upon consideration? May each of 'em dream he sees his Cockatrice in t'others arms; and be stabbing one another in their sleep, to remember 'em of their business when they wake: let 'em be punctual to the point of honour; and if it were possible let both be first at the place of Execution. Let neither of 'em have cogitation enough, to consider 'tis a whore they fight for: and let 'em vallue their lives at as little as they are worth. And lastly let no succeeding fools take warning by 'em; but in imitation of them when a Strumpet is in question,

Let 'em beneath their feet all reason trample;
And think it great to perish by Example. (IV.ii.488)

The extreme malice here distorts both character and plot. Thersites's malignant 'humour' is exaggerated to the detriment of his semi-choric function. Dryden increases the discomfort this character engenders to the point where it ceases to be productive in provoking commentary or

reflection, and merely kills the tragic mood and distracts us from the focus
on and sympathy for the tragic hero which he himself thinks proper.
Dryden goes part-way towards the principles of classical decorum in
tragedy extolled by Thomas Rymer, but in the end he is unwilling to go all
the way.[16]

Dryden has qualified praise for Shakespeare's characterization (237–
40), but also attempts to develop Shakespeare's characters and prune their
number: 'I ... threw out many unnecessary persons; improv'd those
Characters which were begun, and left unfinish'd; as Hector, Troilus,
Pandarus, and *Thersites*; and added that of *Andromache*' (226). It is true
that Dryden has amplified the roles of these characters. For example, the
nobility and tragic potential of Troilus and Hector are increased by a
series of alterations, including a new scene (the latter part of III.ii), in
which Hector persuades Troilus to give up his love for the sake of his
country. Troilus at first resists, but ultimately gives in to the promptings of
friendship: 'let me lean my head / Upon thy bosome; all my peace dwells
there' (III.ii.419). Not to be outdone in friendship, Hector then offers to
defend Troilus's relationship in the arena of war and politics; but now it is
Troilus's turn to be noble, and he refuses the offer.[17]

However, Dryden has not necessarily made his characters more
rounded. Dryden has an extended discussion of character in his Preface,
from which it appears that he does not consider character an end in itself,
and has little interest in any naturalistic urge to depict complex characters
for the sake of interest in their personalities. Dryden does care about pro-
bability and plausibility of character, but he also sees character as related
to the play's moral. He builds characters on the basis of typical characteristics which he says must be apparent each time the characters appear.
What makes the behaviour or manners of characters plausible for Dryden
is not the opacity and perversity which we might consider lifelike but conformity with certain moral, psychological and socio-political assumptions:

The manners arise from many causes: and are either distinguish'd by
complexion, as choleric and phlegmatic, or by the differences of Age or Sex, of
Climates, or Quality of the persons, or their present condition: they are likewise to be gather'd from the several Virtues, Vices, or Passions, and many
other commonplaces which a Poet must be suppos'd to have learn'd from
natural Philosophy, Ethics, and History. (235)

It seems particularly obvious to the modern reader that assumptions about
character based upon class and gender are likely to produce stereotypes.
Dryden does not believe in character types: 'A character ... cannot be

suppos'd to consist of one particular Virtue, or Vice, or passion only'; but 'the characters are no other than the inclinations ... 'tis a composition of qualities which are not contrary to one another in the same person' (236). This removal of contradiction in character makes Dryden's characters seem flatter than Shakespeare's, despite his avowed attempt to flesh them out. Moreover, 'one virtue, vice, and passion, ought to be shown in every man, as predominant over all the rest: as covetousness in *Crassus*, love of his country in *Brutus*' (236). This might serve as an apt description of Ben Jonson's characters, and perhaps explains why, though Dryden praises Shakespeare's characters, he thinks Jonson's better still (238–9). In his new scene III.ii Dryden increases pity and admiration for both Troilus and Hector, but the scene is more *about* idealized friendship, and the ability to privilege both friendship and duty over heterosexual love, than it is about character. Hector draws the moral in the final line: 'That Friendship never gain'd a nobler field' (III.ii.439). Troilus is expressing this ideal rather than his character when he says, 'I love you Brother, with that awful love / I bear to Heav'n, and to superior vertue' (III.ii.246). The characters conform to our expectations, in line with Dryden's thinking on consistency of character: Troilus is ' hot and fiery' with the 'rashness of ... youth' (III.ii.238, 241), as in the debate in Act II. Hector's concern is for 'the general state, / And all our common safety' (288–9), which continues and develops the stance he took in the debate in Act II. Yet this is not to suggest that there is no merit in Dryden's work: the scene, moving from friendship through rage and estrangement to reconciliation, has considerable dramatic tension.

It should be no surprise to us by now that Dryden violates his own precepts on character. For example, he says character must conform to what is 'deliver'd to us by relation or History' (235), but goes against the entire tradition by making Cressida faithful. This alteration to Shakespeare is as startling as any of Shakespeare's alterations to Homer or Chaucer. In a move towards moral refinement, Dryden's Cressida becomes virtuous and misunderstood. She merely feigns love for Diomedes at the instruction of her father, who in Dryden's version, wants to turn his coat again and get back to Troy. This is not to say that fidelity in Dryden's Cressida is a dramatic fault or that the play does not work. On the contrary, the scene in which Troilus observes Cressida feigning love for Diomedes has all the poignancy of misunderstanding, as well as dramatic tension and suspense. Moreover, the perfidy of Shakespeare's Cressida may seem too rapid, and inconsistent with what we have seen of her character. The continuity of character and motivation in Dryden's Cressida has more psychological plausibility.

Dryden's Cressida is more moral. She insists on a promise of marriage, never mentioned in Shakespeare's play (III.ii.84). She considers herself bound to Troilus by 'all those holy vows, / Which, if there be a pow'r above, are binding' (V.ii.242). Troilus's doubts are disastrously inflamed at the end when Cressida begs him to spare Diomedes's life, but her motives are filial piety (her father needs Diomedes's protection) and love: 'my return to you / Wou'd be cut off for ever by his death' (V.ii.215). In the end, Cressida stabs herself to prove her fidelity, Troilus recognizes her 'purest, whitest innocence' (V.ii.268), and she dies blessing him.

Dryden's Cressida is softer and more 'womanly'. The love scenes therefore become more tender and sentimental, in keeping with Restoration taste. For example, Shakespeare's stage direction when the lovers must part is 'she embraces him' (after IV.iv.12). Dryden replaces this with: 'They both weep over each other, she running into his armes' (after IV.i.25). Shakespeare's Cressida trades bawdy witticisms with Pandarus in I.ii, jokes with Troilus about men's poor sexual performance in III.ii and bandies words with the Greeks in between kisses in IV.v, to the admiration of Nestor and the discomfiture of Ulysses. Dryden's Cressida is less bawdy and the kissing scene is reduced in Dryden's play to a speech by Pandarus which gives no account of Cressida's response to the men's kisses (IV.ii.353). Jean Marsden goes a little too far, however, in calling her an 'exemplary pathetic heroine'.[18] Dryden keeps some of the boldness of Shakespeare's character: 'Boldness comes to me now, and I can speak; / Prince *Troilus*, I have lov'd you long' (III.ii.35).

The extent to which Dryden does 'feminize' Cressida might be considered to weaken her, and women generally. Indeed, Dryden's project in *Troilus and Cressida* and the critical material surrounding it seems to be in part a thoroughgoing attack on effeminacy. In his discussion of language in the dedication, Dryden does not confine himself to the written word but says: 'our pronunciation is effeminate' (223). In his preface Shakespeare is praised over Fletcher for having 'a more Masculine, a bolder and more fiery Genius', whereas Fletcher is 'soft and Womanish' (233). Later Dryden extols male friendship over heterosexual love: 'Friendship is both a virtue, and a Passion essentially; love is a passion only in its nature, and is not a virtue but by Accident; good nature makes Friendship; but effeminacy Love' (247). As we have seen, he exalts male friendship in the Trojan camp in the exchange between Hector and Troilus in III.ii. Similarly, in the Greek camp, Patroclus becomes Achilles's 'sweetest, best of friends' (V.ii.142), rather than his catamite, so that in fighting to avenge Patroclus, despite his promise to Polyxena, Achilles is privileging idealized male friendship over heterosexual love.

Many of Dryden's alterations to Shakespeare in the play might be described as 'masculinist'. He makes various additions to Shakespeare which suggest that women are bad for heroes, and that effeminacy, in the Restoration sense of excessive preoccupation with women and love, is incompatible with affairs of state. In the Greek camp Dryden retains Patroclus's critique of Achilles's effeminacy in abstaining from the fight because of his love for the Trojan Polyxena;

> A woman impudent and mannish grown
> Is not more loath'd than an effeminate man,
> In time of action. (IV.ii.38)

Dryden makes slightly more of this point by having Achilles receive Polyxena's letter, and vow to abstain from fighting in response, later in the scene.

In Troy Hector as well as Troilus must struggle to resist effeminacy. When Hector delays fighting in response to the promptings of love, he becomes ashamed, for, as Troilus tells him, 'fondnesse of a wife' is a 'more unpardonable ill' than 'superstition' as a reason for not fighting (V.i.132-4). Moreover, Ulysses is able to manipulate Hector into fighting Achilles by sending through Troilus a specious message that the Greeks think Hector is afraid and that he is relying on his sister Polyxena to intercede for him with Achilles (V.i.135). The appeal to his manhood goads Hector to shun the warnings of his wife Andromache and his sister Cassandra, and to rouse all the manhood of Troy:

> Let us not leave one Man to guard the Walls;
> Both Old and young, the coward and the brave,
> Be summon'd all, our utmost fate to try,
> And as one body move, whose Soul am I. (V.i.181)

Hector here becomes, as it were, the soul of manhood. Since he is the noblest character in the play, Dryden is placing a strong, positive value on manliness. Since Hector is Prince, manliness also becomes a marker of true royalty.

Yet there are some anomalies within Dryden's masculinism. First, manliness is perfectly compatible with sentimentality: Hector is prompted to send his challenge to the Greeks by learning that his little son Astyanax has had the same idea, a proceeding which is described in some mawkish passages (II.i.29–92). Second, it is ironic that one of the chief means by which Dryden dramatizes his challenge to effeminacy is by adding a strong woman character, Hector's wife Andromache. Dryden's Andromache is depicted as heroic for urging Hector to send a challenge to the Greeks against the promptings of her love and womanhood:

> I would be worthy to be Hectors wife:
> And had I been a Man, as my Soul's one,
> I had aspir'd a nobler name, his friend. (II.i.143)

Hector's response is:

> Come to my Arms, thou manlier Virtue come;
> Thou better Name than wife! (II.i.156)

It is clear in this exchange that Andromache's manly qualities are praised in a context which denigrates women in general, a denigration in which she colludes completely.

The morally compromised character of Paris is eliminated by Dryden, but added passages make clear that in jeopardizing his country for a woman he has committed an act of the deepest dishonour. Andromache tells Hector:

> you shall not wear a cause
> So black as *Helens* rape upon your breast,
> Let Paris fight for *Helen*; guilt for guilt:
> But when you fight for Honour and for me,
> Then let our equal Gods behold an Act,
> They may not blush to Crown. (II.i.167)

For Shakespeare's Priam, Paris is 'besotted on your sweet delights' (II.ii.142). Dryden substitutes 'besotted on effeminate joys' (II.i.44).

Dryden's sexual conservatism in these exchanges may have a political motivation. His critique of effeminacy may be intended as a warning to the Stuart brothers, Charles and James, whose libertinism was arousing anxiety and fuelling the fire of the Whig opposition. In the new scene between Troilus and Hector, discussed above, Hector's argument that Troilus should 'bear it like a man' (III.ii.281) is part of a broader argument that argues that irresponsible love must give way to the public good. It seems clear that Dryden's purpose is at least partly political. We can see this as Hector reaches the climax of his argument:

> If parting from a Mistriss can procure
> A Nations happiness, show me that Prince
> Who dares to trust his future fame so farr
> To stand the shock of Annals, blotted thus,
> *He sold his Country for a womans love!* (III.ii.295)

These words, ringing out in the theatre, like the italicized line in the text, would surely recall the King's violently unpopular French Catholic mistresses and the irresponsible 'womanizing' of both Stuart brothers. As Maximillian E. Novak points out in his headnote to the play, Troilus resembles James as he exclaims, 'The publick, is the Lees of vulgar slaves' and asserts 'an Eagles life / Is worth a world of Crows' (III.ii.305, 309–10). He is not allowed to get away with this. Hector rebukes him:

> And what are we, but for such men as these? ...
> Ev'n those who serve have their expectances,
> Degrees of happiness, which they must share,
> Or they'll refuse to serve us. (III.ii.313, 317)

This is not the elitist note of Exclusion Crisis high Toryism. Dryden's masculinism in this play and his criticism of selfish passion in princes cannot but reflect badly upon England's 'effeminate' and self-centred royal brothers.

However, there are several factors which temper the potentially oppositional nature of the scene, and make it clear that Dryden's perspective is one of moderate Toryism, not Whiggery. First, the nobility of the characters tempers the criticism: the Trojan princes are unquestionaly heroic. The choice which is eventually made, putting the public welfare first, might be considered to reassure the English public about Chrales II's intentions. Moreover, the fact that Cressida is faithful in Dryden's version, and that this truth is only found out too late, with tragic consequences, might serves as a warning to those who were too quick to criticize the royal mistresses. It should also be noted that part of Hector's argument to Troilus is Filmerian and patriarchal: Priam has commanded the handing over of Cressida, so Troilus's surrender of her becomes, 'A King, and fathers will!' (III.ii.330).

Jean Marsden is quite wrong when she states that Dryden steadfastly avoids political reference in *Troilus and Cressida*.[19] On the contrary Dryden seems particularly preoccupied with politics in his adaptation, which was written near the beginning of the Exclusion Crisis and performed by the Duke's Company early in 1679. The political perspective offered is a moderate Tory one, compared to the strident Toryism of Dryden's writing later in the Exclusion Crisis. The play's dedicatee Sunderland was principal Secretary of State. Sunderland is said to have 'put a stop to our ruine, when we were just rowling downward to the precipice' because 'his principles were full of moderation, and all his Councils such as tended to heal and not to widen the breaches of the Nation' (221). This is partly a reference to the fact that Sunderland was attempting to lead a government composed of both royalists and opposition figures, partly an attempt to urge political reconciliation through the familiar tactic of exhortation through praise. Dryden's moderation is apparent in his treatment of religion. He was writing at the time of the Popish Plot, when the Whigs were making political capital out of fear of Catholicism. At first it appears that Dryden capitulates to the prevailing anti-Catholic mood. He inserts attacks on priests throughout the play in the form of humorous jibes by Pandarus and Thersites and more sustained diatribes by Troilus.[20] To provide an occasion for Troilus's anti-clerical outbursts, Dryden makes Cressida's father, the traitor Calchas, into a 'fugitive Rogue Priest' (IV.i.16), and makes him a more unpleasant character. When Troilus thinks he is betrayed, his reaction is: 'That I shou'd trust the Daughter of a Priest!' (V.ii.157), and he and Thersites proceed to outdo one another in cursing the priesthood.

However, there are subtle suggestions that a more cautious attitude to anti-Catholicism is advisable, and an implicit critique of Whig scaremongering about Catholic plots. Dryden's subtitle is *Truth Found Too Late*. This refers to Troilus finding out too late that Cressida was true to him all along, in Dryden's version. However, the subtitle also suggests a general need to avoid precipitate action based on hasty assumptions. A close reading of the play shows that Dryden intends to interrogate facile anti-clericalism. It is significant that the first of Troilus's diatribes is an attempt to refute bad omens before battle which are actually accurate; and that the second is based on a betrayal which has not actually taken place. For those who are prepared to think a little more carefully, anti-clericalism is shown to be over-hasty and misplaced.[21] In his epilogue Dryden uses the irreverent Thersites to mock the Popish Plot scare, a stance he also takes in his prologue to Lee's *Caesar Borgia* in the same theatrical season. Dryden therefore has the courage to stand out against anti-Catholicism when most people were still caught up in the hysteria.

The moderation of Dryden's political views is apparent in his balance between criticism of royal sexual incontinence and an attack on political division and trouble-making. Later, his attitude was to harden, as he became reluctant to make concessions to the king's opponents. In his famous Tory poem *Absalom and Achitophel* (1681), for example, Dryden is less critical of Stuart licentiousness, even indulgent towards the king's scattering of his seed throughout the land. In *Troilus and Cressida*, as we have seen, he is unusually tough on selfish passion in princes. However, he is careful to balance this with a strengthening of the attack on 'faction'. 'Faction' was the charge levelled against the parliamentary opposition by royalists who argued that people should be 'quiet' and leave overall government to the King. In Dryden's play this line is argued primarily through the character of Ulysses. Whereas Shakespeare's Ulysses bears some resemblance to scheming Elizabethan politicians such as Burleigh, Cecil and their co-thinkers (just as his Achilles resembles the Earl of Essex), Dryden's Ulysses resembles his play's dedicatee, Sunderland, presented in the play's dedication as a moderate. Sunderland was politically an unknown quantity in 1679, but was already beginning to acquire a reputation for scheming and double dealing.[22] Dryden's Ulysses is the same, and Dryden gives qualified sanction to the use of Machiavellian means by Ulysses to maintain order in the Greek camp. Indeed, Dryden is prophetic: control is enforced by means which resemble the *realpolitik* for which Sunderland was to become famous,[23] rather than by the more elevated virtues for which Sunderland is praised in the dedication. That Dryden might approve of Ulysses is suggested by a reference in the preface to the Ulysses of Ovid's *Metamorphoses* as having 'all the calmness of a reasonable man' (242), and as displaying the same qualities which Dryden admires in a playwright: the ability to understand his audience and to arouse their passions gradually. This is a significant shift from Shakespeare's play. Shakespeare shows Ulysses's machinations as being just as disastrous as the hot-headedness and pride of Achilles or Essex. In Shakespeare the chain of events which culminates in the treacherous murder of the unarmed Hector is directly precipitated by Ulysses's deceitful stratagems. In Dryden's play Hector dies in battle: as Agamemnon puts it, 'mighty Hector fell beneath thy Sword' (V.ii.305). Ajax, grudging Achilles glory, grumbles, '*Troilus* fell by multitudes opprest; / And so fell *Hector*' (V.ii.314); but the fluctuations of battle we have witnessed, whilst arousing pity and admiration for the Trojan heroes, do not suggest any direct dishonour comparable with the murder of an unarmed man in Shakespeare. Diomedes is treacherous because he asserts Cressida's falsity, but Troilus is able to kill him before being killed in his turn by Achilles.

Dryden takes steps, then, to exculpate Ulysses and elevate his character. Through Ulysses, a positive value is placed on 'Peacefull order' (V.ii.323), and respect for sovereignty. This message already appears in Shakespeare's play, and may have been what attracted Dryden in the first place. Dryden alters Shakespeare to draw out the theme that respect for royal rule must be enforced by authoritarian means if necessary. The Greek council of war is made the first scene, rather than the third, as in Shakespeare. This gives greater prominence to Ulysses's famous speech on degree. Dryden shortens the speech and concentrates on subordination to the Crown. Shakespeare's 'O, when degree is shak'd, / Which is the ladder of all high designs, / The enterprise is sick' (I.iii.101) becomes 'Or when Supremacy of Kings is shaken, / What can succeed?' (I.i.38). There is more at stake here than linguistic simplifcation: Dryden sharpens the speech's political force. Shakespeare conveys the dangers of 'appetite, an universal wolf' which 'Must make perforce an universal prey, / And last eat up himself' (I.iii.120, 122). Dryden substitutes 'wild Ambition' (45), a quality Tories routinely attributed to Whigs and 'rebels'. The same phrase occurs in *Absalom and Achitophel* (line 198). Ulysses speaks to more general approval in Dryden's version, since the final part of the speech on degree is given to Diomedes, and Nestor's agreement is strengthened. In Shakespeare Ulysses' assertion of royal authority is immediately balanced by the entrance of the Trojan Aeneas, who claims not to know which of the Greeks is the High King:

> How may
> A stranger to those most imperial looks
> Know them from eyes of other mortals?
> ... Which is the high and mighty Agamemnon? (I.iii.221, 229)

In Dryden this distraction and, for the High King, humiliation, is omitted and the scene ends forcefully, with Agamemnon asking Ulysses and Nestor to 'vindicate the Dignity of Kings' (I.i.108).

The tone of the play's ending is completely altered by replacing Pandarus's cynicism with a speech by Ulysses, celebrating royal authority:

> Hayl *Agamemnon*! truly Victor now!
> While secret envy, and while open pride,
> Among thy factious Nobles discord threw;
> While publique good was urg'd for private ends,
> And those thought Patriots, who disturb'd it most;
> Then, like the headstrong horses of the Sun,

That light which shou'd have cheer'd the World, consum'd it:
Now peacefull order has resum'd the reynes,
Old time looks young, and Nature seems renew'd:
Then, since from homebred Factions ruine springs,
Let Subjects learn obedience to their Kings. (V.ii.316)

The fourth and fifth lines of this speech seem to have a particular topical application. The last two lines express 'the Moral that directs the whole action of the Play to one center' (Preface, 234). If subjects persist in causing trouble and in interfering in government business which they are no more fit to understand than Phaethon was to control the 'horses of the Sun', the King or his ministers will have to act forcefully. 'Peacefull order' can be restored only by decisive political leadership and necessary action to deal with the King's enemies. Thus Dryden's ideal of sovereignty is bound up with the idea that the monarch must act strongly, must 'put his foot down'. He is exhorting his King to restrain his own pleasures and to get tough with the Whig disrupters of the state. This is a Tory perspective. Dryden is moderate in the sense of being balanced in his criticism: priests are mocked, but so are facile attacks on priests; the King and his brother are criticized, but so are quasi-Whiggish faction-mongers. Dryden dedicates the play to a man who seems capable of mediating between the Stuart brothers and their opponents. Yet the play's final word is an assertion of strong royal authority, which is why the overall political tenor of the play is of moderate Toryism, rather than simply moderation.

We began our exploration of Restoration drama with the central figure of Dryden in Chapter 1, and we now end with him. Dryden was the foremost champion of Shakespeare in the Restoration and the prime exponent of adaptation. *Troilus and Cressida* exemplifies Dryden's ideas about adapting Shakespeare, which influenced dramatic practice well into the eighteenth century.

Notes

1 See Dobson, *The Making of the National Poet*; Taylor, *Reinventing Shakespeare*; Bate, *The Genius of Shakespeare*; Marsden (ed.), *The Appropriation of Shakespeare*. Hume in 'Before the Bard' qualfies the views of Dobson and Taylor, arguing that the major shift towards 'bardolatory' happened only after 1730. See also Marsden, *The Re-Imagined Text: Shakespeare, Adaptation, & Eighteenth-Century Literary Theory*. The strength of Marsden's work lies in locating dramatic practice alongside Restoration literary criticism. However, I disagree with her uniform stress on simplification (linguistic, moral and political) in the adaptations, as I feel it makes insufficient allowance for contra-

diction. Her view that women in the plays are depicted as inhabiting the private sphere is problematic and takes no account of the debate about when and how the notion of such a sphere began to develop: see Shoemaker, *Gender in English Society 1650–1850: The Emergence of Separate Spheres?* For a fuller bibliography see Dobson, 233–51.

2 Dryden, Preface to *All For Love* in *Works*, XIII, 18. For the disupte between Dryden and Shadwell see *Dryden and Shadwell: The Literary Controversy and Mac Flecknoe*.

3 All quotations are taken from *Dryden and Shadwell: The Literary Controversy and Mac Flecknoe*.

4 See the discussion of this play in my *Restoration Theatre and Crisis*, 71–82; and Wikander, 'The Spitted Infant: Scenic Emblem and Exclusionist Politics in Restoration Adaptations of Shakespeare', who has shown that Crowne uses 'scenic emblem' and particularly the image and spectacle of dead babies to render Shakespeare 'more politically conservative and more iconographically simplistic' (342).

5 Epistle Dedicatory to the *Life of Plutarch* (1683) in *Works*, XVII, 228.

6 *Works*, XIII, 18.

7 *Works*, XIII, 244. Italics reversed.

8 *Works*, XIII, 20.

9 *Pace* Marsden in *The Re-Imagined Text*. The best reading of Dryden's Cleopatra as a human and complex character mis-read, and either idealized or vilified by all around her, is Hughes 'Art and Life in *All For Love*'.

10 For the heroism of Dryden's Cleopatra see Waith, *The Herculean Hero*, 194.

11 *The Ingratitude of a Common-wealth*, ed. McGugan, sigs A2r–A2v.

12 The politics of various of the adaptations are discussed in my *Restoration Theatre and Crisis*. On the politics of adaptations see also Maguire, 'Factionary Politics: John Crowne's *Henry VI*' and 'Nahum Tate's *King Lear*: "the king's blest restauration"'.

13 *Works*, XIII, 219, 220. Italics reversed here and in all quotations from the preface and prologue.

14 Dryden, however, thinks pity and fear 'must be principally, if not wholly founded' on the tragic hero (236). 'For terror and compassion work but weakly, when they are divided into many persons' (236–7).

15 In the dedication to his tragi-comedy *The Spanish Fryar*, published in 1681, Dryden was to defend the mixing of comedy and tragedy.

16 He offers a partial defence of the practice of Shakespeare and other English dramatists, and a judicious criticism of Rymer's theories in his unpublished *Heads of an Answer to Rymer's Remarks*: see *Works*, XVII.

17 As Dryden notes in his preface, the scene owes something to scenes between male friends in Shakespeare's *Julius Caesar*, Beaumont and Fletcher's *The Maid's Tragedy* and Euripides's *Iphigenia at Aulis*. We may also compare scenes between male friends in Otway's plays, particularly *The Orphan* and *Venice Preserv'd*.

18 *The Re-imagined Text*, 37.

19 *The Re-imagined Text*, 164–5, n. 61. Cf. James Winn, who under-reads the play's political message as fleeting: *John Dryden and His World*, 317. I have discussed the politics of the play in my *Restoration Theatre and Crisis*. See also McFadden, *Dryden the Public Writer*, 211–16; Novak's headnote to the play in *Works of John Dryden*, XIII; and (though mistaken in my view) Moore, 'For King and Country'.

20 E.g. I.ii.208–9; III.ii.96; IV.ii.243, 370; V.i.122;

21 On the political resonance of Dryden's treatment of priests in the play see Moore, 'For King and Country', and my reply, *Restoration Theatre and Crisis*, 146. I discuss Dryden's changing religio-political views at 145–9.

22 See Kenyon, *Robert Spencer, Early of Sunderland*, 21.

23 In addition to Kenyon, *Robert Spencer, Earl of Sunderland*, see Jones, *Country and Court*, 20; Haley, *Shaftesbury*, 350; Hutton, *Charles II*, 367.

BIBLIOGRAPHY

General critical and historical reading

The following texts have influenced the argument of several chapters and are not cited again under each chapter.

Albion 25:4 (1993) contains important debate by leading historians of the Restoration.

Backscheider, Paula (ed.), *Restoration and Eighteenth-century Dramatists: A Dictionary of Literary Biography*, Detriot, Bruccoli Clark Layman, 1989.

Backscheider, Paula, *Spectacular Politics: Theatrical Power and Mass Culture in Early Modern England*, Baltimore, Johns Hopkins University Press, 1993.

Bevis, Richard W., *English Drama: Restoration and Eighteenth Century, 1660–1789*, London, Longman, 1988.

Bevis, Richard W., 'Canon, Pedagogy, Prospectus: Redesigning "Restoration and Eighteenth-century Drama"', *Comparative Drama* 31 (1997), 178–91.

A Biographical Dictionary of Actors, Actresses, Musicians, Dancers, Managers and Other Stage Personnel In London, 1660–1800, ed. Edward A. Langhans, Philip H. Highfill Jr *et al.*, 14 vols, Carbondale, Southern Illinois University Press, 1973–.

Black, Jeremy (ed.), *Culture and Society in Britain, 1660–1800*, Manchester, Manchester University Press, 1997.

Black, Jeremy, and Jeremy Gregory (eds), *Culture, Politics and Society in Britain, 1660–1800*, Manchester, Manchester University Press, 1991.

Boswell, Eleanor, *The Restoration Court Stage, 1660–1702*, New York, Barnes and Noble, 1932 rpt. 1966.

Botica, Allan Richard, *Audience, Playhouse and Play in Restoration Theatre, 1660–1710*, D. Phil. Thesis, Oxford University, 1985.

Braverman, Richard, *Plots and Counterplots: Sexual Politics and the Body Politic, 1660–1730*, Cambridge, Cambridge University Press, 1993.

Brown, John Russell, and Bernard Harris (eds), *Restoration Theatre*, London, Arnold, 1965.

Brown, Laura, *English Dramatic Form, 1660–1760*, New Haven, Yale University Press, 1981.

Cain, T. G. S., and Ken Robinson (eds), *Into Another Mould: Change and Continuity in English Culture 1625–1700*, London, Routledge, 1992.

Canfield, J. Douglas, and Deborah C. Payne (eds), *Cultural Readings of Restoration and Eighteenth-century Theatre*, Athens, University of Georgia Press, 1995.

Chernaik, Warren, *Sexual Freedom in Restoration Literature*, Cambridge, Cambridge University Press, 1995.

Danchin, Pierre (ed.), *The Prologues and Epilogues of the Restoration, 1660–1700*, 4 vols in 7 parts, Nancy, Presses Universitaires de Nancy, 1981–88.

Dharwadker, Aparna, 'Class, Authorship, and the Social Intertexture of Genre in Restoration Theatre', *Studies in English Literature* 37 (1997), 461–82.

Downie, J. A., *To Settle the Succession of the State: Literature and Politics, 1678–1750*, London, Macmillan, 1994.

Ferris, Lesley, *Acting Women: Images of Women in Theatre*, New York, New York University Press, 1989.

Fisk, Deborah Payne (ed.), *The Cambridge Companion to British Restoration Theatre*, Cambridge, Cambridge University Press, 2000.

Hammond, Paul, *John Dryden, A Literary Life*, London, Macmillan, 1991.

Hammond, Paul, 'The King's Two Bodies: Representations of Charles II' in *Culture, Politics and Society in Britian, 1660–1800*, ed. Jeremy Black and Jeremy Gregory, Manchester, Manchester University Press, 1991, 13–48.

Harris, Tim, 'What's New About the Restoration', *Albion* 29 (1997), 187–222.

Hawkins, Harriet, *Likenesses of Truth in Elizabethan and Restoration Drama*, Oxford, Clarendon Press, 1972.

Holland, Peter, *The Ornament of Action: Text and Performance in Restoration Comedy*, Cambridge, Cambridge University Press, 1979.

Howe, Elizabeth, *The First English Actresses: Women and Drama 1660–1700*, Cambridge, Cambridge University Press, 1992.

Hughes, Derek, *English Drama 1660–1700*, Oxford, Clarendon Press, 1996.

Hume, Robert D., *The Development of English Drama in the Late Seventeenth Century*, Oxford, Oxford University Press, 1976, 272–3.

Hume, Robert D. (ed.), *The London Theatre World, 1660–1800*, Carbondale, Southern Illinois University Press, 1980.

Hume, Robert D., 'The Nature of the Dorset Garden Theatre', *Theatre Notebook* 36 (1982), 99–109 (surveys previous debate on this topic).

Hume, Robert D., *The Rakish Stage: Studies in English Drama, 1660–1800*, Carbondale, Southern Illinois University Press, 1983.

Hutton, Richard, *Charles II: King of England, Scotland, and Ireland*, Oxford, Clarendon Press, 1989.

Jones, J. R., *Country and Court: England 1658–1714*, London, Edward Arnold, 1978.

Jose, Nicholas, *Ideas of the Restoration in English Literature, 1660–71*, London and Basingstoke, Macmillan, 1984.

Kaplan, Deborah, 'Representing the Nation: Restoration Comedies in the Early Twentieth-century Stage', *Theatre Survey* 36 (1995), 37–61.

Kavenik, Frances M., *British Drama, 1660–1789*, New York, Twayne, 1995.

Kenny, Shirley Strum (ed.), *British Theatre and the Other Arts*, Washington, Folger Books, 1984.

Kewes, Paulina, *Authorship and Appropriation: Writing for the Stage in England, 1660–1710*, Oxford, Clarendon Press, 1998.

Kroll, Richard, *The Material Word: Literate Culture in the Restoration and Early Eighteenth Century*, Baltimore, Johns Hopkins University Press, 1991.

Lewcock, Dawn, 'Computer Analysis of Restoration Staging, I: 1661–1672', *Theatre Notebook* 47 (1993), 20–9.

Lewcock, Dawn, 'Computer Analysis of Restoration Staging, II: 1671–1682', *Theatre Notebook* 47 (1993), 141–56.

Loftis, John, 'Political and Social Thought in the Drama' in *The London Theatre World, 1660–1800*, ed. Robert D. Hume, Southern Illinois University Press, 1980, 253–85.

Loftis, John, *et al.* (eds), *The Revels History of Drama in English, Vol. V, 1660–1750*, London, Methuen, 1976; rpt Routledge, 1996.

Love, Harold (ed.), *Restoration Literature: Critical Approaches*, London, Methuen, 1972.

Love, Harold, 'Who were the Restoration Audience?', *Yearbook of English Studies* 10 (1980), 21–44.

Lowenthal, Cynthia, 'Sticks and Rags, Bodies and Brocade: Essentializing Discourses and the Late Restoration Playhouse' in *Broken Boundaries*, ed. Katherine M. Quinsey, Lexington, University of Kentucky Press, 1996, 219–33.

Maccubbin, Robert Purks (ed.), *'Tis Nature's Fault: Unauthroized Sexuality During the Enlightenment*, Cambridge, Cambridge University Press, 1985.

McLean, Gerald (ed.), *Culture and Society in the Stuart Restoration*, Cambridge, Cambridge University Press, 1995.

Markley, Robert, 'History, Ideology and the Study of Restoration Drama', *The Eighteenth Century: Theory and Interpretation* 24 (1983), 91–102.

Markley, Robert, and Laurie Finke (eds), *From Renaissance to Restoration: Metamorphoses of the Drama*, Cleveland, Bellflower Press, 1984.

Marshall, W. Gerald (ed.), *The Restoration Mind*, Newark, University of Delaware Press, 1997.

Milhous, Judith, and Robert D. Hume, *Producible Interpretation: Eight English Plays 1675–1707*, Carbondale, Southern Illinois University Press, 1985.

Miner, Earl (ed.), *Restoration Dramatists: A Collection of Critical Essays*, Englewood Cliffs, Prentice Hall, 1966.

Nicoll, Allardyce, *A History of English Drama 1660–1900*, 6 vols, revised edn, Cambridge, Cambridge University Press, 1952–59, vol I: *Restoration Drama 1660–1700*.

Nyberg, Lennart, 'Restoration Comedy in the Modern British Theatre', *Restoration and Eighteenth-Century Theatre Research* 10 (1995), 1–16.

O'Connor, Barry, 'Late Seventeenth-century Royal Portraiture and Restoration Staging', *Theatre Notebook* 49 (1995), 152–64.

Owen, Susan J., 'Interpreting the Politics of Restoration Drama', *Seventeenth Century* 8 (1993), 67–97.

Owen, Susan J., *Restoration Theatre and Crisis*, Oxford, Clarendon Press, 1996.

Owen, Susan J., 'The Lost Rhetoric of Liberty: Marvell and Restoration Drama' in *Marvell and Liberty*, ed. W. Chernaik and M. Dzelzainis, London, Macmillan, 1999, 334–53.

Owen, Susan J. (ed.), *The Blackwell Companion to Restoration Drama*, Oxford, Blackwell (forthcoming 2001).

Pepys, Samuel, *The Diary of Samuel Pepys*, ed. R. Latham and W. Matthews, 11 vols, London, Bell, 1970–83.

Picard, Liza, *Restoration London*, London, Weidenfeld and Nicolson, 1997.

Powell, Jocelyn, *Restoration Theatre Production*, London, Routledge, 1984.

Quinsey, Katherine M. (ed.), *Broken Boundaries: Women and Feminism in Restoration Drama*, Lexington, University Press of Kentucky, 1996.

Scott, Jonathan, *England's Troubles: Seventeenth-century English Political Instability in European Context*, Cambridge, Cambridge University Press, 2000.

Scouten, Arthur H., and Robert D. Hume, '"Restoration Comedy" and its Audiences, 1660–1776', *Yearbook of English Studies* 10 (1980), 45–69.

Staves, Susan, *Players' Scepters: Fictions of Authority in the Restoration*, Lincoln, University of Nebraska Press, 1979.

Straub, Kristina, *Sexual Suspects: Eighteenth-century Players and Sexual Ideology*, Princeton, Princeton University Press, 1992.

Sutherland, James, *English Literature of the Late Seventeenth Century*, Oxford, Clarendon Press, 1969.

Thomas, David, *Restoration and Georgian England, 1660–1788*, Cambridge, Cambridge University Press, 1989.

Turner, James Grantham, 'The Properties of Libertinism' in *'Tis Nature's Fault*, ed. Robert Parks Maccubbin, Cambridge, Cambridge University Press, 1985, 75–87.

Turner, James Grantham, 'The Libertine Sublime: Love and Death in Restoration England', *Studies in Eighteenth-century Culture* 19 (1989), 99–115.

Turner, James Grantham (ed.), *Sexuality and Gender in Early Modern Europe: Institutions, Texts, Images*, Cambridge, Cambridge University Press, 1993.

Van Lennep, William *et al.* (eds), *The London Stage 1660–1800*, vol. I: *1660–1700*, Carbondale, Southern Illinois University Press, 1965.

Weber, Harald M., *Paper Bullets: Print and Kingship Under Charles II*, Lexington, University Press of Kentucky, 1996.

Winn, James Anderson, *John Dryden and His World*, New Haven, Yale University Press, 1987.

Zwicker, Steven (ed.), *The Cambridge Companion to English Literature 1650–1740*, Cambridge, Cambridge University Press, 1998.

Chapter 1: Heroic tragi-comedy: Dryden's *The Conquest of Granada*

PRIMARY TEXTS

Dryden John, *The Conquest of Granada by the Spaniards, Parts I and II*, in *The Works of John Dryden*, ed. E. Niles Hooker *et al.*, 20 vols, Berkeley, University of California Press, 1956–96, vol. XI, ed. John Loftis and David Stuart Rhodes.

Fortescue, Sir John, *De Natura Legis Naturae* in *The Works of Sir John Fortescue, Knight*, ed. Thomas Lord Clermont, London, 1869.

Hobbes, Thomas, *The English Works of Thomas Hobbes of Malmesbury*, ed. Sir William Molesworth, London, 1839, vol. III.

Locke, John, *Treatises on Government*, ed. P. Laslett, Cambridge, Cambridge University Press, 1988.

Marlowe, Christopher, *The Jew of Malta*, Manchester, Manchester University Press (Revels), 1978.

Villiers, George, Duke of Buckingham, *The Rehearsal* (1671), ed. D. E. L. Crane, Durham, University of Durham Press, 1976.

Wilmot, John, Earl of Rochester, *The Farce of Sodom or The Quintessence of Debauchery* in *Rochester: Complete Poems and Plays*, ed. Paddy Lyons, London, J. M. Dent (Everyman), 1993.

CRITICAL AND HISTORICAL READING

Alssid, Michael W., *Dryden's Rhymed Heroic Tragedies: A Critical Study of the Plays and of Their Place in Dryden's Poetry*, Salzburg, Institut für Englische Sprache und Literatur, 1974.

Altieri, Joanne, *The Theatre of Praise: The Panegyric Tradition in Seventeenth-century English Drama*, Newark, University of Delaware Press, 1986

Armistead, J. M., 'The Higher Magic in Dryden's *Conquest of Granada*', *Papers in Language and Literature* 26 (1990), 478–88.

Ashcraft, Richard, *Revolutionary Politics and Locke's Two Treatises of Government*, Princeton, Princeton University Press, 1986.

Barbeau, Anne T., *The Intellectual Design of John Dryden's Heroic Plays*, New Haven, Yale University Press, 1970.

Bawcutt, N. W., 'Some Elizabethan Allusions to Machiavelli', *English Miscellany* XX (1969), 62–4.

Bawcutt, N. W., 'Machiavelli and Marlowe's *The Jew of Malta*', *Renaissance Drama*, n.s. III (1970), 3–49.

Burns, J. H., and Mark Goldie (eds), *Cambridge History of Political Thought, 1450–1700*, Cambridge, Cambridge University Press, 1991, 254–97.

Canfield, J. Douglas, 'The Significance of the Restoration Rhymed Heroic Play', *Eighteenth Century Studies* 13 (1979), 413–39.

Canfield, J. Douglas, 'The Ideology of Restoration Tragicomedy', *ELH* 51 (1984), 447–64.

Cannan, Paul D., 'New Directions in Serious Drama on the London Stage, 1675–1678', *Philological Quarterly* 73 (1994), 219–42,

Coltharp, David, '"Pleasing Rape": The Politics of Libertinism in the Conquest of Granada', *Restoration* 21 (1997), 15–31.

Evans, David R., '"Private Greatness": The Feminine Ideal in Dryden's Early Heroic Drama', *Restoration* 16 (1992), 2–19.

Fisher, Alan S., 'Daring to be Absurd: The Paradoxes of *The Conquest of Granada*', *Studies in Philology* 73 (1976).

Hagstrum, Jean H., *Sex and Sensibility: Ideal and Erotic Love From Milton to Mozart*, Chicago, University of Chicago Press, 1980.

Haley, David B., *Dryden and the Problem of Freedom: The Republican Aftermath, 1649–1680*, New Haven, Yale University Press, 1997.

Haley, K. H. D., *The First Earl of Shaftesbury*, Oxford, Clarendon Press, 1968.

Hughes, Derek, *Dryden's Heroic Plays*, Lincoln, University of Nebraska Press, 1981.

Jefferson, D. W., 'The Significance of Dryden's Heroic Plays', *Proceedings of the Leeds Philosophical and Literary Societies* 5 (1940), 125–39.

Johnson, J. W., 'Did Lord Rochester Write Sodom?', *Papers of the Bibliographical Society of America* 81 (1987), 119–53.

King, Bruce, *Dryden's Major Plays*, Edinburgh, Oliver and Boyd, 1966.

Kirsch, Arthur C., *Dryden's Heroic Drama*, Princeton, Princeton University Press, 1965.

Love, Harold, 'But Did Rochester *Really* Write Sodom?', *Papers of the Bibliographical Society of America* 87 (1993), 319–36.

McFadden, George, *Dryden the Public Writer, 1660–1685*, Princeton, Princeton University Press, 1978.

Maguire, Nancy Klein, *Regicide and Restoration: English Tragicomedy, 1660–1671*, Cambridge, Cambridge University Press, 1992.

Novak, Maximillian E. (ed.), *The Empress of Morocco and its Critics*, Los Angeles, Clark Library, 1968.

Osborn, Scott C., 'Heroical Love in Dryden's Heroic Drama', *Papers of the Modern Language Association* 73 (1958), 480–90.

Pincus, Steven, *Protestantism and Patriotism: Ideologies and the Making of English Foreign Policy, 1650–1668*, Cambridge, Cambridge University Press, 1996.

Pocock, J. G. A., *The Machiavellian Moment: Florentine Political Thought and the Atlantic Republican Tradition*, Princeton, Princeton University Press, 1975.

Quinsey, Katherine M., 'Almahide Still Lives: Feminine Will and Identity in Dryden's *Conquest of Granada*' in *Broken Boundaries*, ed. Katherine M. Quinsey, Lexington, University of Kentucky Press, 1996, 129–49.

Raab, Felix, *The English Face of Machiavelli: A Changing Interpretation, 1550–1700*, London, Routledge, 1964.

Ribner, Irving, 'Marlowe and Machiavelli', *Comparative Literature* VI (1954), 348–56.

Rubidge, Bradley, 'The Code of Reciprocation in *The Conquest of Granada*', *Restoration* 23 (1999), 31–56.

Sherwood, John C., 'Dryden and the Critical Theories of Tasso', *Comparative Literature* 18 (1966), 351–9.

Swedenberg, H. T., Jr, 'Dryden's Obsessive Concern with the Heroic', *Studies in Philology*, extra series 4 (1967), 12–26.

Teeter, Louis, 'The Dramatic Use of Hobbes's Political Ideas', *ELH* 3 (1936), 140–69.

Thompson, James, 'Dryden's *Conquest of Granada* and the Dutch Wars', *The Eighteenth Century: Theory and Interpretation* 31 (1990), 211–26.

Waith, Eugene M., *The Herculean Hero in Marlowe, Chapman, Shakespeare and Dryden*, London, Chatto and Windus, 1962

Waith, Eugene M., *Ideas of Greatness: Heroic Drama in England*, London, Routledge, 1971.

Wallace, John M., 'Dryden and History: A Problem in Allegorical Reading', *English Literary History*, 36 (1969), 265–90.

Wallace, John M., 'John Dryden's Plays and the Conception of a Heroic Society' in Perez Zagorin (ed.), *Culture and Politics: From Puritanism to the Enlightenment*, Berkeley, University of California Press, 1980, 113–34.

West, Michael, 'Dryden and the Disintegration of Renaissance Heroic Ideals', *Costerus* 7 (1976), 192–222.

Winn, James Anderson, 'Heroic Song: A Proposal for a Revised History of English Theater and Opera, 1656–1711', *Eighteenth Century Studies* 30 (1996–7), 113–38.

Winterbottom, John A., 'The Development of the Hero in Dryden's Tragedies', *Journal of English and Germanic Philology* 52 (1953), 161–73.

Winterbottom, John A., 'The Place of Hobbesian Ideas in Dryden's Tragedies', *Journal of English and Germanic Philology* 57 (1958), 665–83.

Chapter 2: Comedy I: Wycherley's *The Country Wife*

PRIMARY TEXTS

The Complete Plays of William Wycherley, ed. Gerald Weales, New York, Anchor, 1966.

The Plays of William Wycherley, ed. Arthur Friedman, Oxford, Clarendon Press, 1979.

The Plays of William Wycherley, ed. Peter Holland, Cambridge, Cambridge University Press, 1981.

The Country Wife, ed. Thomas Fujimura, London, Edward Arnold (Regents Restoration Drama Series), 1965.

The Country Wife, ed. John Dixon Hunt, London, Ernest Benn Ltd (New Mermaids), 1973.

The Country Wife, ed. David Cook and John Swannell, London, Methuen (Revels), 1975.

The Country Wife, ed. James Ogden, London, A. & C. Black (New Mermaids), 1991. All quotations are taken from this edition.

The Country Wife in Scott McMillin (ed.), *Restoration and Eighteenth-century Comedy*, New York, Norton, second edn, 1997.

CRITICAL AND HISTORICAL READING

Alleman, G. S., *Matrimonial Law and the Materials of Restoration Comedy*, Philadelphia, Pennsylvania University Press, 1942.

Avery, Emmet L., *The Reputation of Wycherley's Comedies as Stage Plays, Research Studies of the State College of Washington* 12 (1944), 131–54.

Bacon, Jon Lance, 'Wives, Widows, and Writings in Restoration Comedy', *Studies in English Literature* 31 (1991), 427–43.

Beauchamp, Gorman, 'The Amorous Machiavellianism of *The Country Wife*', *Comparative Drama* 11 (1997–8), 316–30.

Berman, Ronald, 'Wycherley's Unheroic Society', *ELH* 51 (1984), 465–78.

Birdsall, Virginia Ogden, *Wild Civility: The English Comic Spirit on the Restoration Stage*, Bloomington, Indiana University Press, 1970.

Braverman, Richard, 'Libertines and Parasites', *Restoration* 11 (1987), 73–86.

Braverman, Richard, 'The Rake's Progress Revisited: Politics and Comedy in the Restoration' in *Cultural Readings of Restoration and Eighteenth-century Theatre*, ed. J. Douglas Canfield and Deborah C. Payne, Athens, University of Georgia Press, 1995, 141–68.

Bruce, Donald, *Topics of Restoration Comedy*, New York, St Martin's Press, 1974.

Burke, Helen, 'Wycherley's "Tendentious Joke": The Discourse of Alterity in *The Country Wife*', *The Eighteenth Century: Theory and Interpretation* 29 (1988), 227–41.

Burns, Edward, *Restoration Comedy: Crises of Desire and Identity*, London, Macmillan, 1987.

Candido, Joseph, 'Theatricality and Satire in *The Country Wife*', *Essays in Literature* 4 (1977), 27–36.

Canfield, J. Douglas, 'Religious Language and Religious Meaning in Restoration Comedy', *Studies in English Literature* 20 (1980), 285–406.

Canfield, J. Douglas, *Tricksters and Estates: On the Ideology of Restoration Comedy*, Lexington, University Press of Kentucky, 1997.

Cecil, C. D., 'Libertine and *Précieux* Elements in Restoration Comedy', *Essays in Criticism* 9 (1959), 239–53.

Chadwick, W. R., *The Four Plays of William Wycherley: A Study in the Development of a Dramatist*, The Hague, Mouton, 1975.

Cohen, Derek, 'The Revenger's Comedy: Female Hegemony in *The Country Wife*', *Atlantis* 5 (1980), 120–30.

Cohen, Derek, 'The Revenger's Comedy: A Reading of *The Country Wife*', *Durham University Journal* 76 (1983), 31–6.

Cohen, Derek, '*The Country Wife* and Social Danger', *Restoration and Eighteenth-century Theatre Research* 10 (1995), 1–14.

Cope, Kevin L., 'The Conquest of Truth: Wycherley, Rochester, Butler, and Dryden and the Restoration Critique of Satire', *Restoration* 10 (1986), 19–40.

Cordner, Michael, introduction to *Four Restoration Marriage Plays*, Oxford, Oxford University Press, 1995.

Corman, Brian, *Genre and Generic Change in English Comedy, 1660–1700*, Toronto, University of Toronto Press, 1991.

Craik, T. W., 'Some Aspects of Satire in Wycherley's Plays', *English Studies* 41 (1960), 168–79.

Dobrée, Bonamy, *Restoration Comedy, 1660–1720*, Oxford, Oxford University Press, 1924.

Duncan, Douglas, 'Mythic Parody in *The Country Wife*', *Essays in Criticism* 31 (1981), 299–312.

Edgley, R., 'The Object of Literary Criticism', *Essays in Criticism* 14 (1964), 221–36.

Ford, Douglas, '*The Country Wife*: Rake Hero as Artist', *Restoration* 17 (1993), 77–84.

Freedman, William, 'Impotence and Self-destruction in *The Country Wife*', *English Studies* 53 (1972), 421–31.

Fujimura, Thomas H., *The Restoration Comedy of Wit*, Princeton, Princeton University Press, 1952.

Gill, Pat, *Interpreting Ladies: Women, Wit, and Morality in the Restoration Comedy of Manners*, Athens, University of Georgia Press, 1994.

Hallet, Charles, 'The Hobbesian Substructure of *The Country Wife*', *Papers in Language and Literature* 9 (1973), 380–95.

Harwood, John T., *Critics, Values and Restoration Comedy*, Carbondale, Southern Illinois University Press, 1982.

Hawkins, Barrie, '*The Country Wife*: Metaphor Manifest', *Restoration and Eighteenth-century Theatre Research* 11 (1996), 40–63.

Heilman, Robert B., *The Ways of the World*, Seattle, University of Washington Press, 1978.

Hinnant, Charles H., 'Pleasure and the Political Economy of Consumption in Restoration Comedy', *Restoration* 19 (1995), 77–87.

Holland, Norman N., *The First Modern Comedies: The Significance of Etherege, Wycherley, and Congreve*, Cambridge, MA, Harvard University Press, 1959.

Holland, Peter, *The Ornament of Action: Text and Performance in Restoration Comedy*, Cambridge, Cambridge University Press, 1979.

Hughes, Derek, 'Naming and Entitlement in Wycherley, Etherege and Dryden', *Comparative Drama* 21 (1987), 259–89.

Hume, Robert D., 'The Myth of the Rake in Restoration Comedy', *Studies in the Literary Imagination* 10 (1977) 25–55.

Hume, Robert D., 'William Wycherley: Text, Life, Interpretation', *Modern Philology* 78 (1981), 399–415.

Hume, Robert D., '"The Change in Comedy": Cynical Versus Exemplary Comedy on the London Stage, 1678–83', *Essays in Theatre* 1:2 (May 1983), 101–18.

Hume, Robert D., 'The Example of *The Country Wife*' in *Reconstructing Contexts: The Aims and Principles of Archaeo-historicism*, Oxford, Clarendon Press, 1999, 38–41.

Hynes, Peter, 'Against Theory? Knowledge and Action in Wycherley's Plays', *Modern Philology* 94 (1996), 163–89.

Jordan, Robert, 'The Extravagant Rake in Restoration Comedy' in *Restoration Literature*, ed. Harold Love, London, Methuen, 1972, 69–88.

Kaufman, Anthony, 'Wycherley's *The Country Wife* and the Don Juan Character', *Eighteenth Century Studies* 9 (1975–76), 216–31.

Keller, Katherine, 'Re-reading and Re-playing: An Approach to Restoration Comedy', *Restoration* 6 (1982), 64–71.

Knights, L. C., 'Restoration Comedy: The Reality and the Myth', *Scrutiny* 1937 rpt in *Explorations: Essays in Criticism Mainly on the Literature of the Seventeenth Century*, London and New York, New York University Press, 1964, 149–68.

Kowaleski-Wallace, Beth, 'Women, China, and Consumer Culture in Eighteenth-century England', *Eighteenth Century Studies* 29 (1995–96), 153–7.

Love, Harold, 'The Theatrical Geography of *The Country Wife*', *Southern Review* (Adelaide) 16 (1983), 404–15.

Lynch, Kathleen M., *The Social Mode of Restoration Comedy*, 1926, rpt, New York, Biblo and Tannen, 1965.

McCarthy, Eugene B., *William Wycherley: A Biography*, Athens, Ohio University Press, 1979.

McCarthy, Eugene B., *William Wycherley: A Reference Guide*, Boston, G. K. Hall, 1985

McDonald, C. O., 'Restoration Comedy as Drama of Satire: An Investigation into Seventeenth-century Aesthetics', *Studies in Philology* 61 (1964), 522–44.

McNamara, Peter L., 'The Witty Company: Wycherley's *The Country Wife*', *Ariel* 7 (1976), 59–72.

Malekin, Peter, 'Wycherley's Dramatic Skills and the Interpretation of *The Country Wife*', *Durham University Journal*, n.s. 31 (1969), 32–40.

Malekin, Peter, *Liberty and Love: English Literature and Society, 1640–88*, London, Hutchinson, 1981.

Mann, David, 'The Function of the Quack in *The Country Wife*', Restoration 7 (1983), 19–22.

Markley, Robert, *Two Edg'd Weapons: Style and Ideology in the Comedies of Etherege, Wycherley, and Congreve*, Oxford, Clarendon Press, 1988.

Marshall, W. Gerald, 'Wycherley's "Great Stage of Fools": Madness and Theatricality in *The Country Wife*', *Studies in English Literature* 29 (1989), 409–29.

Matalene, H. W., 'What Happens in *The Country Wife*?', *Studies in English Literature* 22 (1982), 395–411.

Matlack, Cynthia, 'Parody and Burlesque of Heroic Ideals in Wycherley's Comedies: A Critical Reinterpretation of Contemporary Evidence', *Papers on Language and Literature* 8 (1972), 273–86.

Morris, David B., 'Language and Honor in *The Country Wife*', *South Atlantic Bulletin* 37 (1973), 3–10.

Muir, Kenneth, *The Comedy of Manners*, London, Hutchinson, 1970.

Neill, Michael, 'Heroic Heads and Humble Tails: Sex, Politics, and the Restoration Comic Rake', *Eighteenth Century: Theory and Interpretation* 24 (1983), 115–39.

Neill, Michael, 'Horned Beasts and China Oranges: Reading the Signs in *The Country Wife*', *Eighteenth-century Life* 12 (1988), 3–17.

Novak, Maximillian E., 'Margery Pinchwife's "London Disease": Restoration Comedy and the Libertine Offensive of the 1670s', *Studies in the Literary Imagination* 10 (1977), 1–23.

Owen, Susan J., 'The Politics of Drink in Restoration Drama' in *A Babel of Bottles: Drink, Drinkers and Drinking Places in Literature*, ed. James Nicholls and Susan J. Owen, Sheffield, Sheffield Academic Press, 2000, 41–51.

Palmer, John, *The Comedy of Manners*, London, Bell, 1913.

Payne, Deborah C., 'Reading the Signs in *The Country Wife*', *Studies in English Literature* 26 (1986), 403–19.

Payne, Deborah C., 'Comedy, Satire, or Farce? Or the Generic Difficulties of Restoration Dramatic Satire', in *Cutting Edges: Postmodern Critical Essays on Eighteenth-century Satire*, ed. James E. Gill, Knoxville, University of Tennessee Press, 1995, 1–22.

Pearson, Jacqueline, *The Prostituted Muse: Images of Women and Women Dramatists 1642–1737*, London, Harvester, 1988.

Peters, Julie Stone, '"Things govern'd by words": Late Seventeenth-century Comedy and the Reformers', *English Studies* 2 (1987), 142–53.

Righter, Anne, 'William Wycherley' in *Restoration Theatre*, ed. John Russell Brown and Bonard Harris, London, Arnold, 1965, 70–91.

Rodway, Allan, 'Restoration Comedy Re-examined', *Renaissance and Modern Studies* 16 (1972), 37–60.

Rogers, Katharine M., *William Wycherley*, New York, Twayne, 1972.

Roper, Alan, 'Sir Harbottle Grimstone and *The Country Wife*', *Studies in the Literary Imagination* 10 (1977), 109–23.

Rothstein, Eric, and Frances M. Kavenik, *The Designs of Carolean Comedy*, Carbondale, Southern Illinois University Press, 1988.

Schneider, Ben Ross, Jr, *The Ethos of Restoration Comedy*, Urbana, University of Illinois Press, 1971.

Scouten, Arthur H., 'Notes Toward a History of Restoration Comedy', *Philological Quarterly* 45 (1966), 62–70.

Sedgwick, Eve Kosofsky, 'Sexualism and the Citizen of the World: Wycherley, Sterne and Male Homosocial Desire', *Critical Inquiry* 11 (1984), 226–45.

Sedgwick, Eve Kosofsky, *Between Men: English Literature and Male Homosocial Desire*, New York, Columbia University Press, 1985 (chapter 3: *The Country Wife*).

Singh, Sarup, *Family Relationships in Shakespeare and the Restoration Comedy of Manners*, New Delhi, Oxford University Press, 1983.

Smith, John Harrington, *The Gay Couple in Restoration Comedy*, Cambridge, MA, Harvard University Press, 1948.

Styan, J. L., *Restoration Comedy in Performance*, Cambridge, Cambridge University Press, 1986.

Thompson, James, 'Providence and Verbal Irony in *The Country Wife*', *South Atlantic Review* 47 (1982), 37–42.

Thompson, James, *Language in Wycherley's Plays: Seventeenth-century Language Theory and Drama*, University, University of Alabama Press, 1984.

Thompson, James, 'Ideology and Dramatic Form: The Case of Wycherley', *Studies in the Literary Imagination* 17 (1984), 49–62.

Thompson, Peggy, 'The Limits of Parody in *The Country Wife*', *Studies in Philology* 89 (1992) 100–14.

Traugott, John, 'The Rake's Progress from Court to Comedy: A Study in Comic Form', *Studies in English Literature* 6 (1966), 381–407.

Underwood, Dale, *Etherege and the Seventeenth-century Comedy of Manners*, New Haven, Yale University Press, 1957.

Vance, John A., *William Wycherley and the Comedy of Fear*, London, Associated University Presses, 2000 (appeared after this book was written).

Velissariou, Aspasia, 'Patriarchal Tactics of Control and Female Desire in Wycherley's *The Gentleman Dancing Master* and *The Country Wife*', *Texas Studies in Langauge and Literature* 37 (1995), 115–26.

Verdumen, J. P., 'Grasping for Permanence: Ideal Couples' in *The Country Wife* and *Aureng-Zebe*', *Huntington Library Quarterly* 42 (1979), 329–47.

Vernon, P. F., 'Marriage of Convenience and the Moral Code of Restoration Comedy', *Essays in Criticism* 12 (1962), 370–87.

Vernon, P. F., *William Wycherley*, London, Longmans, Green & Co., 1965.

Vieth, David M., 'Wycherley's *The Country Wife*: An Anatomy of Masculinity', *Papers on Language and Literature* 2 (1966), 335–50.

Wain, John, 'Restoration Comedy and its Modern Critics', *Essays in Criticism* 6 (1956), 367–85.

Weber, Harold, 'The Rake-hero in Wycherley and Congreve', *Philological Quarterly* 61 (1982), 143–60.

Weber, Harold, 'Horner and his "Women of Honour": The Dinner Party in *The Country Wife*', *Modern Language Quarterly* 43 (1982), 107–20.

Weber, Harold, *The Restoration Rake-hero*, Madison, University of Wisconsin Press, 1986.

Wheatley, Christopher, 'Romantic Love and Social Necessities: Reconsidering Justifications for Marriage in Restoration Comedy', *Restoration* 14 (1990), 58–70.

Young, Douglas M., *The Feminist Voices in Restoration Comedy: The Virtuous Women in the Play-worlds of Etherege, Wycherley and Congreve*, Lanham, MD, University Press of America, 1997.

Zimbardo, Rose A., *Wycherley's Drama: A Link in the Development of English Satire*, New Haven, Yale University Press, 1965.

Zimbardo, Rose A., 'The Semiotics of Restoration Satire' in *Cutting Edges: Postmodern Critical Essays on Eighteenth-century Satire*, ed. James E. Gill, Knoxville, University of Tennessee Press, 1995, 24–42.

Chapter 3: Comedy II: Behn's *The Rover*

See also books listed under Comedy I.

PRIMARY TEXTS

The Rover, ed. Frederick M. Link, Lincoln and London, University of Nebraska Press, 1967.

The Rover in *Restoration Comedy*, ed. A. Norman Jeffares, 4 vols, London, Folio Press, 1974, vol. 2.

The Rover in *Aphra Behn, Five Plays*, introduced by Maureen Duffy, London, Methuen, 1990.

Oroonoko, The Rover and Other Works, ed. Janet Todd, Harmondsworth, Penguin, 1992.

The Rover in *The HBJ Anthology of Drama*, ed. W. B. Worthen, Fort Worth, Harcourt Brace Jovanovich, 1993.

The Rover or the Banished Cavaliers, ed. Anne Russell, Peterborough (Ontario), Broadview, 1994.

Shakespeare, Aphra Behn and the Canon, ed. W. R. Owens and Lizbeth Goodman, London, Routledge, 1996 (collection of essays with edition of *The Rover* by Owens at the end).

The Rover in Scott McMillin (ed.), *Restoration and Eighteenth-century Comedy*, New York, Norton, second edn, 1997.

The Rover and Other Plays, ed. Jane Spencer, Oxford, Oxford University Press, 1995.

The Works of Aphra Behn, ed. Janet Todd, 7 vols, vol. 5, *The Plays 1671–1677*, London, Pickering, 1996. All quotations from this edition, which contains useful notes.

BIOGRAPHIES

Cameron, William J., *New Light on Aphra Behn*, Auckland, University of Auckland Press, 1961.

Caywood, Cynthia L., 'Deconstructing Aphras: Aphra Behn and her Biographers', *Restoration* 24 (2000), 15–34.

Duffy, Maureen, *The Passionate Shepherdess: Aphra Behn, 1640–89*, London, Methuen, 1989.

Goreau, Angeline, *Reconstructing Aphra: A Social Biography of Aphra Behn*, Oxford, Oxford University Press, 1980.

Jerrold, Walter and Clare, 'Aphra Behn: The Incomparable Astraea' in *Five Queer Women*, London, Brentano's, 1929, 1–82.

Jones, Jane, *New Light on the Background and Early Life of Aphra Behn*, Cambridge, Cambridge University Press, 1996.

Mendelson, Sara Heller, *The Mental World of Stuart Women: Three Studies*, Brighton, Harvester, 1987 (chapter 3: 'Aphra Behn').

O'Donnell, Mary Anne, 'Tory Wit and Unconventional Woman: Aphra Behn' in *Women Writers of the Seventeenth Century*, ed. Katharina M. Wilson and Frank J. Warnke, Athens, University of Georgia Press, 1989.

Sackville-West, Vita, *Aphra Behn: The Incomparable Astraea*, London, Gerald Howe, 1927.

Todd, Janet, *The Secret Life of Aphra Behn*, London, André Deutsch, 1996.

Woodcock, George, *The Incomparable Aphra*, London, Boardman, 1948; rpt as *The English Sappho*, New York, Black Rose Books, 1989.

CRITICAL AND HISTORICAL READING

Armistead, J. M., *Four Restoration Playwrights: A Reference Guide to Thomas Shadwell, Aphra Behn, Nathaniel Lee, and Thomas Otway*, Boston, G. K. Hall, 1984.

Artal, Dolores Altaba, *Aphra Behn's English Feminism: Wit and Satire*, London, Associated University Presses, 1999.

Ballaster, Ros, 'The First Female Dramatists' in *Women and Literature in Britain, 1500–1700*, ed. Helen Wilcox, Cambridge, Cambridge Uinversity Press, 1996, 267–90.

Bobker, Danielle, 'Behn: *Auth*-whore or Wri*ter*? Authorship and Identity in *The Rover*', *Restoration and Eighteenth-century Theatre Research* 11 (1996), 32–9.

Boebel, Dagny, 'In the Carnival World of Adam's Garden: Roving and Rape in Behn's *Rover*' in *Broken Boundaries*, ed. Katherine M. Quinsey, Lexington, University of Kentucky Press, 1996, 55–70.

Canfield, J. Douglas, 'Female Rebels and Patriarchal Paradigms in some Neoclassical Works', *Studies in Eighteenth-century Culture* 18 (1988), 153–66.

Carlson, Susan, *Women and Comedy: Rewriting the British Theatrical Tradition*, Ann Arbor, University of Michigan Press, 1991.

Carlson, Susan, 'Cannibalizing and Carnivalizing: Reviving Aphra Behn's *The Rover*', *Theatre Journal* 47 (1995), 517–39.

Clark, Constance, *Three Augustan Women Playwrights*, New York. Peter Lang, 1986.

Copeland, Nancy, 'Re-producing *The Rover*: John Barton's Rover at the Swan', *Essays in Theatre* 9 (1990), 45–59.

Copeland, Nancy, '"Once a whore and ever?": Whore and Virgin in *The Rover* and its Antecedents', *Restoration* 16 (1992), 20–7.

Copeland, Nancy, 'Reviving Aphra Behn: *The Rover* in the "Restoration" Repertoire', *Restoration and Eighteenth-century Theatre Research*, 14 (1999), 1–19.

Corman, Brian, 'Restoration Studies and the New Historicism: The Case of Aphra

Behn' in *The Restoration Mind*, ed. W. Gerald Marshall, Newark, University of Delaware Press, 1997, 252–71.

Cotton, Nancy, *Women Playwrights in England c. 1363–1750*, Lewisburg, Bucknell University Press, 1980.

Cotton, Nancy, 'Aphra Behn and the Pattern Hero' in *Curtain Calls*, ed. Mary Anne Schofield and Cecilia Macheski, Athens, University of Ohio Press, 1991, 211–19.

DeRitter, Jones, 'The Gypsy, *The Rover*, and the Wanderer: Aphra Behn's Revision of Thomas Killigrew', *Restoration* 10 (1986), 82–92.

Dhuicq, Bernard, 'Religion in Aphra Behn's Works: Representation and Misrepresentation', *Studies in English Literature* 71 (1995), 93–112.

Diamond, Elin, '*Gestus* and Signature in Aphra Behn's *The Rover*', *Eighteenth-century Literary History* 56 (1989), rpt in *Aphra Behn: New Casebook*, ed. Janet Todd, London, Macmillan, 1999, 32–56.

Feldwick, Arlen, 'Wits, Whigs, and Women: Domestic Politics as Anti-Whig Rhetoric in Aphra Behn's Town Comedies' in *Political Rhetoric, Power, and Renaissance Women*, ed. Carole Levin and Patricia Sullivan, Albany, State University of New York Press, 1995.

Ferguson, Margaret, 'The Authorial Ciphers of Aphra Behn' in *The Cambridge Companion to English Literature 1650–1740*, ed. Steven Zwicker, Cambridge, Cambridge University Press, 1998, 225–49.

Ferguson, Moira, *First Feminists: British Women Writers, 1578–1799*, Bloomington, Indiana University Press, 1985.

Franceschina, John, 'Shadow and Substance in Aphra Behn's *The Rover*: The Semiotics of Restoration Performance', *Restoration* 19 (1995), 29–42.

Gallagher, Catherine, 'Who Was that Masked Woman? The Prostitute and the Playwright in the Plays of Aphra Behn', *Women's Studies* 15 (1988) 23–42, rpt in Heidi Hutner (ed.), *Rereading Aphra Behn*, Charlottesville, University Press of Virginia, 1993, 65–85.

Gallagher, Catherine, *Nobody's Story: The Vanishing Acts of Women Writers in the Marketplace, 1670–1820*, Berkeley, University of California Press, 1994.

Gardiner, Judith Kegan, 'Aphra Behn: Sexuality and Self-respect', *Women's Studies* 7 (1980), 67–78.

Gill, Pat, *Interpreting Ladies: Women, Wit and Morality in the Restoration Comedy of Manners*, Athens and London, University of Georgia Press, 1994.

Goodman, Lizbeth, 'The Idea of the Canon' in *Shakespeare, Aphra Behn and the Canon*, ed. W. R. Owens and Lizbeth Goodman, London, Routledge, 1996, 3–19.

Goodman, Lizbeth, 'Reviewing the Idea of the Canon' in *Shakespeare, Aphra Behn and the Canon*, ed. W. R. Owens and Lizbeth Goodman, London, Routledge, 1996, 251–8.

Hobby, Elaine, *Virtue of Necessity: English Women's Writing 1649–88*, London, Virago, 1988.

Hume, Robert D., 'Revision of *The Rover*', *Theatre Journal* 31 (1979), 412–13.

Hutner, Heidi (ed.), *Rereading Aphra Behn: History, Theory, and Criticism*, Charlottes-ville, University Press of Virginia, 1993.

Hutner, Heidi, 'Revisioning the Female Body: Aphra Behn's *The Rover, Parts I and II*, in *Rereading Aphra Behn*, Charlottesville, University Press of Virginia, 1993, 102–20.

Jacobs, Naomi, 'The Seduction of Aphra Behn', *Women's Studies* 18 (1991), 395–403.

Kaji, Riwako, 'The Structuring of Desires in Aphra Behn's Plays: Problems of Prostitution and Gender', *Shiron* (Japan) 38 (1999), 37–53.

Kaufman, Anthony, '"The perils of Florinda": Aphra Behn, Rape and Subversion of Libertinism in *The Rover, Part I*', *Restoration and Eighteenth-century Theatre Research* (1996), 1–21.

Kavenik, Frances M., 'Aphra Behn: The Playwright as "Breeches Part"' in *Curtain Calls*, ed. Mary Anne Schofield and Cecilia Macheski, Athens, University of Ohio Press, 1991, 178–91.

Kinney, Suzanne, 'Confinement Sharpens the Invention: Aphra Behn's *The Rover* and Susanna Centilevre's *The Busie Body*' in Gail Finney (ed.), *Look Who's Laughing: Gender and Comedy*, Langhorne, PA, Gordon and Breach, 1994.

Langdell, Cheri Davis, 'Aphra Behn and Sexual Politics: A Dramatist's Discourse with her Audience' in *Drama, Sex and Politics*, ed. James Redmond, Cambridge, Cambridge University Press, 1985, 109–28.

Lewcock, Dawn, 'More for Seeing than Hearing: Behn and the Use of Theatre' in *Aphra Behn Studies*, ed. Janet Todd, Cambridge, Cambridge University Press, 1996, 66–83.

Link, Frederick M., Introduction to *The Rover*, Lincoln and London: University of Nebraska Press, 1967.

Link, Frederick M., *Aphra Behn*, New York, Twayne, 1968.

Lussier, Mark, '"The Vile Merchandize of Fortune": Women, Economy and Desire in Aphra Behn', *Women's Studies* 18 (1991), 379–93.

Lussier, Mark, '"Marrying that Hated Object": The Carnival of Desire in Behn's *The Rover*' in *Privileging Gender in Early Modern England*, ed. Jean R. Brink, special issue of *Sixteenth-century Essays and Studies* XXIII (1993), 225–39.

Markley, Robert, 'Be impudent, be saucy, forward, bold, touzing, and leud': The Politics of Masculine Sexuality and Feminine Desire in Behn's Tory Comedies' in *Cultural Readings of Restoration and Eighteenth-century Theater*, ed. J. Douglas Canfield and Deborah C. Payne, Athens, University of Georgia Press, 1995, 114–40.

Marsden, Jean I., 'Rape, Voyeurism and the Restoration Stage' in *Broken Boundaries*, ed. Katherine M. Quinsey, Lexington, University of Kentucky Press, 1996, 185–200.

Medoff, Jeslyn, 'The Daughters of Behn and the Problems of Reputation' in *Women, Writing, History: 1640–1799*, ed. Isobel Grundy and Susan Wiseman, Athens, University of Georgia Press, 1992.

Morgan, Fidelis, *The Female Wits: Women Playwrights on the London Stage, 1660–1720*, London, Virago, 1981.

Munns, Jessica, 'Barton and Behn's *The Rover* or, the Text Transpos'd', *Restoration and Eighteenth-century Theatre Research* (1988), 11–22.

Munns, Jessica, '"I by a double right thy bounties claim": Aphra Behn and Sexual Space' in *Curtain Calls*, ed. Mary Anne Schofield and Cecilia Macheski, Athens, University of Ohio Press, 1991, 193–219.

Munns, Jessica, '"Good, sweet, honey, sugar-candied reader": Aphra Behn's Foreplay in Forewords' in *Rereading Aphra Behn*, ed. Heidi Hutner, Charlottesville, University Press of Virginia, 1993, 44–64.

Nash, Julie, '"The sight on't would beget a warm desire": Visual Pleasure in Aphra Behn's *The Rover*', *Restoration* 18 (1994), 77–87.

O'Donnell, Mary Anne, *Aphra Behn: An Annotated Bibliography of Primary and Secondary Sources*, New York, Garland, 1986.

Owen, Susan J., '"Suspect my loyalty when I lose my virtue": Sexual Politics and Party in Aphra Behn's Plays of the Exclusion Crisis, 1678–83', *Restoration* 18 (1994), 37–47; rpt in *Aphra Behn: New Casebook*, ed. Janet Todd, London, Macmillan, 1999, 57–72.

Owens, W. R., 'Remaking the Canon: Aphra Behn's *The Rover*' in *Shakespeare, Aphra Behn and the Canon*, ed. W. R. Owens and Lizbeth Goodman, London, Routledge, 1996, 131–91.

Pacheco, Anita, 'Rape and the Female Subject in Aphra Behn's *The Rover*', *ELH* 65 (1998), 323–45.

Pacheco, Anita (ed.), *Early Women Writers, 1600–1720*, London, Longman, 1998.

Payne, Deborah C., '"And poets shall by patron-princes live": Aphra Behn and Patronage', in *Curtain Calls*, ed. Mary Anne Schofield and Cecilia Macheski, Athens, University of Ohio Press, 1991, 105–19.

Payne, Linda R., 'The Carnivalesque Regeneration of Corrupt Economies in *The Rover*', *Restoration* 22 (1988), 40–9.

Pearson, Jacqueline, *The Prostituted Muse: Images of Women and Women Dramatists, 1642–1737*, London, Harvester, 1988.

Potter, Lois, 'Transforming a Super-rake', review of *The Rover* at the Swan Theatre, *Times Literary Supplement*, 25 July 1986, 817.

Karen J. Ray, '"The yielding moment": A Woman's View of Amorous Females and Fallen Women', *Restoration and Eighteenth-century Theatre Research* 11 (1996), 39–48.

Rogers, Katharine M., *Feminism in Eighteenth-century England*, Urbana, University of Illinois Press, 1982.

Root, Robert L., Jr, 'Aphra Behn, Arranged Marriage, and Restoration Comedy', *Women and Literature* 5 (1977), 3–14.

Schofield, Mary Anne, and Cecilia Macheski (eds), *Curtain Calls: British and American Women and the Theater, 1660–1820*, Athens, University of Ohio Press, 1991.

Spencer, Jane, '*The Rover* and the Eighteenth Century' in *Aphra Behn Studies*, ed. Janet Todd, Cambridge, Cambridge University Press, 1996, 84–106.

Stewart, Ann Marie, 'Rape, Patriarchy, and the Libertine Ethos: The Function of Sexual Violence in Aphra Behn's "The Golden Age" and *The Rover, Part I*', *Restoration and Eighteenth-century Theatre Research* 12 (1997), 26–39.

Straznicky, Marta, 'Restoration Women Playwrights and the Limits of Professionalism', *ELH* 64 (1997), 703–26.

Sullivan, David M., 'The Female Will in Aphra Behn', *Women's Studies* 22 (1993), 335–47.

Taetzsch, Lynne, 'Romantic Love Replaces Kinship Exchange in Aphra Behn's Restoration Drama', *Restoration* 17 (1993), 30–8.

Thompson, Peggy, 'Closure and Subversion in Behn's Comedies' in *Broken Boundaries*, ed. Katherine M. Quinsey, Lexington, University of Kentucky Press, 1996.

Todd, Janet, 'Reconstructing Aphra', *Yale Review* 70 (1981), 631–7.

Todd, Janet, *The Sign of Angellica: Women, Writing, and Fiction 1660–1800*, London, Virago, 1989.

Todd, Janet (ed.), *Aphra Behn Studies*, Cambridge, Cambridge University Press, 1996.

Todd, Janet, *The Critical Fortunes of Aphra Behn*, Columbia, SC, Camden House, 1998.

Todd, Janet (ed.), *Aphra Behn: New Casebook*, London, Macmillan, 1999.

Wiseman, S. J., *Aphra Behn*, Plymouth, Northcote House, 1996.

Zook, Meilinda, 'Contextualizing Aphra Behn: Plays, Politics, and Party' in *Women Writers and the Early Modern British Political Tradition*, ed. Hilda Smith, Cambridge, Cambridge University Press, 1998.

Chapters 4 and 5: Tragedy: Lee's *Lucius Junius Brutus* and Otway's *Venice Preserv'd*

PRIMARY TEXTS

Crowne, John, *The Ambitious Statesman*, London, 1679.

Dryden, John, *The Vindication [of] … the Play Called The Duke of Guise*, London, 1683.

Filmer, Sir Robert, *Patriarcha and Other Writings*, ed. Johann P. Sommerville, Cambridge, Cambridge University Press, 1991.

Jordan, Thomas, *London's Glory*, London, 1680.

Lee, Nathaniel, *The Works of Nathaniel Lee*, ed. Thomas B. Stroup and Arthur L. Cooke, 2 vols. New Brunswick, NJ, Scarecrow Press, 1954.

Lee, Nathaniel, *Lucius Junius Brutus*, ed. John Loftis, Lincoln, University of Nebraska Press, 1967. All quotations from this edition.

Machiavelli, Niccolo, *The Discourses*, ed. L. J. Walker, 2 vols, London, Routledge, 1950.

Marvell, Andrew, *An Account of the Growth of Popery and Arbitrary Government in England*, 'Amsterdam', 1677.

Otway, Thomas, *Venice Preserv'd*, ed. Malcolm Kelsall, Lincoln, University of Nebraska Press, 1969. All quotations from this edition.

The Works of Thomas Otway, ed. J. C. Ghosh, 2 vols, Oxford, Clarendon Press, 1932.

Settle, Elkanah, *The Female Prelate*, London, 1680.

Shakespeare, William, *Complete Works*, ed. Stanley Wells and Gary Taylor, Oxford, Clarendon Press, 1988.

Tate, Nahum, *The Loyal General*, London, 1680.

Tate, Nahum, *The Ingratitude of a Common-wealth* (1682) also in R. McGugan, *Nahum Tate and the Coriolanus Tradition in English Drama with a Critical Edition of Tate's The Ingratitude of a Common-wealth*, New York, Garland, 1987.

Whitaker, William, *The Conspiracy*, London, 1680.

CRITICAL AND HISTORICAL READING

Works are not cited again here if already listed in 'General' or 'Heroic Drama' sections above.

Armistead, J. M., *Nathaniel Lee*, Boston, Twayne, 1979.

Barbour, Frances, 'The Unconventional Heroic Plays of Nathaniel Lee', *University of Texas Studies in English* 20 (1940), 109–16.

Brown, Laura, 'The Defenseless Woman and the Development of English Tragedy', *Studies in English Literature* 22 (1982), 429–43.

Brown, Richard E., 'Nathaniel Lee's Political Drama, 1679–1683', *Restoration* 10 (1986), 41–53.

Bywaters, David, 'Venice, Its Senate, and Its Plot in Otway's *Venice Preserv'd*', *Modern Philology* 80 (1983), 256–63.

Canfield, J. Douglas, 'Royalism's Last Dramatic Stand: English Political Tragedy, 1679–1689', *Studies in Philology* 82 (1985), 234–63.

Canfield, J. Douglas, *Word as Bond in English Literature from the Middle Ages to the Restoration*, Philadelphia, University of Pennsylvania Press, 1989.

Canfield, J. Douglas, *Heroes and States: On the Ideology of Restoration Tragedy*, Lexington, The University Press of Kentucky, 2000.

DePorte, Michael, 'Otway and the Straits of Venice', *Papers on Language and Literature* 18 (1982), 245–57.

Dobrée, Bonamy, *Restoration Tragedy, 1660–1720*, Oxford, Clarendon Press, 1929 rpt 1954.

Fink, Zera S., *The Classical Republicans: An Essay in the Recovery of a Pattern of Thought in Seventeenth-century England*, Evanston, Northwestern University Press, 1945.

Flores, Stephan P., 'Patriarchal Politics Under Cultural Stress: Nathaniel Lee's Passion Plays', *Restoration and Eighteenth-century Theatre Research* 8 (1993), 1–28.

Gill, Pat, 'Pathetic Passions: Incestuous Desire in Plays by Otway and Lee', *Eighteenth Century: Theory and Interpretation* 39 (1998), 192–208.

Hagstrum, Jean, *Sex and Sensibility: Ideal and Erotic Love from Milton to Mozart*, Chicago, University of Chicago Press, 1980.

Ham, Roswell G., *Otway and Lee: Biography from a Baroque Age*, 1931 rpt New York, Greenwood Press, 1969.

Hammond, Antony, '"The greatest action": Lee's *Lucius Juius Brutus*' in *Poetry and Drama, 1570–1700: Essays in Honour of Harold F. Brooks*, ed. Antony Coleman and Antony Hammond, London, Methuen, 1981, 173–85.

Harth, Philip, 'Political Interpretations of *Venice Preserv'd*', *Modern Philology* 85 (1988), 345–62.

Hauser, David R., 'Otway Preserved; Theme and Form in *Venice Preserv'd*', *Studies in Philology* 55 (1958), 481–93.

Hayne, Victoria, '"All language then is vile": The Theatrical Critique of Political Rhetoric in Nathaniel Lee's *Lucius Junius Brutus*', *ELH*, 63 (1996), 337–66.

Hughes, Derek, 'A New Look at *Venice Preserv'd*', *Studies in English Literature* 11 (1971), 437–57.

Hume, Robert D., 'The Satiric Design of Nathaniel Lee's *The Princess of Cleve*', *Journal of English and Germanic Philology* 75 (1976), 117–38.

Hume, Robert D., 'Otway and the Comic Muse', *Studies in Philology* 73 (1976), 87–116.

Hume, Robert D., 'The Unconventional Tragedies of Thomas Otway' in *Du Verbe au Geste: Mélanges en l'honneur de Pierre Danchin*, Nancy, Presses Universitaires de Nancy, 1987.

McBurney, William H., 'Otway's Tragic Muse Debacuhed: Sensuality in *Venice Preserv'd*', *Journal of English and Germanic Philology* 58 (1959), 380–99.

MacKenzie, Aline, 'A Note on Pierre's White Hat', *Notes and Queries* 192 (1947), 90–3.

Marshall, Gerald, *Restoration Serious Drama*, Norman, University of Oklahoma Press, 1975.

Moore, John Robert, 'Contemporary Satire in Otway's *Venice Preserv'd*', *Publications of the Modern Language Association* 43 (1928), 166–81.

Munns, Jessica, '"Plain as the light in the Cowcumber": A Note on the Conspiracy in Thomas Otway's *Venice Preserv'd*', *Modern Philology* 85 (1987), 54–7.

Munns, Jessica, *Restoration Politics and Drama: The Plays of Thomas Otway, 1675–1683*, Newark, University of Delaware Press, 1995.

Nenner, Howard, *By Colour of Law: Legal Culture and Constitutional Politics in England, 1660–1689*, Chicago, University of Chicago Press, 1977.

Owen, Susan J., '"Partial tyrants"' and "Freeborn people" in *Lucius Junius Brutus*', *Studies in English Literature* 31 (1991), 463–82.

Owen, Susan J., '"He that should guard my virtue has betrayed it": The Dramatization of Rape in the Exclusion Crisis', *Restoration and Eighteenth-century Theatre Research* 9 (1994), 59–68.

Owen, Susan J., 'The Politics of John Dryden's *The Spanish Fryar; or, The Double Discovery*', *English* 43 (1994), 97–113.

Owen, Susan J., 'Chaos Theory, Marxist Dialectics and Literature', *new formations*, special 'Technoscience' issue, 19 (November 1996), 84–112.

Parker, Gerald D., 'The Image of Rebellion in Thomas Otway's *Venice Preserv'd* and Edward Young's *Busiris*', *Studies in English Literature* 21 (1981), 389–408.

Parker, Gerald D., '"History as nightmare" in Nevil Payne's *The Siege of Constan-tinople* and Lee's *Lucius Junius Brutus*', *Papers on Language and Literature* 21 (1985), 3–18.

Perdue, Danielle, 'The Male Masochist in Restoration Drama', *Restoration and Eighteenth-century Theatre Research* 11 (1996), 10–21.

Pocock, J. G. A., *The Machiavellian Moment*, Princeton, Princeton University Press, 1975.

Rogers, Katherine, 'Masculine and Feminine Values in Restoration Drama: The Distinc-tive Power of *Venice Preserv'd*', *Texas Studies in Literature* 27 (1985), 390–404.

Rothstein, Eric, *Restoration Tragedy: Form and the Process of Change*, Madison, Univer-sity of Wisconsin Press, 1967.

Schille, Candy B. K., 'Reappraising "Pathetic" Tragedies: *Venice Preserv'd* and *The Massacre of Paris*', *Restoration* 12 (1988), 33–45.

Solomon, Harry M., 'The Rhetoric of Redressing Grievances: Court Propaganda as the Hermeneutical Key to *Venice Preserv'd*', *ELH* 53 (1986), 289–310.

Stroup, Thomas B., 'Otway's Bitter Pessimism' in *Essays Presented to Douglas Mac-Millan, Studies in Philology* (extra series 1967), ed. D. W. Patterson and A. B. Strauss, 54–75.

Taylor, Aline McKenzie, *Next to Shakespeare: Otway's* Venice Preserv'd *and* The Orphan *and Their History on the London Stage,* Durham, NC, Duke University Press, 1950.

Teeter, Louis, *Political Themes in Restoration Tragedy*, Ph.D. dissertation, Baltimore, Johns Hopkins University, 1932.

Vieth, David M., 'Psychological Myth as Tragedy: Nathaniel Lee's *Lucius Junius Brutus*', *Huntington Library Quarterly* 39 (1975), 57–76.

Warner, Kerstin P., *Thomas Otway*, Boston, Twayne, 1982.

Williams, Gordon, 'The Sex-death Motive in Otway's *Venice Preserv'd*', *Trivium* 2 (1969).

Wootton, David, 'Ulysses Bound? Venice and the Idea of Liberty from Howell to Hume' in *Republicanism, Liberty and Commercial Society, 1649–1776*, ed. David Wootton, Stanford, Stanford University Press, 1994.

Chapter 6: Shakespeare adapted: Dryden's *Troilus and Cressida*

PRIMARY TEXTS

Crowne, John, *The Misery of Civil-War*, London, 1680.

Dryden, John, *All For Love* in *The Works of John Dryden*, vol. XIII, ed. George R. Guffey, Maximillian E. Novak and Alan Roper, Berkeley, University of California Press, 1984.

Dryden, John, *Troilus and Cressida* in ibid.

Dryden, John, and Thomas Shadwell, *Dryden and Shadwell: The Literary Controversy and Mac Flecknoe (1668–1679), Facsimile Reproductions*, ed. Richard L. Oden, New York, Delmar, 1977.

Ravenscroft, Edward, *Titus Andronicus; or, The Rape of Lavinia* (1687).

Shakespeare, William, *Troilus and Cressida*, ed. Kenneth Muir, Oxford University Press, rpt World's Classics, 1994.

Tate, Nahum, *The History of King Lear* (1681); also in *Five Restoration Adaptations of Shakespeare*, ed. Christopher Spencer, Urbana, University of Illinois Press, 1965.

Tate, Nahum, *The Ingratitude of a Common-wealth* (see Tragedy bibliography above).

CRITICAL AND HISTORICAL READING

See also works cited under previous chapter headings.

Bate, Jonathan, *The Genius of Shakespeare*, Oxford, Oxford University Press, 1998.

Bate, Jonathan, and Russell Jackson (eds), *Shakespeare: An Illustrated Stage History*, Oxford, Oxford University Press, 1996.

Branam, George C., *Eighteenth-century Adaptations of Shakespearean Tragedy*, Berkeley, University of California Press, 1956.

Hughes, Derek, 'Art and Life in *All For Love*', *Studies in Philology* 80 (1983), 84–107.

Dobson, Michael, *The Making of the National Poet: Shakespeare, Adaptation and Authorship, 1660–1769*, Oxford, Clarendon Press, 1992.

Dobson, Michael, 'Improving on the Original: Actresses and Adaptations' in *Shakespeare: An Illustrated Stage History*, ed. Jonathan Bate and Russell Jackson, Oxford, Oxford University Press, 45–68.

Dobson, Michael, 'Adaptations and Revivals' in *The Cambridge Companion to British Restoration Theatre*, ed. Fisk (see p. 172), 40–51.

Hume, Robert D., 'Before the Bard: "Shakespeare" in Early Eighteenth-century London', *ELH* 64 (1997), 41–75.

Kenyon, J. P., *Robert Spencer, Earl of Sunderland*, Cambridge, Cambridge University Press, 1958.

Maguire, Nancy Klein, 'Nahum Tate's *King Lear*: "the king's blest restauration"' in *Appropriation of Shakespeare*, ed. Jean I. Marsden, Hemel Hempstead, Harvester Wheatsheaf, 1991, 29–43.

Maguire, Nancy Klein, 'Factionary Politics: John Crowne's Henry VI' in *Culture and Society in the Stuart Restoration*, ed. Gerald MacLean, Cambridge, Cambridge University Press, 1995, 70–92.

Marsden, Jean I. (ed.), *The Appropriation of Shakespeare: Post-Renaissance Reconstruction of the Works and the Myth*, Hemel Hempstead, Harvester Wheatsheaf, 1991.

Marsden, Jean I., *The Re-imagined Text: Shakespeare, Adaptation, & Eighteenth-century Literary Theory*, Lexington, University Press of Kentucky, 1995.

Merchant, W. Moelwyn, 'Shakespeare Made Fit' in *Restoration Theatre*, ed. John Russell Brown and Bernard Harris, Stratford-upon-Avon Studies 6, London, Edward Arnold, 1965.

Moore, Lewis D., 'For King and Country: John Dryden's *Troilus and Cressida*', *College Language Association Journal* 26 (1982), 98–111.

Odell, G. C., *Shakespeare From Betterton to Irving*, 2 vols, London, Constable, 1920–21.

Rosenthal, Laura J., 'Reading Masks: The Actress and the Spectatrix in Restoration Shakespeare' in *Broken Boundaries*, ed. Katherine M. Quinsey, Lexington, University of Kentucky Press, 1996, 201–18.

Shoemaker, Robert, *Gender in English Society 1650–1850: The Emergence of Separate Spheres?*, London, Longman, 1998.

Sorelius, Gunnar, *'The Giant Race Before the Flood': Pre-Restoration Drama on the Stage and in the Criticism of the Restoration*, Uppsala, Almquist and Wiksells, 1966.

Spencer, Hazleton, *Shakespeare Improved*, Cambridge, MA, Harvard University Press, 1925.

Taylor, Gary, *Reinventing Shakespeare: A Cultural History From the Restoration to the Present*, London. The Hogarth Press, 1990.

Vickers, Brian, *Shakespeare: the Critical Heritage*, vol. I: *1623–1692*, London, Routledge and Kegan Paul, 1974.

Wikander, Matthew, 'The Spitted Infant: Scenic Emblem and Exclusionist Politics in Restoration Adaptations of Shakespeare', *Shakespeare Quarterly* 37 (1986), 340–58.

INDEX